John Bloundelle-Burton, Frank Hazen, S. Herbert

Across the Salt Seas

A Romance of the War of Succession

John Bloundelle-Burton, Frank Hazen, S. Herbert

Across the Salt Seas
A Romance of the War of Succession

ISBN/EAN: 9783744675987

Printed in Europe, USA, Canada, Australia, Japan

Cover: Foto ©ninafisch / pixelio.de

More available books at **www.hansebooks.com**

ACROSS
THE SALT SEAS

A ROMANCE OF THE
WAR OF SUCCESSION

BY

JOHN BLOUNDELLE-BURTON

AUTHOR OF "IN THE WAY OF ADVERSITY,"
"THE HISPANIOLA PLATE," "A GEN-
TLEMAN ADVENTURER," ETC.

HERBERT S. STONE & CO.
CHICAGO & NEW YORK
MDCCCXCVII

COPYRIGHT, 1897, BY
HERBERT S. STONE & CO.

Across the Salt Seas.

CHAPTER I.

Dreams he of cutting foreign throats, of breaches, ambuscadoes, Spanish blades; of healths five fathoms deep.—Shakespeare.

"Phew!" said the captain of *La Mouche Noire*, as he came up to me where I paced the deck by the after bittacle. "Phew! It is a devil in its death agonies. What has the man seen and known? Fore Gad! he makes me shudder!"

Then he spat to leeward—because he was a sailor; also, because he was a sailor, he squinted into the compass box, then took off his leather cap and wiped the warm drops from his forehead with the back of his hand.

"Death agonies!" I said. "So! it is coming to that. From what? Drinking, old age, or——"

"Both, and more. Yet, when I shipped him at Rotterdam, who would have thought it! Old and reverend-looking, eh, Mr. Crespin? White haired — silvery. I deemed him some kind of a minister — yet, now, hearken to him!"

And as he spoke he went to the hatchway, bent his head and shoulders over it, and beckoned me to come and do likewise; which gesture I obeyed.

Then I heard the old man's voice coming forth from the cabin where they had got him, the door of it being open for sake of air, because, in this tossing sea, the ports and scuttles were shut fast — heard him screaming, muttering, chuckling and laughing; calling of healths and toasts; dying hard!

"The balustrades!" he screamed. "Look to them. See! Three men, their hands stretched out, peering down into the hall; fingers touching. God!" — he whispered this, yet still we heard — "how can dead men stand thus together, gazing over, glancing into dark corners, eyes rolling? See how yellow the mustee's eyes are! But still, all dead! Dead! Dead! Dead! Yet there they stand, waiting for us to come in from the garden. Ha! quick — the passado — one — two — in — out — good! through his midriff. Ha! Ha! Ha!" and he laughed hideously, then went on: "The worms will have a full meal. Or "—after a pause, and hissing this: "Was he dead before? Hast run a dead man through?"

"Like this all day long," the captain muttered in my ear, "from the dawn. And now the sun is setting; see how its gleams light up the hills inland. God's mercy! I hope he dies ere long. I want not his howlings through my ship all night. Mr. Crespin," and he laid his hand on my arm, "will you go down to him, to service me? You are a gentleman. Maybe can soothe him. He is one, too. Will you?"

I shrugged my shoulders and hitched my sea cloak tighter round me; then I said:

"To do you a service—yes. Yet I like not the job. Still, I will go," and I put my hand on the brass rail to descend. Then, as I did so, we heard him again— a-singing of a song this time. But what a song! And to come from the dying lips of that old, white-haired, reverend-looking man! A song about drinkings and carousings, of girls' eyes and lips and other charms, which he should have thought no more of for the past two score years! and killing of men, and thievings and plunder. Then another change, orders bellowed loudly, as though he trod on deck—commands given to run out guns—cutlasses to be ready. Shrieks, whooping and huzzas!

"He has followed the sea some time in his life," the captain whispered as I descended the companion steps. "One can tell that. And I thought him a minister!"

I nodded, looking up at him as I went below, then reached the open door of the cabin where the man lay.

He was stretched out upon his berth, the bedding all dishevelled and tossed beneath him, with, over it, his long white hair, like spun flax, streaming. His coat alone of all his garments was off, so that one saw the massive gold buttons to his satin waistcoat; could observe, too, the richness of his cravat, the fineness of his shirt. His breeches, also, were of satin, black like his waistcoat—the stuff of the very best; his buckles to them gold; his shoes fastened with silver latchets. That he was old other things than his hair showed—the white face was drawn and pinched with age, the body lean and attenuated, the fingers almost fleshless, the backs of his hands naught but sinews and shrivelled skin. And they were strange hands, too, for one to gaze upon; white as the driven snow, yet with a thickness at the tips of the fingers, and with ill-shapen, coarse-looking nails, all seeming to say that, once, in some far off time, those hands had done hard, rough work.

By the side of the berth, upon one of the drawers beneath it, pulled out to make a seat, there squatted a mulatto—his servant whom he had brought on board with him when we took him into the ship in the Maas. A mulatto, whose brown, muddy looking eyeballs rolled about in terror, as I thought, of his master's coming death, and made me wonder if they had given his distempered brain that idea of the "mustee's yellow eyes," about which he had been lately shrieking. Yet, somehow, I guessed that 'twas not so.

"How is 't with him now?" I asked the blackamoor, seeing that his master lay quiet for the time being; "is this like to be the end?"

"Maybe, maybe not," the creature said in reply. "I have seen him as far gone before—yet he is alive."

"How old is he?"

"I know not. He says he has seventy years."

"I should say more," I answered. Then I asked: "Who is he?"

"The captain has his name."

"That tells nothing. When he is dead he will be committed to the sea unless we reach Cadiz first. And he has goods," casting my eye on two chests, one above the other, standing by the cabin bulkhead. "They will have to be consigned somewhere. Where is he going?"

"To Cadiz."

"Ha! Well, so am I. He is English?"

"Yes—he is English."

'Twas evident to me that this black creature meant to tell nothing of his master's affairs—for which there was no need to blame him—and I desisted from my enquiries. For, in truth, this old man's affairs were not my concern. If he died he would be tossed into the sea, and that would be the end of him. And if he did not die— why still 'twas no affair of mine. I was but a passenger, as he was.

Therefore, I turned me on my heel to quit the cabin, when, to my astonishment, nay, almost my awestruck wonderment, I heard the old man speaking behind me as calmly as though there were no delirium in his brain nor any fever whatever. Perhaps, after all, I thought, 'twas but the French brandy and the Geneva he had been drinking freely of since we took him on board, and which he brought with him in case bottles, that had given him his delirium, and that the effect was gone now with his last shriekings and ravings.

But that which caused most my wonderment was that he was speaking in the French — which I had very well myself.

"What brings you here, Grandmont?" he asked, his eyes, of a cold grey, fixed on me.

"So," thinks I, "you are not out of your fever yet, to call me by a name I never heard of." But aloud, I answered:

"I have taken passage the same as you yourself. And we travel the same road — toward Cadiz."

Meanwhile the negro was a-hushing of him — or trying to — saying: "Master, master, you wander. Grandmont is not here. This gentleman is not he"; and angered me, too, even as he said it, by a scornful kind of laugh he gave, as though to signify: "Not anything like him, indeed."

But the old man took no heed of him — pushing him aside with a strength in the white coarse hand which you would not have looked to see in one so spent — and leaned a little over the side of the berth, and went on:

"Have you heard of it, yet, Grandmont?"

Not knowing what to do, nor what answer to make, I shook my head — whereon he continued: "Nineteen years of age now, if a day. Four years old then — two hundred crowns' worth of good wood burnt, — all burnt — a mort o' money! But we have enough left and to serve, 'tis true. A plenty o' money — though 'tis soaked in blood. Nineteen years old, and like to be a devil — like yourself, Grandmont!"

"Grandmont is dead," the negro muttered. "Drownded dead, master. You know."

This set the old man off on another tack, doubtless the words "drownded dead" recalling something to him; and once more he began his chantings — going back to the English — which were awful to hear, and brought to my mind the idea of a corpse a-singing:

>"Fishes' teeth have eat his eyes;
>His limbs by fishes torn."

Then broke off and said: "Where am I? Give me to drink."

This the negro did, taking from out the drawer he sat upon a bottle of Hungary water, and pouring a draught into a glass, which, when the old man had tasted, set him off shrieking curses.

"Brandy!" he cried, "Brandy! French brandy, not this filth. Brandy, dog!" and as he spoke he raised his hand and clutched at the other's wool. "If I had you in Martinique——" then, exhausted, fell back on his pillows and said no more, forgetting all about the desired drink.

Now, that night, when I sat with the captain after supper, he being a man who had roamed the world far and wide, and had not always been, as he was now, a carrier of goods only, with sometimes a passenger or two, from London to the ports of France, Spain and Portugal, we talked upon that hoary-headed old sinner lying below in the after-starboard cabin; I telling him all that had passed in my hearing.

And he, smoking his great pipe, listened attentively, nodding his head every now and again, and muttering much to himself; then said:

"Spoke about two hundred crowns' worth of good wood being burnt, eh? That would be at Campeachy. Humph! So! So! We have heard about that. Told the black, too, that he wished he had him in Martinique, did he? Also knew Grandmont. Ha! 'tis very plain." Then he rose and went to his desk, lifted up the sloping lid and took out a book and read from it—I observing very well that it was his log.

"See," he said, pushing it over to me, "that's what he calls himself now. Yet 'tis no more his name than 'tis mine—or yours."

Glancing my eye down the column, I came to my own name—after a list of things by way of cargo which he had on board, such as a hundred and seventy barrels of potash, sixty bales of hemp, a hundred bales of Russia leather, twenty barrels of salted meat, twenty-eight barrels of whale oil and many other things. Came to my own name, Mervyn Crespin, officer, passenger to Cadiz. Then to the old man's:

"John Carstairs, gentleman, with servant, passenger to Cadiz."

"No more his name than 't is mine—or yours," the captain repeated.

"What then?" I asked.

"It might be—anything," and again he mused. "Martinique," he went on, "Campeachy. A friend of Grandmont's. Let me reflect. It might be John Cuddiford. He was a friend of Grandmont's. It might be Alderly. But no, he was killed, I think, by Captain Nicholas Crafez of Brentford. Dampier, now—nay, this one is too old; also William Dampier sailed from the Downs three years ago. I do believe 't is Cuddiford."

"And who then is Grandmont, Captain? And this Cuddiford—or Carstairs?"

"Ho!" said he, "'t is all a history, and had you been sailor, or worn that sword by your side for King William as you wear it now for Queen Anne, you would have known Grandmont's name. Of a surety you would have done so, had you been sailor."

"Who are they, then?"

"Well now, see. Grandmont was — for he is dead, drowned coming back from the Indies in '96 — that's six years agone — with a hundred and eighty men, all devils like himself."

As he said this I started, for his words were much the same as those which the old man had used an hour or so before when he had spoken of something — a child, as I guessed — that had been four years old, and was now nineteen and "like to be a devil" like himself — Grandmont. It seemed certain, therefore, that this man, Grandmont, was a friend in life, and that now there was roaming about somewhere a son who had all the instincts of its father, and who was known to Carstairs, or Cuddiford.

This made the story of interest to me, and caused me to listen earnestly to the captain's words.

"Coming back from the Indies, and not so very long, either, after the French king had made him a lieutenant of his navy — perhaps because he was a villain. He does that now and again. 'T is his way. Look at Bart, to wit. There's a sweet vagabond for you. Has plagued us honest merchants and carriers more than all Tourville's navy. Yet, now, he is an officer, too."

"But Grandmont, Captain! Grandmont."

"Ah! Grandmont. Well, he was a filibuster—privateer—buccaneer—pirate—what you will! Burnt up all their woods at Campeachy—the old man spake true—because the commandant wouldn't pay the ransom he and his crew demanded; also because the commandant said that when he had slaughtered them all, if he did so, he would never find out where their buried wealth was. Then he took a Pink one day with four hundred thousand francs' worth of goods and money on board, and slew every soul in the ship. Tied dead and living together, back to back, and flung them into the sea. Oh! He was a devil," he concluded. "A wicked villain! My word! If only some of our ships of war could have caught him."

"Yet he is dead?"

"Dead enough, the Lord be praised."

"And if this is a friend of his—this Cuddiford, or Carstairs—he must needs be a villain, too."

"Needs be! Nay, is, for a surety.

And, Mr. Crespin," he said, speaking slowly, "you have heard his shrieks and singings—could you doubt what he has been?"

"Doubt? No," I answered. "Who could? Yet, I wonder who were the dead men looking down the stairs, as they came in from the garden."

"Who? Only a few of their victims. If he and Grandmont worked together they could not count 'em. Well, one is dead; good luck when the other goes too. And, when he does, what a meeting they will have there!" and he pointed downward.

CHAPTER II.

SECRET SERVICE.

It seemed not, however, as though this meeting were very likely to take place yet, since by the time we were off Cape St. Vincent—which was at early dawn of the second morning following the old man's delirium—that person seemed to have become very much restored. 'T is true he was still very weak, and kept his berth; but otherwise seemed well enough. Also all his fever and wanderings were gone, and as he now lay in his bunk reading of many papers which the negro handed to him from the open uppermost chest, he might, indeed, have passed for that same reverend minister which the captain had, at the beginning, imagined him to be.

Both of us—the captain because he was the captain, and I because I was the only other passenger—had been in and out to see him now and again and to ask him how he did. Yet, I fear, 't was not charity nor pity that induced either of us to these Christian tasks. For the skipper was prompted by, I think, but one desire, namely, to get the man ashore alive out of his ship, and, thereby, to have done with him. He liked not pirates, he said, "neither when met on the high seas, nor when retired from business"; while as for myself, well! the man fascinated me. He seemed to be, indeed, so scheming an old villain, and to have such a strange past behind him, that I could not help but be attracted.

Now in these visits which I had paid him at intervals, he had told me that he was on his way to Cadiz, where he had much business to attend to; sometimes, he said, in purchasing goods that the galleons brought in from the Indies, sometimes in sending out other goods, and so forth. Also he said —which was true enough, as I knew very well—the galleons were now due; it was for this reason he was on his way to the south of Spain.

"So," said the captain, when I repeated this, "the devil can speak truth sure enough when he needs. To wit, it is the truth that the galleons are on their way home. What else has he said to you, Mr. Crespin?"

"He has asked me what my business may be."

"And you have told him?"

"Nay. I tell no one that," I replied, "It

is of some consequence, and I talk not of it."

Yet here, and with a view to making clear this narrative which I am setting down, 'tis necessary that I should state who and what I am, and also the reason why I, Mervyn Crespin, am on my road to Cadiz on board a coasting vessel, *La Mouche Noire*—once a French ship of merchandise, now an English one. She was taken from that nation by some of our own vessels of war, sold by public auction, and bought by her present captain, who now is using her in his trade between England and Holland, and Holland and Spain—a risky trade, too, seeing that war has broken out again, that England and Austria are fighting the French and Spanish, and that the sea swarms with privateers; yet, because of the risk, a profitable trade, too, for those who can make their journeys uncaught by the enemy.

However, to myself.

I am, let me say, therefore, an officer of the Cuirassiers, or Fourth Horse, which, a short time before the late King William's death, has been serving in the Netherlands under the partial command of Ginkell, Earl of Athlone. The rank I hold is that of lieutenant—aspiring naturally to far greater things—and already I have had the honor of taking part in several sieges, amongst others Kaiserswerth, with which the war commenced, as well as in many skirmishes. Now, 'twas at this place, where my Lord the Earl of Athlone commanded, that I had the extreme good fortune, as I shall ever deem it, of being wounded, and thereby brought under his Lordship's notice. As for the wound, 'twas nothing, one of M. Bouffler's lancers having run me through the fleshy part of my arm, and it was soon healed; but the earl happened to see the occurrence, as also the manner in which I cut the man down a second later, and from that moment he took notice of me — sent for me to his quarters when the siege was over, spoke with commendation of my riding and my sword play, and asked me of my family, he being one who, although a Dutchman who came only into England with his late master, knew much of our gentry and noble homes.

"Of the Crespins of Kent, eh?" he said. "The Crespins — a fair, good family. I knew Sir Nicholas, who fell at the Boyne. What was he to you?"

"My uncle, sir. The late king gave me my guidon in the Cuirassiers because of his service."

"Good! He could do no less. Your

uncle was a solid man — trustworthy. If he said he would do a thing, he did it — or died. 'Twas thus in Ireland. You remember?"

"I remember, sir. He said he would take prisoner Tyrconnel with his own hands, and would have done it had not a bullet found his brain."

"I do believe he would. Are you as trustworthy as he?"

"Try me," and I looked him straight in the face.

"Maybe I will. A little later," and even as he spoke fell a-musing, while he drank some schnapps, which was his native drink, and on which, they say, these Hollanders are weaned — from a little glass. Then soon spake again:

"What languages have you? Any besides your own?"

"I have the French. Also some Spanish. My grandmother was of Spanish descent, and dwelt with us in Kent. She taught me."

"Humph!" And again he mused, then again went on, though now — doubtless to see if my French was any good, and to try me — he spoke in that tongue.

"Could you pass for a Frenchman,

think you, amongst those who are not French, say in Spain itself?"

"Yes, amongst those who are not French, I am sure I could. Even amongst those who are French, if I gave out that I was, say, a Dutchman speaking with an accent," and I laughed, for I could not help it. The earl had a bottle nose and eyes like a lobster's, and made a queer grimace when I said this boldly. Then he, too, laughed.

"So I've an accent, eh, when I speak French? You mean that?"

"I mean, sir, that however well one speaks a language not their own, there is some accent that betrays them to those whose native tongue they are speaking. A Dutchman, a Swiss, most Englishmen and many Germans can all speak French, and 't would pass outside France for French. But a native of Touraine, or a Parisian, or any subject of King Louis could not be deceived."

"True. Yet you or I could pass, say in Spain, for Frenchmen."

"I am sure."

"Humph! Well, we will see. And, perhaps, I will, as you say, try you. Only if I do, 't will be a risky service for you. A lieutenant-colonelcy or a gibbet. A regiment or a bullet. How would you like that?"

"I risk the bullet every moment that the Cuirassiers are in action, and there is no lieutenant-colonelcy in the other scale if I escape. I prefer the 'risky service,' when there is one. As for the gibbet; well, one death is the same as another, pretty much, and the gibbet will do as well as any other, so long as 't is not at Tyburn—which would be discreditable."

"You are a man of metal!" the Dutchman exclaimed, "and I like you, although you don't approve of my accent. You will do. I want a man of action, not a courtier——"

"I meant no rudeness," I interposed.

"Nor offered any. Tush! man, we Dutch are not courtiers, either. But we are staunch. And I will give you a chance of being so. Come here again to-morrow night. You shall have a throw for that colonelcy—or that gibbet."

"My Lord, I am most grateful to you."

"Good day. Come to-morrow night. Now I must sleep." And he began to divest himself of his wig and clothes, upon which I bowed and withdrew.

Be sure I was there the next night at the same time, exchanging my guard with Bertram Saxby, who, alas! was killed shortly afterward at Ruremonde. The day I had passed in sleeping much, for I had a suspicion that it was like enough Ginkell would send me on the service he had spoken of that very night; might, indeed, order me to take horse within the next hour, and I was desirous of starting fresh—of beginning well. He was a rough creature, this Dutch general—or English, rather, now!—and would be as apt as not to give me my instructions as I entered the room, and bid me be miles away ere midnight struck. Therefore I went prepared. Also my horse was ready in its stall.

He was not alone when I did enter his quarters. Instead, he was seated at a table covered with papers and charts, on the other side of which there sat another gentleman, a man of about fifty, of strikingly handsome features; a man who, in his day, I guessed, must have played havoc with women's hearts—might, indeed, I should think, have done so now had he been inclined that way. Those soft, rounded features, and those eyes, themselves soft and liquid—I saw them clearly when he lifted them to scan my face!—would, I guessed, make him irresistible to the fair sex.

He spoke first after I had saluted the

Earl of Athlone—and I observed that, intuitively, he also returned my salute by a bend of his head, so that I felt sure he was used to receive such courtesies wherever he might be and in whatever company—then he said to the Dutchman, in a voice that, though somewhat high, was as musical as a chime of bells.

"This is the gentleman, Ginkell?"

"This is the gentleman. A lieutenant of the Fourth Horse."

"Sir," said the other, "be seated," and he pointed with a beautifully white hand to a chair by the table. "I desire some little conversation with you. I am the Earl of Marlborough." And as he mentioned his name he put out that white hand again and offered it to me, I taking it with all imaginable respect. He was at this time the most conspicuous subject of any sovereign in the world; his name was known from one end of Europe to the other. Also it was the most feared, although he had not yet put the crowning point to his glory nor risen to the highest rank for which he was destined. But he was very near his zenith now—his greatness almost at its height—and, I have often thought since, there was something within him at this time which told him it was close at hand. For he had an imperturbable calmness, an unfailing quiet graciousness, as I witnessed afterward on many occasions, which alone could be possessed by one who felt sure of himself. In every word he spoke, in his every action, he proclaimed that he was certain of, and master of, his destiny!

"My Lord Athlone tells me," he continued, when I was seated, the soft voice flowing musically, "that you have the fitting aspirations of a soldier—desire a regiment, and are willing to earn one."

I bowed and muttered that to succeed in my career was my one desire, and that if I could win success I would spare no effort. Then he went on:

"You speak French. That is good. Also Spanish. That, too, is good. Likewise, I hear, can disguise your identity as an Englishman if necessary. That is well, also. Mr.——" and he took up a piece of paper lying before him, on which I supposed my name was written, "Mr. Crespin, I—we—are going to employ you on secret service. Are you willing to undertake it?"

"I am willing, my Lord, to do anything that may advance my career. Anything that may become a soldier."

"That is as it should be. The light in which to regard matters—anything that may become a soldier. That before all. Well, to be short, we are going to send you to Cadiz."

"To Cadiz, my Lord!" I said, unable to repress some slight feeling of astonishment.

"Yes. To Cadiz, where you will not find another English soldier. Still that will, perhaps, not matter very much, since we do not desire you when there to appear as a soldier yourself. You are granted leave from your regiment indefinitely while on this mission, and, at the first at least, you will be a private gentleman. Also, when at Cadiz, you will please to be anything but an *English* gentleman."

"Or a Dutch one," put in the other earl with a guttural laugh. "Therefore, assume not the Dutch accent."

Evidently my Lord Marlborough did not know of the joke underlying this remark, since he went on:

"As a Frenchman you will have the best chance. Or, perhaps, as a Swiss merchant. But that we leave to you. What you have to do is to get to Cadiz, and, when there, to pass as some one, neither English nor Dutch, who is engaged in ordinary mercantile pursuits. Then when the fleet comes in——"

"The fleet, my Lord!"

"Yes. The English fleet. I should tell you—I must make myself clear. A large fleet under Admirals Rooke and Hopson, as well as some Dutch admirals, are about to besiege Cadiz. They will shortly sail from Portsmouth, as we have advices, and it is almost a certainty that they will succeed in gaining possession of the island, which is Cadiz. That will be of immense service to us, since, while we are fighting King Louis in the north, the Duke of Ormond, who goes out in that fleet in command of between thirteen and fourteen thousand men, will be able to attack the Duke of Anjou, or, as he now calls himself, King Philip V of Spain, in the south. But that is not all. We are not sending you there to add one more strong right arm to His Grace's forces—we could utilize that here, Mr. Crespin," and he bowed courteously, "but because we wish you to convey a message to him and the admirals."

I, too, bowed again, and expressed by my manner that I was listening most attentively, while the earl continued:

"The message is this: We have received information from a sure source that the galleons now on their way back to Spain from the Indies have altered their plan of arrival because they, in their turn, have been informed in some way, by some spy or traitor, that this expedition will sail from England. Therefore they will not go near Cadiz. But the spot to which they will proceed is Vigo, in the north. Now," and he rose as he spoke, and stood in front of the empty fireplace, "your business will be to convey this intelligence to Sir George Rooke and those under him, and I need not tell you that you are like enough to encounter dangers in so conveying it. Are you prepared to undertake them?"

CHAPTER III.

I FIND A SHIP.

"You see," the Earl of Marlborough continued, while Ginkell and I stood on either side of him, "that neither your risks nor your difficulties will be light. To begin with, you must pass as a Frenchman, or, at least, not an Englishman, for Cadiz, like all Spanish ports and towns, will not permit of any being there. Therefore, your only way to get into it is to be no Englishman. Now, how, Mr. Crespin, would you suggest reaching the place and obtaining entry? It is far away."

I thought a moment on this; then I said:

"But Portugal, my lord, is not closed to us. That country has not yet thrown in its lot with either France or Austria."

"That is true. And the southern frontier of Portugal is very near to Spain—to Cadiz. You mean that?"

"Yes. I could proceed to the frontier of Portugal, could perhaps get by sea to Tavira—then, as a Frenchman, cross into Spain, and so to Cadiz."

He pondered a little on this, then said: "Yes, the idea is feasible. Only, how to go to Tavira?" and he bent over a chart lying on the table, and regarded it fixedly as he spoke. "How to do that?" running his finger down the coast line of Portugal as he spoke, and then up again as far north as the Netherlands, stopping at Rotterdam.

"All traffic is closed," he muttered, "between Spain and Holland now, otherwise there would be countless vessels passing between Rotterdam and Cadiz which would doubtless put you ashore on the Portuguese coast. But now — now — there will scarce be any."

Ginkell had been called away by one of his aides-de-camp as his lordship bent over the chart and mused upon it, or, doubtless, his astute Dutch mind might have suggested some way out of the difficulty that stared us in the face; but even as we pondered over the sheet an idea occurred to me.

"My Lord," I said, "may I suggest this: That I should make my way to Rotterdam to begin with — by some chance there may be a ship going south — through some part of the bay at least. But even if it is not so — if all traffic is stopped — why then I could at least get to England, might arrive there before the fleet sails for Cadiz."

"Nay," his Lordship interrupted; "you would be too late. They may have sailed by now."

"I know not what further to propose, my Lord."

"We must risk it," he said, promptly. "Chance your finding some vessel by which you can proceed, even if only part of the way. The hope is a poor one, yet 'tis worth catching at. King Louis wants the money those galleons are bringing; his coffers are empty; he hardly knows where to turn for the wherewithal to pay his and his grandson's men; we want it, too, if we can get it. Above all, we want to prevent the wealth falling into the hands of Spain, which now means France. Mr. Crespin, on an almost forlorn chance you must start for Rotterdam."

"When shall I go, my Lord? To-night? At once?"

"You are ready?"

"I am ready."

"Good! You have the successful soldier's qualities. Yes, you must go at once—at once."

* * * * * * * * *

"That night I was on the road for Rotterdam, which is fifty leagues and more to the northeast of Kaiserswerth, so that I had a fair good ride before me ere I reached what might prove to be the true outset of my journey.

I did not go alone, however, since at this time I rode in the company of my Lord Marlborough, who was returning to the Hague, to which he had come in March as Ambassador Extraordinary and Plenipotentiary to the States General, as well as Captain General of all Her Majesty's forces, both at home and abroad. Also, his Lordship had been chosen to command the whole of the allied forces combined against the King of France and his grandson, the King of Spain, whom we regarded only as the Duke of Anjou; and he was now making all preparations for that great campaign, which was already opened, and was soon to be pushed on with extreme vigour and with such success that at last the power and might of Louis were quite crushed and broken. This concerns not me, however, at present.

Nor did my long ride in company with his Lordship and a brilliant staff offer any great incident. Suffice it, therefore, if I say that on the evening of the second day from my setting out, and fifty hours after I had quitted Kaiserswerth, I rode into Rotterdam, and, finding a bed for the night at the "Indian Coffee House," put up there.

This I did not do, however, without some difficulty, since, at this time, Rotterdam was full of all kinds of people from almost every part of Europe, excepting always France and Spain, against the natives of which countries very strict laws for their expulsion had been passed since the declaration of war which was made conjointly by the Queen, the Emperor and the States General, against those two countries on the 4th of May of this year, 1702.

But of other peoples the town was, as I say, full. In the river there lay coasting vessels, deep sea vessels, merchant ships, indeed every kind of craft almost that goes out to sea, and belonging to England, to Holland, to Denmark and other lands. Also there were to be seen innumerable French vessels; but these were prizes which had been dragged in after being taken prisoners at sea, and would be disposed of shortly, as well as their goods and merchandise, by the Dyke-Grauf, or high bailiff. And of several of these ships, the captains and the seamen, as well as in many cases the passengers who were belated on their journeys, were all ashore helping to fill up the inns and taverns. Also troops were quartered about everywhere, these being not only the

Dutch, or natives, who were preparing to go forward to the Hague and thence to wheresoever my Lord Marlborough should direct, but also many of our own, brought over by our great ships of war to Helvetsluys, and, themselves, on their way to serve under his command.

The room, therefore, which I got at the Indian Coffee House, was none of the best, yet, since I was a soldier, I made shift with it very well, and in other ways the place was convenient enough for my purpose. It may be, indeed, that I could scarce have selected a better house at which to stop, seeing that the "ordinary" below was the one most patronized by the merchant captains who flocked in daily for their dinner, and for the conversation and smoking and drinking which succeeded that meal.

And now, so that I shall arrive as soon as may be at the description of all that befell me, and was the outcome of the mission which the Earl of Marlborough confided to me, let me set down at once that it was not long before I, by great good chance, stumbled on that very opportunity which I desired, and which was so necessary to the accomplishment of what his Lordship wanted.

This is how it happened:

After the ordinary, at which I myself

took a seat every day at one o'clock, the drinking and the smoking and the conversation began, as I have said, and none, however strange they might be at first to the customers of the place, could be there long without the making of acquaintances; for all the talk ran on the one subject in which all were interested and absorbed, namely, the now declared war and the fighting which had been done, and was also to do; on the stoppage to trade and ruin to business that must occur, and such like. And I can tell you that many an honest sea captain and many a burly Rotterdam burgher drank down his schnapps or his potato brandy or seidel of brown beer, as his taste might be, while heaving also of sighs, or muttering pious exclamations or terrible curses—also as his taste might direct—at the threatened ruin, and also at the fear which gripped his heart, that soon he would not have the wherewithal left for even these gratifications, humble as they were.

"Curse the war!" said one, to whom I had spoken more than once. He was, indeed, my captain of *La Mouche Noire*, in whose ship you have already found me; "it means desolation for me and mine if it lasts, hunger and shoelessness for my wife and little ones at home in Shadwell. Above all I curse the ambition of the French king, who has plunged all Europe into it; placed all honest men 'twixt hawk and buzzard, as to fortune. Curse him, I say."

"Ay, gurse him!" chimed in a fat Friesslander captain, who sat at his elbow. "Gurse him, I say, too. I was now choost maging for Chava; should have peen out of the riffer mit meine vreight if his vleet had not gorne along mit that von gursed Chean Part in it, ven I had to put pack. And here I am mit all mein goots——"

"And here am I, mit all mein!" broke in my captain, a-laughing in spite of himself, "yet—yet I know not if I will not make a push for it. I think ever of the home at Shadwell and the little ones. I could not abide to think also of their calling for bread, and of their mother having none to give them. Yet 'twill come to that ere long. And the war may last for years."

"Where were you for?" I asked him, using indeed what had become a set phrase in my mouth since I had consorted with all these sailors. For by enquiring of each one with whom I conversed what his destination had been, or would be if he had courage to risk the high seas outside, I thought that at last I might strike upon one whose way was mine. For all were not afraid to go forth; indeed there was scarcely a dark night in which one or two did not get down the river and sneak out into the open, thinking that, when there, there was a chance of escaping the French ships of war and privateers and of reaching their destination, while by remaining here there was no chance of earning a brass farthing. And I had known of several ships going out since I had been in Rotterdam, only they were of no use to me. One was bound for Archangel, another one for the Indies, a third for our colony of Massachusetts.

"I," said my captain, whose name I knew afterward to be Tandy. "I? Oh, I was freighted for Cadiz. But of course, that can never be now. Yet if I could but get away I might do much with my goods. At Lisbon they would sell well, or even farther south. Though, 't is true, there 's not much money below that till one comes to Spain."

Though I had thought the time must come when I should hear one of these sailors say that Cadiz was, or had been, his road (I knew that if it did not come soon 't would be no good for me, and I might as well make my way back to my regiment), yet now, when I did so hear it, I almost started with joyful surprise. Yet even in so hearing, what had I gained? The captain had but said that at one time, before the declaration of hostilities, he had been ready to sail for Cadiz. He did not say that at this moment — almost three months later — he was still likely to go. Instead, had said it could never be now.

But — for it meant much to me! — my heart beat a little faster as I asked, leaning across the beer and spirit-slopped table to him:

"Do you ever on your cruises carry passengers?"

He gave me a quick glance. I read it to mean that he would be glad to know what my object could be in such a question, put seriously and in a somewhat low tone, as though not intended for other people's ears. Then he said:

"Oh! ay! I carry 'em, when I can get 'em, if they will pay fairly. But who do you think would trust themselves aboard a coaster now, in such times as these, unless she was under convoy of one of the queen's ships in company with others?"

"I would," I replied, leaning even a little more forward than before, and speaking in a still lower tone. "I would, to get

ACROSS THE SALT SEAS. 39

as near to Cadiz as might be. And pay well, too."

He did not speak for a moment; instead, he glanced his eye over me as though scanning my outward gear for proof of what I had said as to paying handsomely. Yet I did not fear this scrutiny, for I was well enough appareled at all points, having when I left Venloo put off my uniform and donned a very fair riding suit of blue cloth, well faced and passemented; also my plain sword and wig were of the best, such as befitted a gentleman.

"Pay well," he said, when he had concluded this inspection, "pay well. Humph! That might induce me, since I am like enough to lose my goods ere I sight Cape Finisterre. Pay well. You mean it? Well, now see! What would you pay? Come. A fancy price? To be put as near Cadiz as can be compassed. And no questions asked," and he winked at me so that I wondered what he took me for. Later on I found that he supposed me to be one of the many spies in the pay of France, who, because they had both the English and French tongue, were continually passing from one part of the continent of Europe to another.

"As to the questions," I replied, "you might ask as many as you desired. They would not be answered. As to the pay, what will you take?"

He thought a moment, and again his eye ranged over my habiliments; then he said, sharply:

"A hundred guineas. Fifty down, on the nail, the rest at the end of the journey. You to take all risks. That is, I mean, even though we get no further than the mouth of the Scheldt — which is like enough. Say, will you give it?"

"'T is, indeed, a fancy price, yet, on conditions, yes," I answered promptly.

"Those conditions being —— "

"That you weigh within twenty-four hours; that if we are chased you run, or even fight, till there is no further hope, and that if we escape capture you approach to the nearest point to Cadiz possible. Tavira to be that point."

He got up and went out of the door into the street, and I saw him looking up into the heavens at the clouds passing beneath the sun. Then he came back and resumed his seat, after which he said:

"If the wind keeps as 'tis now I will weigh ere twenty-four hours are past. The conditions to be as you say. And the fifty guineas to be in my hands ere we up anchor. They," he added, half to himself, "will be something for the home even though I lose my ship."

And this being settled and all arrangements concluded, we went off in his boat, which was lying at the steps of the Boömjes, to see the ship. Then, I having selected my cabin out of two which he had unoccupied, returned to the coffee house to write my Lord Marlborough word of what I had done, to dispose of my horse — which I was sorry enough to do, since it was a good, faithful beast that had carried me well; yet there was no use in keeping it, I not knowing if I should ever see Rotterdam again — to make one or two other preparations, and to write to my mother at home.

As to the hundred guineas — great as the demand was, I felt justified in paying it, since, if I succeeded in my task, the result might be splendid for England. Also I had a sufficiency of money with me, the earl having ordered two hundred guineas to be given me out of the regimental chest (which was pretty full, seeing that at Venloo eight great chests of French gold were taken possession of by us on gaining the town), and had also given me bills for three hundred more guineas, signed by his own hand, which the money changers would be only too glad to pay anywhere. And, besides this, I had some money of my own, and should have more from the sale of the horse.

There remains one thing, however, to mention, which I have almost forgot to set down, namely, that at the Indian Coffee House I had given my name accurately, his Lordship, who was perfectly acquainted with France—indeed, he had once served her under Turenne, in his capacity of colonel of the "English Regiment" sent out by King Charles the Second—having said that Crespin was as much a French as an English name. And although no questions had as yet been asked as to what my business was, there being, indeed, none who had any right or title to so ask, I had resolved that, if necessary, I would do this: namely, here in Holland I would be English, since, at the time, and we being allies, it was almost one and the same thing; and that in Spain I would be French, which was also at the period one and the same thing. And if we were to be captured by any of Louis' privateers or ships of war also I should be French, in that case possibly a Canadian, to account for any strangeness in my accent.

And with this all fixed in my mind I made my preparations for going to sea in *La Mouche Noire.*

CHAPTER IV.

AN ESCAPE.

The wind shifted never a point, so that, ere sunset the next day, we were well down the river and nearing the mouth, while already ahead of us we could see the waves of the North Sea tumbling about. Also, we could see something else, that we could have done very well without, namely, the topmasts of a great frigate lying about three miles off the coast, or rather cruising about and keeping off and on, the vessel being doubtless one of Louis' warships, bent on intercepting anything that came out of the river.

"Yet," said Captain Tandy, as he stood on the poop and regarded her through his perspective glass, "she will not catch us. Let but the night fall, and out we go, while, thanks to the Frenchman who built our little barky, we can keep so well in that she can never come anear us."

"She can come near enough, though, to send a round shot or two into our side," I hazarded, "if she sees our lights."

"She won't see our lights," the captain made answer, and again he indulged in that habit which seemed a common one with him—he winked at me; a steady, solemn kind of a wink, that, properly understood, conveyed a good deal. And, having favoured me with it, he gave orders that the light sail under which we had come down the river should be taken in, and, this done, we lay off the little isle of Rosenberg, which here breaks the Maas in two, until nightfall.

And now it was that Tandy gave me a piece of information which, at first, I received with anything but satisfaction; the information, to wit, that at the last moment almost—at eleven o'clock in the morning, and before I had come on board—he had been fortunate enough to get another passenger, this passenger being the man Carstairs—or Cuddiford, as he came to consider him—whom, at the opening of this narrative, you have seen in a delirium.

"I could not refuse the chance, Mr. Crespin," he said, for he knew my name by now. "Things are too ill with me, owing to this accursed fresh war, for me to throw guineas away. So when his blackamoor accosted me at the 'Indian' and said that he heard I was going a voyage south—God,

He knows how these things leak out, since I had never spoke a word of my intention, though some of the men, or the ship's chandler, of whom I bought last night, may have done so—and would I take his master and him? I was impelled to do it! There are the wife and the children at home."

"And have you got another hundred guineas from him?" I asked.

"Ay, for him and the black. But they will not trouble you. The old gentleman —who seems to be something like a minister— tells me he is not well, and will not quit his cabin. The negro will berth near him; they will not interfere with you."

"Do they know there is another passenger aboard?"

"I have not spoken to the old man; maybe, however, some of the sailors may have told the servant. Yet none know your name; but I—it can be kept secret an you wish." And again he winked at me, thinking, of course, as he had done before, that my business was of a ticklish nature, as indeed it was, though not quite that which he supposed. Nay, he felt very sure it must be so, since otherwise he would have got no hundred guineas out of me for such a passage.

"I do not wish it known," I said. "It

must be kept secret. Also my country. There must be no talking."

"Never fear," he replied. "I know nothing. And I do not converse with the men, most of whom are Hollanders, since I had to pick them up in a hurry. As for the old man, you need not see him; and, if you do, you can keep your own counsel, I take it."

I answered that I could very well do that; after which the captain left me — for now the night had come upon us, dark and dense, except for the stars, and we were about to run out into the open. But even as I watched the men making sail, and felt the little ship running through the water beneath me — I could soon hear her fore foot gliding through it with a sharp ripple that resembled the slitting of silk — I wished that those other passengers had not come aboard, that I could have made the cruise alone.

Yet we were aboard, he and I, and there was no help for it; it must be endured. But still I could not help wondering what any old minister should want to be making such a journey as this for; especially wondered, also, why he should be attended by a black servant; and why, again, it should be worth his while to pay a hundred guineas for the passage.

But you know now as well as I do that this man was no minister, but rather, if Tandy's surmises were right, some villainous old filibuster who had lived through evil days and known evil spirits; my meditations are, therefore, of no great import. Rather let me get on to what was the outcome of my journey.

When we were at sea we showed no light at all; no! not at foremast, main or mizzen; so that I very well understood now why the captain had winked as he said that the Frenchman, if she was that, would not see us; and especially I understood it when, on going below, I found that the cabin windows were fastened with dead lights so that no ray could steal out from them. Also, the hatches were over the companions so that neither could any light ascend from below. In truth, as we slapped along under the stiff northeast breeze that blew off the Holland coast, we seemed more like some dark flying spectre of the night than a ship, and I could not but wonder to myself what we should be taken for if seen by any passer-by. Yet, had I only known, there were at that time hundreds of ships passing about in all these waters in the same manner —French ships avoiding the English war vessels, and English and Dutch avoiding the French war vessels; and—which, perhaps, it was full as well I did not know—sometimes two of them came into contact with each other, after which neither was ever more heard of. Only, in different ports there were weeping women and children left, who—sometimes for years!—prayed for the day to come when the wanderers might return, they never knowing that, instead of those poor toilers of the sea having been made prisoners (as they hoped) who would at last be exchanged, they were lying at the bottom of the sea.

"'T is a gay minister, at any rate," I said to Captain Tandy when I returned to the deck—for all was so stuffy down below, owing to the closing up of every ingress for the fresh air, that I could not remain there—"and he at least seems not to mind the heat."

"What is he doing, then?" the captain asked.

"He is singing a little," I replied, "and through the half open door of his cabin one may hear the clinking of bottle against glass. A merry heart."

"The fiend seize his mirth! I hope he will not make too much turmoil, nor set the ship afire. If he does we shall be seen easy enough."

I hoped so, too, and as each night the old man waxed more noisy and the clink of the bottle was heard continuously — until at last his drinking culminated as I have written — the fear which the captain had expressed took great hold of me, so that I could scarce sleep at all. Yet those fears were not realized, the Lord be praised! or I should scarcely be penning this narrative now.

The first night passed and, as 't was summer, the dawn soon came, by which time we were running a little more out to sea, though — since to our regret we saw that the frigate was on our beam instead of being left far behind, as we had hoped would be the case — we now sailed under false colours. Therefore at our peak there flew at this time the lilies of France, and not our own English flag. Yet 't was necessary — imperative, indeed — that such should be the case if we would escape capture. And even those despised lilies might not save us from that. If the frigate, which we knew by this time to be a ship of war, since her sides were pierced three tiers deep for cannon, and on her deck we could observe soldiers, suspected for a moment those colours to be false she would slap a shot at us; the first, perhaps, across our bows only, but the second into our waist, or, if that missed, then the third, which would doubtless do our office for us.

At present, however, she did nothing, only held on steadily on her course, which nevertheless was ominous enough, for this action told plainly that she had seen us leave the river, or she would have remained luffing about there still. And, also, she must have known we were not French, for what French ship would have been allowed to come out of the Maas as we had come?

She did nothing, I have said; yet was not that sleuth-like following of hers something? Did it not expound the thoughts of her captain as plainly as though he had uttered them in so many words? Did it not tell that he was in doubt as to who and what we were; that he set off against the suspicious fact of our having quitted the river, which bristled with the enemies of France, the other facts, namely, that our ship was built French fashion, that maybe he could read her French name on her stern, and that she flew the French flag?

Yet what puzzled us more than aught else was, how had the frigate known that we had so got out? The night had been dark and black, and we showed no lights.

ACROSS THE SALT SEAS. 51

Still she knew it.

The day drew on and, with it, the sea abated a little, so that the tumbling waves, which had often obscured the frigate from us for some time, and, doubtless, us from it, became smoother, and Tandy, who had never taken his eye off the great ship, turned round and gave now an order to the men to hoist more sail. Also another to the man at the wheel to run in a point.

Then he came to where I was standing, and said:

"She draws a little nearer; I fear they will bring us to. Ha! as I thought." And even as he spoke there came a puff from the frigate's side; a moment later the report of a gun; another minute, and, hopping along the waves went a big round shot, some fifty yards ahead of us.

"What will you do?" I asked the captain. "The next will not be so far ahead."

"Run for it," he said. "They may not hit us—short of a broadside—and if I can get in another mile or so they cannot follow. Starboard, you below," he called out again to the man at the wheel, and once more bellowed his orders to the men aloft.

This brought the ship's head straight for where the land was—we could see it plain enough with the naked eye, lying flat and low, ten miles away—also it brought our stern to the frigate, so that we presented nothing but that to them—a breadth of no more than between twenty and twenty-five feet.

"'T will take good shooting to hit us this way," said Tandy very coolly. "Yet, see, they mean to attempt it."

That this was so, one could perceive in a moment; then came three puffs, one after the other, from their upper tier; then the three reports; then the balls hurtling along on either side of us, one just grazing our larboard yard-arm—we saw the splinters fly like feathers!—the others close enough, but doing no harm.

"Shoot, and be damned to you," muttered Tandy; "another ten minutes more, and you can come no further. Look," and he pointed ahead of us to where I saw, a mile off, the water crisping and foaming over a shoal bank, "'tis eight miles outside Blankenberg, and is called 'The Devil's Bolster.' And we can get inside it, and they cannot." Then again he bellowed fresh orders, which even I, a landsman, understood well enough, or, at least, their purport. They were to enable us to get round and inside the reef, and so place it between us and the frigate.

They saw our move as soon as it was made, however, whereupon the firing from their gun-ports grew hotter, the balls rattling about us now in a manner that made me fear the ship must be struck ere long; nay, she was struck once, a round shot catching her on her starboard quarter and tearing off her sheathing in a long strip. Yet, at present, that was all the harm she had got, excepting that her mizzen shroud was cut in half.

But now we were ahead of the reef and about half a mile off it; ten minutes later we were inside it, and, the frigate being able to advance no nearer because of her great draught, we were safe. They might shoot, as the captain said, and be damned to them; but shoot as much as they chose, they were not very like to hit us, since we were out of range. We were well in sight of each other, however, the reef lying like a low barricade betwixt us, and I could not but laugh at the contempt which the sturdy Dutch sailors we had on board testified for the discomfited Frenchmen. There were three of them at work on the fo'castle head at the time the frigate left off her firing, and no sooner did she do so and begin to back her sails to leave us in peace—though doubtless she meant lying off in wait for us when we should creep out—than these great Hollanders formed themselves into a sort of dance figure, and commenced capering and skipping about, with derisive gestures made at the great ship. And as we could see them regarding us through their glasses, by using our own, we knew very well that they saw these gestures of contempt. Tandy, however, soon put a stop to these, for, said he, "They may lie out there a week waiting for us, and if then they catch us, they will not forget. And 't will go all the harder with us for our scorn. Peace, fools, desist." Whereon the men left off their gibes.

"Lie out there a week," thinks I to myself. "Fore Gad! I trust that may not be so. For if they do, and one delay follows another, heaven knows when I shall see Cadiz. Too late, anyway, to send the fleet after the galleons, who will, I fear, be in and unloaded long before the admiral can get up to Vigo."

Yet, as luck would have it, the frigate was not to lie there very long—not even so long as an hour. For, see, now, how Providence did intervene to help me on my way, and to remove at least that one obstacle to my going forward on my journey.

Scarce had those lusty Dutch sailors

been ordered off the head by Tandy than, as I was turning away from laughing at them, my attention was called back by a shout from the same quarter, and on looking round, I saw two of them spring up the ladder again to the very spot they had left, and begin pointing eagerly away beyond the frigate. And following their glances and pointing, this is what I saw:

Two other great ships looming large on the seascape, rising rapidly above the water, carrying all their canvas, coming on at a mighty rate. Two great ships sailing very free but near together, which in a few moments spread apart, so that they put me in mind of some huge bird opening of its wings—I know not why, yet so it was!—and then came on at some distance from each other, their vast black hulls rising every moment, and soon the foam becoming visible beneath their bows as their fore feet flung it asunder.

"Down with that rag," shouted Tandy, squinting up at the lilies on our peak, and hardly shifting his perspective glass to do so. "Down with it, and up with our own. My word! The Frenchman will get a full meal now. Look at their royal masts and the flag of England flying on them."

I did look, and, after a hasty glance, at

something else—the French frigate, our late pursuer!

Be very sure that she had seen those two avengers coming up in that fair breeze—also that she was making frantic efforts to escape. But her sails were all laid aback as I have said, also, she was off the wind. The glasses showed the confusion that prevailed on board her. And she had drifted so near the shoal that her danger was great. Unless she boldly ran out to meet those two queen's ships she would be on it ere long, and that was what she dared not do.

For now from the others we saw the puff of smoke, like white balls of wool, come forth; we saw the spits of flame; saw the Frenchman's mainmast go down five minutes later, and hang over the side nearest us like some wounded creature all entangled in a net. And still she neared the shoal, and still the white balls puffed out till they made a long fleecy line, through which the red flames darted; borne on the air we heard shouts and curses; amidst the roaring of the English cannon firing on the helpless, stricken thing, we heard another sound, a grinding, crashing sound, and we knew she was on the bank. Then saw above, at her mizzen, the French flag pulled down upon the cap, and heard through their trumpets their loud calls for assistance from the conquerors.

"Humph! Humph!" said Tandy. "Old Lewis," for so he spoke of him, "has got one ship the less—that's all. Loose the foresheet, there, my lads; stand by the mainsail halyards. Good. That's it; all together!"

And away once more we went.

CHAPTER V.

THE ENGLISH SHIPS OF WAR.

After that we met with no further trouble or interference, not even, so far as we knew, being passed by anything of more importance than a few small carrying craft similar to ourselves, who bore away from us on sighting with as much rapidity as we were prepared to bear away from them, since in those days, and for long after, no ship passing another at sea but dreaded it as though it was the Evil One himself; dreaded that the cabin windows, with their clean dimity cloths run across them, might be, in truth, nothing but masked gun ports with the nozzles of the cannon close up against the other side of those running curtains; dreaded, also, that, behind the bales of goods piled up in the waist, might be lurking scores of men, armed to the teeth, and ready for boarding!

Also, as though to favour us — or me, who needed to get to the end of my journey as soon as might be — the wind blew fresh and strong abaft us from the north, so that by the evening of the fifth day from leaving Rotterdam we were drawing well to our journey's end, and were, in fact, rounding Cape St. Vincent, keeping in so near the coast that we could not only see the cruel rocks that jut out here like the teeth of some sea monster, but also the old monks sitting sunning themselves in front of their monastery above the cliffs.

And now it was at that time, and when we were getting very near to Tavira — which must be our journey's end, unless the English fleet, of which Lord Marlborough had spoken, was already into Cadiz, and masters of the place — that the old man who called himself Carstairs was taken with his delirium, of which I have written already.

But, as also I have told, he was better the next day, by noon of which we were well into the Bay of Lagos, and running for Cape Santa Maria; and 'twas then that he told me that story of his having much business to attend to at Cadiz, and that, the galleons being now due there, he was on his way to meet them.

That I laughed in my sleeve at the fool's errand on which this old man had come — this old man, who had been a thieving buccaneer, if his wanderings and Tandy's suspicions were true — you may well believe. Also, I could not help but fall a-wondering how he would feel if, on nearing Tavira, we learnt that our countrymen were masters of Cadiz. For then he would do no business with his precious galleons, even should my Lord Marlborough be wrong — which, however, from the sure way in which he had spoken, I did not think was very like to be the case — and even if they had made for Cadiz, since they would at once be seized upon.

It was, however, of extreme misfortune that just at this time when all was so well for my chances, and when we were nearing our destination, the weather should have seen fit to undergo a sudden change, and that not only did the wind shift, but all the summer clearness of the back end of this fair August month should have departed. Indeed, so strange a change came over the elements that we knew not what to make of it. Up to now the heat had been great, so great, indeed, that I — who could neither endure the stuffiness of my cabin below nor the continual going and coming of the negro in the gangway which separated his master's cabin from mine, nor the stench of some drugs the old man was continually taking—had been sleeping on the deck. But now the tempest became so violent that I was forced to retreat back to the cabin, to bear the closeness as best I might, to hear the flappings of the black creature's great feet on the wooden floor at all hours of the night, and, sometimes again, the yowlings of the old man for drink.

For with the shifting of the wind to the east, or rather east by south, a terrible storm had come upon us; across the sea it howled and tore, buffetting our ship sorely and causing such destruction that it seemed like enough each moment that we should go to the bottom, and this in spite of every precaution being taken, even to striking our topmasts. Also we lay over so much to our starboard, and for so long, that again and again it seemed as though we should never right, while as we thus lay, the sea poured into us from port and scuttle. But what was worse for me—or would be worse if we lived through the tempest we were now in the midst of—we were being blown not only off our course, but back again the very way we had come, and out into the western ocean, so that to all else there had to be added the waste of most precious time. Time that, in my case, was golden!

Meanwhile Carstairs, who during the

whole of our passage from Rotterdam had carefully kept his cabin — not even coming on deck during the time we were chased by the French frigate nor, later, when the two ships of war had battered and driven her on to the shoal bank — now saw fit to appear on deck and to take a keen interest in all that was going on around.

"A brave storm," he said, shrieking the words in my ear — I having at last struggled up again to get air — amidst the howling of the wind and the fall of the sea upon our deck, each wave sounding as though a mountain had fallen, "a brave storm! Ha! I have seen a-many, yet I know not if ever one worse than this."

"What think you of our chances?" I bawled back at him, while I noticed that his eye was brighter and clearer than I had seen it before, and that in his face there was some colour.

"We shall do very well," he answered, "having borne up till now. That fellow knows his work," and he nodded toward where Tandy was engaged in getting the foreyard swayed up. "We shall do."

His words were indeed prophetic, for not an hour after he had uttered them the wind shifted once more, coming now full from the south, which was, however, of all

ACROSS THE SALT SEAS. 63

directions the very one we would not have had it in; and with the change the sea went down rapidly, so that in still another hour the waves, instead of breaking over our decks, only slapped heavily against the ship's sides, while the vessel itself wallowed terribly amongst them. Yet so far we were saved from worse.

But now to this there succeeded still another change — the sea began to smoke as though it were afire; from it there rose a cold steaming vapour, and soon we could not see twenty yards ahead of us, nor was the man at the wheel able to see beyond the forehatch. So that now we could not move in any direction for fear of what might be near, and were forced to burn lights and fire guns at intervals to give notice of our whereabouts in chance of passers by.

Again, however — this time late at night — the elements changed, the mist and fog thinned somewhat and rose some feet from the surface of the now almost tranquil sea; it was at last possible to look ahead somewhat, though not possible to proceed, even if the light wind which blew beneath the fog would have taken us the way we desired to go.

And still the mist cleared so that we could see a mile—or two miles—around, and then we observed a sight that none of us could comprehend, not even Cuddiford, who whispered once to himself, though I heard him plain enough, "What in the name of the devil does it mean? What? What?"

Afar off, on our starboard quarter, we saw in the darkness of the night—there was no moon—innumerable lights dotting the sea; long lines of light such as tiers of ports will emit from ships, also lights higher up, as though on mastheads and yards—numbers of them, some scores each in their cluster.

Cuddiford's voice sounded in my ear. Cuddiford's finger was laid on my arm.

"You understand?" he asked.

"No."

"'T is some great fleet."

I started—hardly could I repress that start or prevent myself from exclaiming: "The English fleet for Cadiz!"

Yet even as I did so, the water rippled on the bows where we were standing. It sounded as if those ripples blended with the man's voice and made a chuckling laugh.

"A large fleet," he said slowly, "leaving Spain and making for the open."

Then a moment later he was gone from my side.

Leaving Spain and making for the open!

What then did that mean? "Leaving Spain and making for the open!" I repeated to myself again. Was that true? And to assure myself I leant further forward into the night—as though half a yard nearer to those passing lights would assist my sight! —and peered at those countless clusters.

Was it the English fleet that was leaving Spain? Whether that was or not—whether 't was in truth the English fleet or not—it *was* leaving Spain; I could understand that. We in our ship were almost stationary; that body was rapidly passing out to sea.

What did it mean? Perhaps that the English had done their work—destroyed Cadiz. I did not know if such were possible, but thought it might be so. Perhaps that the galleons had been on their way in, after all, and had been warned of those who were there before them, and so had turned tail and fled.

Yet I feared—became maddened and distraught almost at the very idea—that, having done their work, my countrymen should have left the place, gone out to the open on, perhaps, their way back to England. Became maddened because, if such were the case, there was no opportunity left me of advising them about the galleons. While, on the other hand, if that passing fleet was in truth the galleons, then were they saved, since never would they come near the coast of Spain again while British ships remained there. Rather would they keep the open for months, rather put back again to the Indies than run themselves into the lion's jaws.

Truly I was sore distressed in pondering over all this; truly my chance of promotion seemed very far off now. Yet I had one consolation: I had done my best; it was not my fault.

That night, to make things more unpleasant than they already were—and to me it seemed that nothing more was wanting to aid my melancholy!—Cuddiford began his drinkings and carousals again, shutting off himself with the negro in his cabin, from whence shortly issued the sounds of glasses clinking, of snatches of songs—in which the black joined—of halloaing and of toasts and other things. Ribald bawlings, too, of a song of which I could catch only a few words now and again, but which seemed to be about a mouse which had escaped from a trap and also from a great fierce cat ready to pounce on it. Then, once more, clappings and clinkings of glasses together—an intolerable noise, be sure!—and presently, with an oath, confusion drank to England.

"So," thinks I, "my gentleman, that is how you feel, is it? Confusion to England! Who and what are you, then, in the devil's name? Spy of France or Spain, besides being retired filibuster, or what? Confusion to England, eh?"

And even as I thought this and heard his evil toast, I determined to hear more. Whereon I slipped quietly off my bunk, got out into the gangway and listened across it to his cabin opposite, feeling very sure as I did so that both he and his black imagined I was up on deck.

Then I heard him say, going on, evidently, with a phrase he had begun:

"Wherefore, I tell you, my lily, my white pearl, that those accursed seamen and soldiers—this Rooke, who chased me once so that I lost all my goods in my flight—are tricked, hoodwinked, *embustera; flanqués comme une centaine d'escargots!* Done for—and so is this white-livered Englishman over there in t'other cabin—who I do believe is an English spy. Ho! that we had him in Maracaibo or Guayaquil. Hein! Hey! my snowball?"

"Hoop! Hoop!" grunted the brute, his companion. "Hoop! Maracaibo! Hoop!

But, but, John "—"John," thinks I, "and to his master!"—"don't speak so loud. Perhaps they hear you."

"Let them hear and be damned to them. What care I?" Yet still he lowered his voice, though not so low but what I made out his words:

"Fitted out a fleet, did they, to intercept the galleons? Oh! the beautiful galleons! Oh! the sweet and lovely galleons! Oh, my beautiful *Neustra Senora de Mercedes*. You remember how she sits on the water like a swan, Cæsar? And the beautiful *Santa Susanna!* What ships! what lading! Oh! I heard it all in London. I know. Thought they would catch 'em in Cadiz, did they? Ha! Very well. Now, see, my lily white. They have been too quick; got in too soon — and — and what's the end on 't? Those are the galleons going out—back again to the sea—and the English fleet can stop in Cadiz till the forts sink 'em or they rot. Give me some more drink. 'Of all the girls that there can be, the Indy girl's the girl for me,'" and he fell a-singing.

"If he is right, my Lord Marlborough has been deceived," I whispered to myself. "Yet which knows the most? Still this old ruffian must be right. Who else could

ACROSS THE SALT SEAS. 69

be putting to sea but the galleons?" and I went back once more to my cabin to ponder over matters.

But now — all in a moment — there arose such an infernal hubbub from that other cabin that one might have thought all the fiends from below had been suddenly let loose; howls from the negro, so that I thought the other must be killing of him in his drunken frenzy; peals of laughter from the old man, bangings and kickings of bulkheads and the crash of a falling glass. And, in the middle of it all, down ran Tandy from the deck above, with, as I thought, a more concerned look upon his face than even such an uproar as this called for. Then he made at once for the cabin where those two were; yet, even as he advanced swiftly, he paused to ask me if I had heard him speak a passing picaroon a quarter of an hour back.

"Not I," I replied. "Who could hear aught above in such a din as this below? What did they tell you?"

"Bad! Bad news. But first to quell these brutes," and he ran on as he spoke, and kicked against the fast-closed cabin door.

"Bad news!" I repeated to myself, even as I followed him. "Bad news. My God!

the old villain is right and the galleons have escaped. Farewell, my hopes of promotion; I may as well get back to the regiment by the first chance that comes."

But now I had to listen to Tandy setting his other passenger to his facings, which he did without more ado, since, the cabin door not being opened quick enough, he applied his brawny shoulder to it and soon forced it to slide back in its frame, the lock being torn out by his exertion. Then after a few oaths and curses, which need not be set down here, he roared as follows:

"See here, you drunken, disreputable old vagabond, out you go from this ship tomorrow morning, either ashore in Lagos bay or in the first Guarda Costa or sailing smack that comes anigh us carrying the Portygee colours. And as for you, you black, shambling brute," turning to the negro and seizing him by the wool, whereby he dragged him into the gangway, after which he administered to him a rousing kick, "get you forward amongst the men, and, by God! if you come back aft again I'll shoot you like a dog."

"My friend," said old Carstairs, speaking now with as much sobriety and dignity as though he had been drinking water all these days; "my good friend, you forget.

I have paid my passage to Cadiz, and to Cadiz I will go, or the nearest touching point. Also, there are laws——"

"There are," roared Tandy, "and 't will not suit you to come within a hundred leagues of any of them. To-morrow you go ashore."

"I have business with the in-coming galleons," said Carstairs, leering at him. "Those galleons going out now will come in again, you know. Soon!" and still he leered.

"Galleons, you fool!" replied the captain. "Those are the English warships. Your precious galleons may be at the bottom of the ocean. Very like are by now."

And then that old man's face was a sight to see, as, suddenly, it blanched a deathly white.

"The English warships," he murmured. "The English warships," and then fell back gasping to his berth, muttering: "Out here! Out here!"

"Is this true?" I asked him a moment later, as we went along forward together. "Is it true?"

"Ay, partly," he replied. " Partly. They are the English ships of war, but, my lad, I have had news which I did not tell him. They are in retreat. Have failed.

Cadiz is not taken, and they are on their way back to England."

"My God!" I exclaimed. And I know that as I so spoke I, too, was white to the lips.

"On their way back to England!" I repeated.

"Ay—that's it," he said.

CHAPTER VI.

GALLEONS ABOUT!

"What's to do now? That's the question," said Tandy, an hour later, as he and I sat in his little cabin abaft the mainmast, while, to hearten ourselves up, we sipped together a bottle of Florence wine which he had on board, and he sucked at his great pipe. "What now? No use for me to think of Cadiz, though what a chance I would have had if our countrymen had only made themselves masters of it! And for you, Mr. Crespin? For you? I suppose, in truth, you knew of this—had some affair of commerce, too, which brought you this way, on the idea that they would be sure to capture the place."

"Ay, I had some idea," I answered, moodily, thinking it mattered very little what I said now, short of the still great secret that the galleons were going into Vigo, and never did mean coming into these more southern regions. This secret I still kept, I say—and for one reason. It was this, namely, that I thought it very likely that, even though the fleet under Rooke might be driven back from Cadiz, they yet had a chance of encountering the galleons making their way up to Vigo, and, if they did so, I felt very sure that they would attack those vessels, even in their own hour of defeat. Therefore, I said nothing about the real destination of the Spanish treasure ships, though I knew well enough that all hope was gone of my being the fortunate individual to put my countrymen on their track.

Also, I remembered that that hoary-headed old ruffian, Carstairs, had spoken of two at least of those galleons as being of importance to him — and you may be sure that I had no intention whatever of enlightening him as to anything I knew.

"What did the Portuguese picaroon tell you?" I asked of Tandy, now; "what information give? And — are they sure of their news?"

"Oh, very sure," he answered. "No doubt about that. No doubt whatever that we have failed in the attack on Cadiz — abandoned the siege, gone home. They were too many for us there, and — 'tis not often that it happens, God be praised! — we are beaten."

"But why so sure? And are they—these Portuguese—to be trusted?"

"What use to tell lies? They *are* Portuguese, and would have welcomed a victory."

I shrugged my shoulders at this—then asked again what the strength of their information was.

To which the captain made reply:

"They came in, it seems, early in the month, and called on the governor to declare for Austria against France, to which he returned reply that it was not his custom to desert his king, as many of the English were in the habit of doing, he understood; whereon—the Duke of Ormond being vexed by such an answer, which, it seems, did reflect on him—the siege of Port St. Mary's commenced, the place being taken by our people and being found to be full of wealth——"

"Taken and full of wealth!" I exclaimed. "Yet you say we are defeated!"

"Listen," went on Tandy, "that was as nothing; for now the German Prince of Hesse-Darmstadt, who had come too, in the interests of his Austrian master, interfered, begging of Rooke and that other not to destroy the town, since it would injure their cause forever with the Spaniards, and—and—well, the Portygee captain of that picaroon I spoke says that they were only too willing to fall in with his desires and retire without making further attempt."

"And these are English seamen and soldiers!" I muttered furiously. "My God! To turn tail thus!"

"Ormond agreed not with these views, it seems," Tandy went on, "but he could not outweigh the admirals—and that is all I know, except that he will perhaps impeach 'em when they get back to England. And, anyway, they are gone."

"And with them," I thought to myself, "go all my hopes. The galleons will get in safe enough; there is nothing for it but to make back for Holland and tell the earl that I have failed. No more than that," and my bitterness was great within me at these reflections, you may be sure.

Tandy, I doubted not, observed these feelings which possessed me, for a minute later he said—while I observed that in a kindly way he filled up my glass for me, as I sat brooding with my head upon my hands by the side of the cuddy table:

"I see this touches you nearly, Mr. Crespin, and am grieved. Yet what will you do now? Since you have missed your chance—I know not what—will you return with me? If so you are very welcome, and—and," he spoke this with a delicacy I should scarce have looked for, "and there will be no—no—passage money needed. *La Mouche Noire* is at your service to Rotterdam, or, for the matter of that, to Deal or London, or where you will. I shall but stay to go in to Lagos for wood and water, and, perhaps, sell some of my goods, if fortune serves so far, and then— why then, 't is back again to Holland or England to see what may be done. I have the passage moneys of you and that old ribald aft. For me things might be worse, thank God!"

At first I knew not what answer to make to this kindly offer—for kindly it was, since there was according to our compact no earthly reason whatsoever why he should convey me back again, except as a passenger paying highly for the service. In truth, I was so sick and hipped at the vanishing of this, my great opportunity, that I had recked nothing of what happened now. All I knew was that I had failed; that I had missed, although through no fault of mine own, a glorious chance. Therefore I said gloomily:

"Do what you will—I care not. I must

get me back to Holland somehow, and may as well take passage there with you as go other ways. In truth there is none that I know of. Yet, kind as your offer is to convey me free of charge, it must not be. I cannot let you be at a loss, and I have a sufficiency of money."

"Oh! as for that, 'tis nothing. However, we will talk on this later. Now let's see for getting into Lagos—there is nothing else to be done. 'Specially as I must have wood and water."

Then he went away to study his chart and compass, while I sought my bed again, and, all being perfect silence at this time in Carstairs' cabin—doubtless he was quite drunk by now!—I managed to get some sleep, though 'twas uneasy at the best.

In the morning when I again went on deck I saw that we were in full sail, as I had guessed us to be from the motion of the ship while dressing myself below; also, a look at the compass box told me we were running due north—for Lagos. And, if aught could have cheered the heart of a drooping man, it should have been the surroundings of this fair, bright morning. It was, I remember well, September 22—the glistening sea, looking like a great blue diamond sparkling beneath the bright sun, the white spume flung up forward over our bows, the equally white sheets above. Also, near us, to add to the beauty of the morn, the sea was dotted with a-many small craft, billander rigged, their sails a bright scarlet—and these, Tandy told me, were Portuguese fishing boats out catching the tunny, which abounds hereabout. While, away on our starboard beam, were—I started as I looked at them—what were they?

Three great vessels near together, their huge white sails bellied out to the breeze, sailing very free; the foam tossed from their stems, almost contemptuously, it seemed, so proudly did they dash it away from them; vessels full rigged, and tightly, too; vessels along the sides of which there ran tier upon tier of gun-ports; vessels also, from each of whose mastheads there flew a flag—the flag of England!

"What does it mean?" I asked Tandy, who strolled along the poop toward me, his face having on it a broad grin, while his eye drooped into that wink he used so. "What does it mean? They are our own ships of war; surely they are not chasing us!"

"Never fear!" said he. "They are but consorts of ours just now. Oh! it's a brave talk we have been having together with the flags this morning. They are of the fleet—are Her Majesty's ships *Eagle*, *Stirling Castle* and *Pembroke*—and are doing exactly the same as ourselves, are going into Lagos for water. Also those transports behind," and he pointed away aft, where half a dozen of those vessels were following.

"The fleet," I gasped, "the fleet that has left Cadiz—the great fleet under Sir George Rooke—and going into Lagos!"

"Some of them—those you see now on our beam, and the transports coming up."

"And the others," I gasped again, overcome by this joyful news, "the others? What of them?"

"Oh! they will lie off till these go out with the fresh water casks. Then for England."

"Never," I said to myself. "Not yet, at least," and I turned my face away so that Tandy should not perceive the emotion which I felt sure must be depicted on it.

For think, only think, what this meant to England—to me!

It meant that I—the only man in the seas around Spain and Portugal who knew of where the galleons would be, or were by now—I who alone could tell them, tell this great fleet, which I had but lately missed, of the whereabouts of those galleons—had by God's providence come into communication with them again; meant that the instant we were in Lagos bay I could go aboard one of those great warships and divulge all—tell them to make for Vigo, tell them that it was in their power to deal so fierce a blow to Spain and France as should cripple them.

I could have danced and sung for very joy. I could have flung my arms around Tandy's sun-burned and hairy neck in ecstasy, have performed any act of craziness which men indulge in when a great happiness falls upon them; nay, would have done any deed of folly, but that I was restrained by the reflection of how all depended on me now, and of how — since I was the bearer of so great a piece of news from so great a man as the Earl of Marlborough — it behooved me to act with circumspection and decorum. Therefore I calmed myself, instead of indulging in any transports whatever. I recollect that I even forced myself to make some useless remark upon the beauty of the smiling morn; that I said also that I thought *La Mouche Noire* was making as good seaway as the great frigates themselves, then asked coldly and indifferently, with the same desire for disguise, when Tandy thought we might all be in the bay and at anchorage.

He glanced up at the sun—he had a big tortoise-shell watch in his pocket, but, sailor-like, never looked at it during the day, and when he had the sun for horloge—then leaned over the high gunwale of the ship and looked between his hands toward the north, and said:

"The old castle of Penhas is rising rapidly to view. 'T is now eight of the clock. By midday we shall have dropped anchor."

"And the frigates?" I asked, with a nod toward the queen's great ships, which still were on our beam, in the same position to us as before.

"About the same. Only they will go in first to make choice of their anchorage." Then he added: "But they will not stay long; no longer than to fill the casks. Perhaps a day, or till nightfall."

"'T will be long enough for me," I thought. "An hour would suffice to get on board one of them, ask to be taken off and sent to the admiral's ship to tell my tale. Long enough."

And now I went below again—with what different feelings from those which possessed me when I went on deck, you may well suppose—and began hastily to bestow my necessaries, such as they were, into the bag I had carried behind me on my horse from Venloo to Rotterdam: a change of linen, some brushes, a sleeping gown and a good cloak, carried either around me or the bag, if warm and dry weather, my powder flask and a little sack of bullets for my cavalry pistols — that was all. Also I counted my pieces, took out my shagreen bill case and saw that my Lord Marlborough's money drafts were safe, as well as my commission to the regiment, which must now serve as a passport and letter of presentation, and I was ready to go ashore at any moment, and to transfer myself to one of the ships if they would take me with them after I had told my news, as my Lord had said I was to demand they should do. Yet, little while enough as I had been a-doing of these things, 't was not so quickly finished but that there was time for an interruption; interruption from Mr. Carstairs, who, a moment or so after I had been in my cabin, tapped gently, almost furtively, it seemed to me, upon the door, and on my bidding him come in — I suspecting very well who it was — put his head through the opening he had made by pushing it back.

"Are we in danger?" he asked, while as he spoke, I could not but observe that he looked very badly this morning — perhaps from the renewals of his drinkings. His face was all puckered and drawn, and whiter, it seemed to me, than before; his eyes were hideously bloodshot—that must, I guessed, be the drink—while the white, coarse hand with which he grasped the panel shook, I observed.

"Danger!" I repeated coldly, as well as curtly, for, as you may be sure, I had come to thoroughly despise, as well as cordially to detest, this dissolute old man who, besides, had a black and fearful past behind him, if his feverish wanderings of mind were to be trusted. "Danger! From what?"

"There are war frigates by us," he whispered. "Do you not know?"

"Yes, I know. But you who have been, it seems, a sailor, should also know our own flag, I think."

"Our own flag! Our English flag!"

"Can you not see?"

"They are on the other side of the ship. I cannot see aught through my port."

"Look through mine, then," I answered, pointing to it, and he, with many courteous excuses for venturing to intrude—he was much changed now, I thought—went over to my window, and gazed at the queen's vessels.

"True," he said. "True. They are

English—our—ships. Where could they come from, do you suppose?"

"From the Cadiz fleet. And they are going into Lagos, as we are."

"And then—do you know where to, then—afterward—noble sir?"

"Then they will go north."

He drew a long breath at this—I guessed it to be a sigh of satisfaction at the thought that the English fleet should be going north, while the galleons, in which he had seemed to be so concerned, should either be going into, or gone into, Cadiz—as he supposed. Then he said:

"Oh, sir, this is, indeed, good news. For—for—I have business at Cadiz—very serious business, and—if they had remained here in the south they might have done much harm to honest traders, might they not? Do you not think so?"

"They may do harm elsewhere," I answered, again curtly. And my brevity caused him to look at me enquiringly.

"What harm? What can they do?"

"Oh! as for that," I said, unable to resist the temptation of repaying him somewhat for all the discomfort he had caused in the ship, and also because I so much despised him, "as for that, they might do much. They say there are some galleons about.

Supposing they should meet them. 'T is a great fleet; it could be fateful to a weaker one."

"Galleons! Galleons about!" he repeated—shrieked, almost. "Nay! Nay! Nay! The galleons are safe in Cadiz by now."

"Are they?" I said, shrugging of my shoulders.

"Are they not?" And now his face was death itself.

"We spoke a ship last night which did not say so," I answered. "No galleons have passed this way, gone in yet."

I almost regretted my words, seeing, a moment later, their effect on him. For that effect was great—I had nigh written terrible.

He staggered back from the port-hole by which he had been standing, gazing out at the *Pembroke* and her consorts, his face waxy now from the absence of blood; his lips a bluish purple, so that I could see the cracks in them; his coarse white hands twitching; and his eyes roving round my cabin lighted on my washing commode, on which stood the water ewer; then he seized it and the glass, poured out from one to the other—his hand shook so that the neck of the vessel clinked a tune upon the rim of the glass—and drank, yet not without some sort of a murmured apology for doing so—an apology that became almost a whine.

"Not passed this way—not gone in yet? My God! Where are they? And—and—with that fleet here—here—here—'twixt here and Cape St. Vincent! Where are they?"

"Probably coming in now—on their way," I made answer. "Or very near." Then next said, quietly: "You seem concerned about this?"

"Concerned!" he wailed. "Concerned! I have my fortune, my all—'t is not much, yet much to me—on board two of the galleons, and—and—ah!" and he clutched at his ruffled shirt front. "The English fleet is there—across their path! My God!"

CHAPTER VII.
LAGOS BAY.

Tandy had timed our arrival in the bay with great exactness, since, soon after midday, both the queen's ships and ourselves had dropped anchor within it, the former saluting, and being saluted in return, by some artillery from the crazy old castle that rose above the shore. And now from those three frigates away went pinnaces and jolly boats, as well as the great long boats and launches, all in a hurry to fetch off the water which they needed, while also I could see very well that from the *Pembroke* they were a-hoisting overboard their barge, into which got some of the land officers — as the sailors call the soldiers — and also a gentleman in black who was, I supposed, a chaplain.

And then I considered that it was time for me to be ashore, too, since I knew not how long 't would take for the ships of war to get in what they wanted, and to be off and away again; though Tandy told me I need be in no manner of hurry, since they had let down what he called their shore anchors, which they would not have done had they intended going away again in a moment, when they would have used instead their kedge, or pilot, anchors.

However, I was so impatient that I would not be stayed, and consequently begged the captain to let me have one of the shore boats, which had come out on our arrival and were now all around us, called alongside; and into this I jumped the instant it touched our ship. My few goods I left on board, to be brought on land when the captain himself came, which he intended to do later; nor did I make my farewells to him, since I felt pretty sure we should meet again shortly, while it was by no means certain that the admiral would take me with him, after I had delivered my news; but, instead, might order me to return at once to the earl with some reply message. Yet I hoped this would not be so, especially since his Lordship had bidden me see the thing out and then bring him, as fast as I could make my way back to the Netherlands, my account of what had been done.

As for that miserable old creature, Carstairs, I clean forgot all about him; nor even if I had remembered his existence, should I have troubled to pay him any adieux, for in truth, I never supposed that I should see him again in this world, and for certain, I had no desire to do so; yet as luck would have it — but there is no need to anticipate.

I jumped into the shore boat, I say, as soon as it came alongside *La Mouche Noire*, and was quickly rowed into the port, observing as I went that there was a considerable amount of craft moored in the bay, many of which had doubtless run in there during the storms of a night or two ago, while, also, there were some sheltering in it which would possibly have been lying in other harbors now—and those, Spanish ones—had it not been for the war and the consequent danger of attack from the English and Dutch navies in any other waters than those of Portugal, she being, as I have said, neutral at present, though leaning to our—the allies'—side. To wit, there were at this moment some German ships, also a Dane or two, a Dutchman and a Swedish bark here.

And now I stepped ashore on Portuguese ground, and found myself torn hither and thither by the most ragged and disorderly crowd of beggars one could imagine, some of them endeavouring to drag me off to a dirty inn at the waterside, in front of which there sat two priests a-drinking with some scaramouches, whom I took to be Algarvian soldiers, while others around me had, I did believe, serious intentions on my pockets had I not kept my hands tight in them. Also—which hearted me up to see—there were many of our English sailors about, dressed in their red kersey breeches with white tin buttons, and their grey jackets and Welsh kersey waistcoats, all of whom were bawling and halloaing to one another—making the confusion and noise worse confounded—and using fierce oaths in the greatest good humour. And then, while I stood there wondering how I should find those whom I sought for, I heard a voice behind me saying in cheery tones in my own tongue:

"Faith, Tom, 't is an Englishman, I tell you. No doubt about that. Look to his rig; observe also he can scarce speak a word more of the language of the country he is in than we can ourselves. Does not that proclaim him one of us? Except our beloved friends, the French, who are as ignorant of other tongues as we are, we are the worst. Let's board him—we are all in the same boat."

Now, knowing very well that these remarks could hardly be applied to any one but me, I turned round and found close to my elbow a fat, jolly-looking gentleman, all clad in black, and with a black scarf slung across him, and wearing a tie-wig, which had not been powdered for many a day—a gentleman with an extremely red face, much pitted with the small-pox. And by his side there stood four or five other gentlemen, who, 'twas easy to see at a glance, were of my own trade—their gold laced scarlet coats, the aiguillettes of one, the cockades in all their hats, showed that.

"Sir," said the one who had spoken, taking off his own black hat, which, like his wig, would have been the better for some attention, and bowing low. "I fear you overheard me. Yet I meant no offense. And, since I am very sure that you are of our country, there should be none. Sir, I am, if you will allow me to present myself, Mr. Beauvoir, chaplain of her Majesty's ship, *Pembroke*. These are my friends, officers serving under his Grace of Ormond, and of my Lord Shannon's grenadiers and Colonel Pierce's regiment"; whereon he again took off his hat to me, in which polite salutation he was followed by the others, while I returned the courtesy.

And now I knew that I had found what I wanted — knew that the road was open to

ACROSS THE SALT SEAS. 93

me to reach the admiral, to tell my tale. I had found those who could bring me into communication with the fleet; be very sure I should not lose sight of them now. But first I had to name myself, wherefore I said:

"Gentlemen, I am truly charmed to see you. Let me in turn present myself. My name is Mervyn Crespin, lieutenant in the Cuirassiers, or Fourth Horse, and it is by God's special grace that I have been so fortunate as to encounter you. For," and here I glanced round at the filthy crowd which environed us, and lowered my voice a little, "I am here on a special mission to your commander from my Lord Marlborough. Yet I thought I had failed when I heard you were off and away from Cadiz."

Now, when I mentioned the position which I held in the army all looked with increased interest at me, and again took off their hats, while when I went on to speak of my mission from the Earl of Marlborough there came almost a dazed look into some of their faces, as though 't was impossible for them to understand what the Captain-General of the Netherlands could have to say with the fleet that had been sent forth from England to Cadiz.

"A message to our commander," Mr,

Beauvoir said. "A message to our commander. By the Lord Harry, I am afraid 'tis even now a bootless quest, though. Our commander with all his fleet is on his way back to England — and pretty well dashed, too, through being obliged to draw off from Cadiz, I can tell you. I fear you will not see him this side of Spithead, even if you go with us, who are about to follow him."

That I was also "pretty well dashed" at this news needs no telling, since my feelings may be well enough conceived; yet I plucked up heart to say:

"I do think, if your captain but hears the news I bring, that he will endeavour to catch the fleet and turn it from its homeward course — ay, even though he sets sail again to-night without so much as a drop of fresh water in his casks. 'T is great news — news that may do much to cripple France."

"Is it private, sir?" the chaplain asked. "For the ears of the admirals alone?"

"Nay," said I; "by no means private from English ears; yet," I continued, with still another glance around, "not to be spoken openly. Is there no room we can adjourn to?"

"We have been trying ourselves for half an hour to find an inn," said one of the grenadiers, with a laugh, "which swarms not with vermin of all sorts. Yet, come, let us endeavour again. Even though there is naught for gentlemen to eat or drink, we may, at least, be alone and hear this news. Come, let us seek for some spot," and he elbowed his way through the waterside crowd which still stood gaping round us, and which, even when we all moved away, hung on our heels, staring at us as though we were some strange beings from another world. Also, perhaps, they thought to filch some scrap of lace or galloon from off our clothes.

"Away, vagabonds! What in heaven's name is Portuguese for 'away, vagabonds'?" muttered Mr. Beauvoir, making signs to the beggarly brood, who — perhaps because often our ships put in here for water, and they were accustomed to seeing the English — held out their dirty, claw-like hands, and shrieked: "Moaney! Moaney! Englase moaney!" "Away, I say, and leave us in peace!"

And gradually, seeing there was nothing more to be gotten after one or two of us had flung them a coin or so, they left us to our devices, so that we were able to stroll along the few miserable streets which the town possessed; able to observe, also, that there was no decent inn into which a person, who valued his future comfort and freedom from a month or so of itching, could put his foot in safety.

But now we reached a little open spot, or *plaza*, a place which had a melancholy, deserted look — there being several empty houses in this gloomy square — while, on another, we saw the arms of France stuck up, a shield with a blazing sun upon it, — the emblem of Louis! — and the lilies on it, also — and guessed it must be the consul's place of business. And here it seemed to me as if this was as fitting an opportunity as I should find for making the necessary disclosures — disclosures which, when these gentlemen had heard them, might induce them to hurry back to the *Pembroke*, bring me into communication with the captain, and lead him to put to sea, in the hopes of picking up the remainder, and chief part, of the English fleet, which was but twenty-four hours ahead of them.

"Gentlemen," I said, "here is a quiet spot" — as indeed it was, seeing that there was nothing alive in this mournful *plaza* but a few scraggy fowls pecking among the stones, and a lean dog or two sleeping in the sun. "Let me tell you my news."

Whereupon all of them halted and stood

round me, listening eagerly while I unfolded my story and gave them the intelligence that the galleons had gone into Vigo, escorted, as the earl had said while we rode toward Rotterdam, by a large French fleet.

" 'Fore George, Harry," said Mr. Beauvoir, turning toward the elder of the officers with him, a captain in Pierce's regiment, "but this is mighty fine news. Only —can it be true? I mean," he went on with a pleasant bow to me, "can it be possible that the Earl of Marlborough is not mistaken? For, if 't is true and we can only communicate with Sir George Rooke and get him back again, 't will be a fine thing; wipe out the scandal and hubbub that will arise over our retreat from Cadiz, go far to save Parliament enquiries and the Lord knows what—to say nothing of court martials. Humph?"

"Why should the earl be mistaken in this?" asked one of the others. At least he was right in judging they would not go into Cadiz."

"We must take you at once to Captain Hardy, of our ship," said the chaplain. "'T is for him to decide when he has heard your story. Come, let us get back to the pinnace—no time must be wasted."

"With the very greatest will in the

world," said I. "'T is for that I have travelled from Holland, and, pray God, I have not come too late. Success means much for me."

Then we turned to go, while the officers attacked me on all sides for an account of the siege of Kaiserswerth, of which they had not yet heard full accounts, and we were just leaving the square when there appeared at the door of the French consul's house a man who, no sooner did he observe us and our English appearance — which betrays us all over Europe, I have noticed, though I know not why — and also the brilliancy of the officers' dress, than he set to work bowing and grimacing like a monkey; also he began calling out salutations to us in French, and asking us how the English did now in the wars? and saying that, for himself, he very much regretted that France and England had got flying at one another's throats once more, since if they were not fools and would only keep united, as they had been in the days of him whom he called *le grand roi Charles Deux*, they might rule the world between them; which was true enough as regarded their united powers (if not the greatness of that late king of ours), as many other people more sensible than he have thought.

"'T is a merry heart," said Mr. Beauvoir, smiling on the fantastic creature as he gibbered and jumped about on his doorstep, while the others looked contemptuously at him, for we soldiers had but a poor opinion of the French, though always pleased to fight them; "a joyous blade! Let us return his civility"; whereupon he took off his hat, which courtesy we all imitated, and wished him "Good day" politely in his own language.

"Ha! you speak French, monsieur," the other said at this; "also you have the *bonne mine.* English gentlemens is always gentlemens. Ha! I ver' please see you." —he was himself now speaking half English and half French. "*Je vous salue.* Lagos ver' *triste.* I always glad see gentlemens. *Veuillez un verre de vin? C'est Français, vrai Français!* Ver' goot."

"'T is tempting," said the chaplain of the *Pembroke*, his face appearing to get more red than before at the invitation. "Well, we can do no harm in having a crack with him. Only—silence, remember," and he glanced at the officers. "Not a word of our doings —lately, now, or to come."

"Never fear," said the eldest. "We can play a better game than that would be," whereon the chaplain, after bowing gracefully to our would-be host, said in very fair French that, if he desired it, we would all drink a glass of wine with him—only he feared we were too many.

"Not a jot, not a jot," this strange creature cried, beckoning all of us into the house and forthwith leading us into a whitewashed room, in the middle of which was a table with, upon it, a great outre of wine, bound and supported by copper bands and flanked with a number of glasses, so that one might have thought he was ever offering entertainment to others. Then, with great dexterity, he filled the requisite number of glasses, and, after making us each touch his with ours, drank a toast.

"*A la fin de la guerre*," he said, after screaming, first, "*Attention, messieurs*," and rapping on the table with his glass to claim that attention, "*à l'amitié incassable de la France et de l'Angleterre. Vivent, vivent, vivent la France et l'Angleterre*," and down his throat went all the wine.

"A noble toast," said Mr. Beauvoir, with a gravity which—I know not why!—I did not think, somehow, was his natural attribute, "a noble toast. None—be he French or English—could refuse to pledge that," and, with a look at the others, away went his liquor, too, while my brother officers, with a queer look upon their faces, which seemed to express the thought that they scarce knew whether they ought to be carousing in this manner with the representative of an enemy, swallowed theirs.

"Ha! goot, ver' goot," our friend went on, "we will have some more." And in a twinkling he had replenished the glasses and got his own up to, or very near to, his lips. And catching a glance of Mr. Beauvoir's grey eye as he did this, I felt very sure that the reverend gentleman knew as well as I did, or suspected as well as I did, that these were by no means the first potations our friend had been indulging in this morning.

"Another toast," he cried now, "*sacré nom d'un chien!* we will drink more toasts. A la santé"—then paused, and muttered: "No, no. I cannot propose that. No. *Ce n'est pas juste.*"

"What is not just, monsieur?" asked Mr. Beauvoir, pausing with his own uplifted glass.

"Why, *figurez-vous*, I was going to commit an *impolitesse*—what you call a *rudesse*—rudeness—in your English tongue. To propose the continued prosperity of France —no! *vraiment il ne faut pas ça.* Because you are my guests—I love the English gentlemens always—and it is so certain—so very certain."

"The continued success of France is very certain, monsieur?" said one of the grenadiers, looking darkly at him. "You say that?"

"*Sans doute.* It cannot be otherwise. On sea and land we must triumph now—and then—then we shall have *la paix incassable.* Oh! yes, now that Chateaurenault is on the seas, we must perforce win there—win every—everything. And for the land, why ——."

"Chateaurenault is on the seas!" exclaimed the chaplain, looking very grave. "And how long has that been, monsieur?"

"Oh, some time, some time." Then he put his finger to his nose and said, looking extremely cunning in his half drunkenness. "And soon now he will be free to scour them, turn his attention to you and the Dutch—curse the Dutch always, they are *cochons!*—soon, ver' soon. Just as soon as the galleons are unloaded at Vigo—when we need protect them no more."

Swift as lightning all our eyes met as the good-natured sot said this in his boastfulness; then Mr. Beauvoir, speaking calmly again, said:

"So he is protecting them at Vigo, eh? 'T is not often they unload there."

"*Ah, non, non.* Not ver' often. But, you see, you had closed Cadiz against them, so, *naturellement,* they must go in somewhere."

"Naturally. No — not another drop of wine, I thank you."

CHAPTER VIII.

ON BOARD H. M. S. PEMBROKE.

A good snoring breeze was ripping us along parallel with the Portuguese coast a fortnight later, every rag of canvas being stretched aloft—foretop gallant royals, mizzentop gallant royals and royal staysails. For we had found the main body of the fleet at last, after eleven days' search for them, and we were on the road to Vigo.

Only, should we be too late when we got there? That was the question!

Let me take up my tale where I left off. Time enough to record our hopes and fears when that is told.

Our French friend, whose boastfulness had increased with every drop of Montrâchet he swallowed (and 'twas real good wine, vastly different, the chaplain, who boasted himself a fancier, said afterward, from the filthy concoctions to be obtained in that part of Portugal), had been unable to hold his tongue, having got upon the subject of the greatness of his beloved France, and the consequence was that every word he let fall served but to corroborate the Earl of Marlborough's information and my statement. Nay! by the time he allowed us to quit his house, which was not for half an hour after he had first divulged the neighborhood of Chateaurenault and the galleons, and during which period he drank even more fast and furious than before, he had given us still further information. For, indeed, it seemed that once this poor fool's tongue was unloosed, there were no bounds to his vaunts and glorifications, and had it not been that he was our host and, also, that every word he said was of the greatest value to us, I do, indeed, believe that one or other of the officers would have twisted his neck for him, so exasperating was his bragging.

"*Pauvre Angleterre! Pauvre Angleterre!*" he called out, after we had refused to drink any more, though he himself still kept on unceasingly; "Poor England. Ah, *mon Dieu*, what shall become of her! Beaten at Cadiz——"

"Retired from Cadiz, if you please, monsieur," one of Pierce's officers said sternly, "because the Dutch ships had run out of provisions, and because, also, the admiral and his Grace could not hope to win Spain to the cause of Austria by bombarding their towns and invading their country. Remember that, sir, if you please."

"*Oh, la la! C'est la même chose.* It matters not." Then the talkative idiot went on: "I hope only that the fleet is safe in England by now. Ver' safe, because otherwise——"

"Have no fear, sir," the officer said again, though at a sign from Mr. Beauvoir, he held his peace and allowed the Frenchman to proceed.

"Ver' safe, because, otherwise, Chateaurenault will soon catch them — poof! like a mouse in grimalkin's claws. The *débarquement* must be over by now — oh yes, over by now! — *l'amiral* will be free to roam the seas with his great fleet. *Tiens! c'est énorme!* There is, for instance, *La Sirène, L'Espérance, La Superbe, Le Bourbon, L'Enflame* — all terrible vessels. Also many more. *Le Solide, Le Fort, Le Prompte — Fichtre!* I cannot recall their names — they are fifteen in all. What can you do against that?"

"What did we do at La Hogue?" asked Mr. Beauvoir quietly.

"Ha! La Hogue! *Voilà — faute de bassesse — faute de*——"

"Sir," said the chaplain, interrupting,

"let us discourse no more on this subject. If we do we shall but get to quarrelling — and you have been polite and hospitable. We would not desire that to happen. Sir, we are obliged to you," and he held out his hand.

The strange creature took it — he took all our hands and shook them; he even seemed about to weep a little at our departure, and muttered that Lagos was "ver' triste." He loved to see any one, even though a misguided enemy.

"And," said Mr. Beauvoir, as we made our way down to the quay where the pinnace was to take them off, "to chatter to them as well as see them. Forgive him, Lord, he is a madman! Yet, I think," turning to me, "you should be satisfied. He corroborates you, and he has told us something worth knowing. Fifteen ships of war in all, eh?" whereon he fell a-musing. "A great fleet, in truth; yet ours is larger and we are English. That counts."

It took us a very little while to fetch off to the *Pembroke*, and on arriving on board, Mr. Beauvoir instantly sent to know if he could see the captain, since he brought great news from the shore. The sentry would not, however, by any means undertake to deliver the message, since Captain

Hardy was now abed, he having been on the poop all night while the ships were coming in; whereupon Mr. Beauvoir, saying that the business we were now on took precedence of sleep and rest, pushed his way into the great cabin and instantly knocked at the door outside the captain's berth. Also, he called to him to say that he had news of the galleons and the French admiral's fleet, and that there waited by his side an officer of the land forces charged with a message to him from the Earl of Marlborough.

"What!" called out the captain as we heard him slip his door open, after hearing also a bound as he leaped from his bunk to the floor. "What!" and a minute after he stood before us, a fine, brave-seeming gentleman, without his coat or vest on.

"What! News of the galleons! Are you the messenger, sir?" looking at me and returning my salute. "Quick! Your news; in as few words as may be."

And in a few words I told him all while he stood there before me, the chaplain supplementing of my remarks in equally few words by a description of what the drunken French consul had maundered on about in his boastings.

And the actions of this captain showed me at once that I was before one of those sea commanders who, by their daring and decision, had done so much to make our power on the ocean feared, notwithstanding any checks such as that of Cadiz, which they might now and again have to submit to.

"Sentry!" he called out, running into his cabin to strike upon a gong by his bedside at the same time. "Sentry!" And then, when the man appeared, went on: "Send the yeoman of the signals to me at once. Away with you."

"Make signal," he said to the lad, who soon came tumbling down the companion ladder, his glass under his arm, "to Captain Wishart in the *Eagle*, and all the captains in the squadron, to repair here for consultation without loss of time. Up! and waste no moment."

And sure enough—for in Her Majesty's navy they are as prompt as we of the sister service, if not prompter, since to a sailor, minutes are sometimes of as much importance as an hour on land—ere a quarter of an hour had passed the waters of the harbour were dotted with the barges of the other captains making for our ship, and, five minutes after that, all were assembled in the great cabin listening to my tale.

And all were at once agreed on what must be a-doing.

"'T is of vast importance," said Captain Wishart, who I think was the senior, since he presided, "that the admiral be acquainted with this. 'T is for him to decide what shall be done when he has heard the mission on which this officer has come, and heard also the words of the Frenchman. Now, who has the fastest sailer? You, I think, Hardy."

"True enough," replied that captain, "as to speed, I can sail two feet to every one of all the rest. Yet the head of the ship is somewhat loose, which may endanger the masts; she is also leaky, and our food is short. Nevertheless, since the intelligence has been by good luck brought to my hands I am loth indeed to resign the honor of finding Sir George."

"Nor shall you resign it," exclaimed the other captains. "The chance is yours. Succeed in it and you will get your flag. Hardy, you must take it."

Enough that I say he took it — had he not done so he would not have been worth one of his ship's biscuits, the cases of which were, as it happened, now running extremely low. Took it, too, in spite of the murmurings of some of his men, who said that they had signed for the expedition to Cadiz, and for that alone, and, therefore, it was plainly his duty to return to England. But Captain Hardy had a short way with such as these — a way well enough known to sailors! — while to others, with whom he thought it worth while to explain at all, he pointed out that there must be in the galleons, if they could only get alongside of them, sufficient prize money for all.

Off we went, therefore, to find the admiral and the main body of the fleet, while, as luck would have it, there blew from off the Portuguese coast a soft, brisk wind which took us along on the course we desired, namely, that in which we supposed and hoped that Sir George Rooke and the Dutch fleet had gone. All the same, it was no very pleasant cruise; the food ran lower and lower as day after day passed and we could not see so much as a topsail anywhere, until at last we came to two biscuits a day, officers and men. Then, to make matters worse, the weather came on rough and boisterous, so that the captain said for sure the fleet would separate; that though we might find one or two of the number 't was scarce likely we should find more, and that even those which we might by chance come across would possibly not have the *Royal Sovereign*, which was Rooke's ship, amongst them.

Briefly, however, we did find them after eleven days, and when we had begun to give up all hope, and while another terrible fear had taken possession of our minds — the fear that even should we come together and proceed to Vigo, we might find the galleons unloaded and their treasure removed inland. However, as I have now to tell — and, indeed, as you have read of late in the published accounts of our attack upon those galleons — that was not to be.

We found, therefore — to hurry on — the two fleets very close to one another, and no sooner had Sir George communicated the news to the Dutch admiral, Vandergoes, and to the Duke of Ormond, than it was determined to at once proceed on the way to Vigo to see if the galleons were there, and if — above all things — they still had their goods in them; for, though 't was like enough that we should destroy them if we could, and crush Chateaurenault as well, 't would be but half a victory if we could not wrench away the spoils from the enemy and profit by it ourselves.

And now off went two frigates to scout in the neighbourhood of the Bay of Vigo and see how much truth there was in the information my Lord Marlborough had sent; and on the night of October 9, to which we had come by this time, they returned; returned with the joyful intelligence that the treasure ships were drawn up as far as possible in a narrow strait in the harbour; that outside and guarding them, were some twenty French and Spanish ships of war, and that across the harbour was stretched a huge boom of masts and spars, protected on either side by great batteries of cannon.

Also they brought another piece of good news: The galleons, they thought, were still *unloaded.*

And still another piece of intelligence, equally welcome: The frigates had sighted Sir Cloudesley Shovel's fleet in the neighbourhood of Cape Finisterre, had communicated with him, and brought back word that as we drew near to Vigo he would combine with us.

That night we kept high revels on board all our ships — those only whose duty it was to take the watches being prevented from joining in the delirium of joy. Casks were broached and healths were drunk, suppers eaten joyously — we of the *Pembroke* having now all we could desire given us from our consorts — songs sung. And, if there was one who more than others was the hero of the evening, it was the simple gentleman who had brought the first intimation of the whereabouts of those whom we now meant to "burn, plunder, and destroy," as the old naval motto runs; the man who now pens these lines — myself.

Perhaps 't was no very good preparation for a great fight that, on the night before the day when we hoped to be gripping French and Spaniards by the throat, blowing up, burning or sinking their ships, and seizing their treasures, we should have been wassailing and carousing deeply all through that night. Yet, remember, we were sailors and soldiers; we were bent on an errand of destruction against the tyrant who had crushed and frighted all Europe for now nigh sixty years; the splendid despot who, but a few months ago, had acknowledged as King of England one whom every Englishman had sworn deeply should never sit on England's throne, nor inherit the crown of his ancestors — if, indeed, the Stuarts were the ancestors of the youth whom the late James called his son.

For this remembrance we may be forgiven — forgiven for hating Louis and all his brood — hating him, the tyrant of Versailles, and the fat booby, his grandson, who aspired to grasp the throne of Spain by the help of Versailles and its master, that great, evil King of France!

Through that night, I say, we drank and caroused, called toasts to our good queen, prayed God that we might do her credit on the morrow, and exalt the name of great Anna? And even the watch, coming off duty in turns, ran into the main cabin ere they sought their berths, seized cans and cannikins brimming high, and drank her health and that of our own dear land.

'T was a great night, yet it came to an end at last, and the autumn morning dawned, thick, hazy, damp — still, not so thick or hazy but that we could see through it the mountains over and around Vigo looming up, and, at their feet, the entrance to the bay.

Also, we saw, away to the northwest, the fleet of Sir Cloudesley Shovel coming up toward us, escorted and led by our scouts.

CHAPTER IX.

THE TAKING OF THE GALLEONS.

Looking back upon that great day—it was October 11—it seems to me that many of the events which happened must have been due to the mercy and goodness of God, so incredible were they.

For see now what fell out at the very first, namely, that the haze and mist were so thick that we were enabled to anchor at the mouth of the great river and harbour without so much as even our presence being known, so that when the sun set and the fog lifted, the surprise of those snared and trapped creatures was great, and they at once began firing wildly upon us, without, however, doing any harm whatever. But the lifting of that fog showed us what we had to encounter, the work that was to be done.

For, first, it enabled us to see that, across the river, or narrow strait, as indeed it was, the French admiral had laid a tremendous boom, made up of cables, yards and masts, topchains and casts, some nine feet in circumference, while the whole was kept fixed and steady by anchors at either side. This, too, we perceived, was constructed between two forts known as the Ronde and the Noot, one on the left bank and the other on the right, while far up the harbour, where we saw the galleons all a-lying tucked in comfortably under the cliffs, with a line of French ships of battle, and some Spanish ones, ahead of and guarding them, we perceived a great fort, which is known as the Fort of Redondella.

And now the night came down upon us, and we knew that for this day there would be no fighting, though, since all through it the admiral went from ship to ship in his barge, giving orders, 't was very certain that at daybreak it would begin.

And so it did, as now I have to describe.

For on the morrow, and when, as near six o'clock as may be, the sun came up swiftly over the great hills, or mountains, which abound here, we made our first preparations for the attack by the landing of the Duke of Ormond with two thousand five hundred and fifty men on the side of the Fort Redondella, they marching at once toward it on foot.

As for myself, although a soldier, it had

been decided that I should remain in the *Pembroke*, and this for more than one reason.

"You have," said Captain Hardy to me, "no uniform with you; therefore, if you fall into the hands of those on shore it may go hard with you. Yet here you can be of service; help train a gun, if need be, issue orders, take part in the boarding, which must surely occur, perhaps take part in sacking of the galleons. There's business for you—such, indeed as, as a soldier, you are not very like to ever see again. My lad!" he went on—and in truth I was a lad to him, though I esteemed myself a very full-fledged man—"you are to be congratulated. You will have much to talk about in years to come—if you survive this day—which falls not often to a landsman's lot," and he ran away as gay as a lad himself, all grizzled with service though he was, to prepare for assisting in breaking the boom.

So I stayed in the *Pembroke* and, as you shall see, if you do but read, the doing so led to all that happened to me which I have now to set down, and all of which—had it not so happened—would have prevented this narrative from ever being penned, since it is not to describe only the siege of Vigo and the taking of the Spanish galleons that I am a-writing of this story.

Therefore I proceed:

Down from the hills already the smoke was rolling fast, obscuring the beauteous morn by now; white smoke from the cannon in the fort—through which there leapt every moment great spits of flame from the big guns' mouths!—dun-coloured smoke from the grenades carried by Lord Shannon and Colonel Pierce's grenadiers; black, greasy smoke vomited forth from the fuzees. And it came down to the water and poured across it in clouds, enveloping the galleons in its wreaths and the great French ships of battle; clinging around our own topsails and masts, almost obscuring each of our vessels from the other.

Yet not so much, neither, but that—a breeze having sprung up after a calm which had enforced us to drop our anchors for a while—we, of the *Pembroke*, could see glide by us a great ship, with her men on yards and masts and in fighting tops, all cheering lustily, and some a-singing—a vessel that rushed forward as a tiger rushes to its prey. At first we thought it was the *Royal Sovereign*—that great, noble ship which transmits a name down from Bluff Harry's days—then knew we were mistaken. It was the

Torbay, Vice-Admiral Hopson's own, in which he flew his flag, her sails all clapt on, her cable training at her side, where he had cut it, so as to lose no precious time, her course direct for the boom. And after her went ourselves, as hound let loose from leash follows hound. Captain Hardy had spoken true—'t was a day not to be missed!

We heard a snapping, a crashing—'t was awful, too, to hear!—we heard roar upon roar from hundreds of lusty throats in that great ship—we knew the boom was gone—cut through as a woodsman's axe cuts through a sapling. Amidst all the enemy's fire—fire from the French ships and those Spanish forts on shore—we heard it. And we, too, cheered and shouted—sent up our queen's name to the smoke-obscured heavens above. Some cried the old watchword of past days, "St. George and England"; some even danced and jumped upon the decks for glee—danced and jumped, even though the hail of ball was scattering us like ninepins, or a hundred pins!—even though some lay writhing on those decks, and some were lying there headless, armless, legless! What mattered? The enemy were there behind that boom, and it was broken. We were amongst them now. Let those die who must; those live who were to conquer.

Between the *Bourbon* and *L'Espérance* the noble *Torbay* rushed — to the jaws of death she went, as though to a summer cruise on friendly seas, her anchor cables roared through her hawse-holes — Hopson had anchored 'twixt those two great French ships! He was there; there was to be, could be, no retreat now; 't was death or victory.

At first it seemed as though it could alone be the first. The cannon grinned like teeth through tier upon tier of gunboats in the Frenchman's sides; the balls crashed into the *Torbay;* they did the same with us and Vandergoes' ship, now ranged on the other side of the *Bourbon* — a French fireship had clapt alongside of her, and set her rigging alight; her foretopmast went by the board; her sails were all aflame; her foreyard burnt like a dry log; her larboard shrouds burnt at the dead-eyes.

Yet still she fought and fought — vomited forth her own flames and destruction; still from the throats of those left alive came shouts of savage exultation, for, all afire as she was, we saw that she was winning. And not only she, but all of us. We had sunk one Frenchman ourselves. Vandergoes had mastered the *Bourbon*—she was done for! The *Association* had silenced a battery ashore. And now a greater thing than all happened—Chateaurenault saw that he was beaten, set his flagship, *Le Fort*, on fire, and fled to the shore, calling on all his captains to follow him.

Yet still one awful dread remained! The *Torbay* was burning fiercely, charred masts and yards were falling to the deck—itself aflame—blocks burning like tarred wood crashed down, too. What if her powder magazine exploded! If it did, all in her neighbourhood would be destroyed, hurled to atoms, as she herself would be.

Almost it seemed as if that had happened now. There came a hideous roar, a belch of black, suffocating smoke; it set all sneezing and coughing as though a sulphur mine were afire. Yet that explosion, that great cloud of filthy blackness, those masses of burnt and charred wood hurled up into the air and falling with a crash on every deck around, amidst shrieks and howls and curses terrible to hear, though drowned somewhat by the booming of the cannon all about, was to be the salvation of the *Torbay*, of ourselves, and of the Dutchmen.

ACROSS THE SALT SEAS. 123

For it was the fireship itself that had exploded. It was, in truth, a merchantman laden with snuff, which had been hastily fitted up as one of those craft. And in so doing the density of the fumes which it emitted, and its falling *débris* when it was burst asunder, helped to put out the flames that raged in the *Torbay* and in us.

The firing began to cease even as this happened; the enemy began to recognise that 't was useless. They would have been blind not to have so recognised. On shore 't was easy enough to perceive that the forts of Redondella, Noot and Ronde, with their platforms, had been captured by Ormond and Captain Bucknam, of the *Association;* on the water the *Bourbon* was ours. The lilies were hauled down, in their place floated the banner of England; the fireship had vanished into the elements, the great boom lay in pieces on the water like some long, severed snake. Yet might one have wept to gaze upon the *Torbay* — the queen and victress of this fight — and upon ourselves.

There she lay — Hopson by now in the *Monmouth*, to which he had been forced to transfer his flag, so sad a ruin was she — listing over to her wounded starboard side, into which the water poured in volumes, it becoming tinged as it mixed with the blood in her scuppers; her yards and masts were charred sticks; black bits of sooty, greasy matter, which had once been her white sails, floated down slowly to the waves and fell upon and dissolved into them. Also her shrouds were but burnt pieces of rope and twine now. Upon her deck there were stretched a hundred and twenty men, dead or dying. And with the *Pembroke* it was almost as bad. We were shattered and bruised, our foremast gone, our own sails shot through and through, and hanging over the sides like winding sheets, our own decks charnel houses. Yet we had won the fight, the day was ours, the galleons our booty.

But were they? That was the question!

'T was true, they were all as we had first seen them, though some, we noticed, had been run ashore, perhaps to give them a chance of hurriedly landing some of their cargo; but, alas! we noticed now that they were all aflame, were burning fiercely.

And we knew well enough what this meant — meant that the French and Spaniards had set them on fire so that we should benefit nothing through their falling into our hands. And all of us saw it at the same time — Rooke saw it, Hopson saw it — every man on board our English decks who was still alive saw and understood.

By God's mercy the breeze was still blowing into the strait. Some of us still had some sail left clinging to our bruised and battered yards; enough to take us farther in, enough to enable the boarding parties to row ashore, to reach those burning ships, to save something, surely!

From all the ships' sides as we ran up as far as we could toward where they lay, came now the hoarse grating of the ropes running through the blocks as the boats were lowered. Into those boats leaped swarms of men, their cutlasses ready, their pistols in their hands, their eyes inflamed with the lust of plunder, wild oaths and jokes, curses—and, sometimes, prayers that we were not too late—upon their lips.

And in our cutter I went, too—appointed to the command of her in place of the lieutenant who should have taken that command, but who now lay dead upon the *Pembroke's* deck, a dozen balls in his body.

Jostling one another—for there were scores of boats lowered by now, and all making their way, under either sail or the seamen's brawny arms, to where those burning galleons lay—we rushed through the half mile of water that separated us from them, all eager to board and be amongst the spoil. And woe, I thought, to him or them who, when we were there, should strive to bar our entrance! Our blood was up, fevered by the carnage of the earlier hours; woe to them who endeavoured to prevent our final triumph! Through wreckage of all kinds we went, spars, yards and masts, military tops floating like tubs, dead men face upward, living men clinging to oars and overturned boats and shrieking to be saved, while ever still, in front of us, the galleons burned and blazed—one blew up as we neared it, another, spouting flames from port and window and burning to the water's edge, sank swiftly and in a moment beneath the water.

But at last we were up to them, were beneath their bows, could see their great figureheads and read their names—most of them so terribly sacred that one wondered that even Spaniards should so dare to profane those holy words by using them for their ships!

And now some orders were issued by a grey-haired officer to those close by. The boarding parties were told off in boats of twos and threes to the different vessels flaming before our eyes. The one which I commanded was directed to a great vessel of three decks, having above her upper one a huge poop-royal, and named—heavens, what a name for a ship!—*La Sacra Familia*. And as we swept toward them all we saw that one mercy was now to be vouchsafed. There would be no further slaughter here; no need for more shedding of blood. The vessels were not defended; those who had set fire to them had undoubtedly fled.

Yet up on the poop-royal of that galleon, to which we now clambered by aid of rope and ladder—with cutlass in mouth and pistol in belt—as well as by chains and steps, we saw there was still some human life left. We saw a tall monk standing there, gazing down curiously at us, his shaven crown glistening in the autumn sun. Also, it seemed as though he smiled a welcome to us, was glad to see us; perhaps regarded us as men who might save him from that burning mass.

We rushed on board, and first, before all other things, except a salutation which I made to the monk by a touch of the finger to my hat, I directed those under my command to endeavour to stifle the fire, which seemed at present to be entirely confined to the after part of the ship. "For," said I to those of my own following, and also to those who had come in the other boats under the command of two bo'suns, "if this is not done there will be no getting at the goods whatever. Where generally is the storage made?" I asked, turning to one of these officers.

"Faith, sir, I know not," he said, with a harsh laugh. "My account has been ever with the king's—and now the queen's—ships. We sailors know little of such things as stored treasure. Yet," and he again laughed, "we have our opportunity now. If we can but quench this fire, we may learn something."

"Perhaps," said a voice behind me, musical and deep, and greatly to my astonishment—when I turned round and saw who its owner was, namely, the monk—speaking in very good English, "I may be of some service here. I have been a passenger in her since she loaded at Guayaquil," and his eyes met mine boldly.

They were large, roving eyes, too, jet-black and piercing, and looked out from a dark, handsome face. A face as close-shaven as the crown, yet with the blue tinge all over upper lip and chin and cheeks which showed where there grew a mass of hair beneath.

"I am obliged to you, sir," I answered,

touching my hat again — for his manner proclaimed that this was no common peasant who had become a monk because the life was easier than that of a hedger and ditcher; but, instead, a man who knew something of the world and its courtesies. Then, he having told me that all the plate and coin was in the middle of the ship, and the merchandise, such as skins and leather, Campeachy wood, quinquina, silks, indigo and cochineal in the after part, I sent off all the men to endeavour at once to extinguish the flames below; to cut off communication between the atmosphere and that part of the ship which was already in flames; to close all hatches and bulkhead doors; to stop up the crevices by which the air could pass to the burning part, and, if possible, to separate the one half of the vessel from the other, as well as to pour down water on the flames.

And, half an hour later — while still I stood gazing down on the men at their work, and still by my side stood the monk, uttering no word, but regarding with interest all that was doing — one of the bo'suns called up to me, saying:

"We have scotched it now, sir. There is no more fire left."

CHAPTER X.

SEÑOR JUAN BELMONTE.

And now I made my way below by the main hatch — for the after-companion was all burnt, so that there was no descent by that, I being intent on the men finding out — and setting to work at once on getting at and landing — the specie there might be in the ship; for, although the galleons were ours now, and 't was a certainty that neither French nor Spaniards could make any attempt whatsoever to recover possession of them, there was another matter to be thought about, namely, that this one, of which I was, so to speak, in chief command, might be so badly injured that she might sink at any moment; and, if she did that, then it would be goodbye to any bars of silver and gold, pistoles or crusadoes which she might have stowed away in her, ready for the Castile mint. And with this apprehension in my mind, I decided that the unloading must at once begin.

But as I came down the main companion it was apparent that I must make my way

ACROSS THE SALT SEAS. 131

aft through the great cabin, since my men were all at work in the hinder part of the ship; and, consequently, I put my hand to the cabin door to open it, when I discovered that it was closed — shut fast. Yet, even as I perceived this, while still I moved the catch about between my fingers, wondering what I should do, and whether I must not go back and fetch some of the sailors up from the after part to burst open the door, I heard a footstep, light, yet firm, tapping on the cabin deck; a footstep that, I could very well perceive, was coming toward the closed door; and then, a moment later, I heard a voice on the other side say something in Spanish, of which I could not catch one word; yet I doubted not that a question had been asked as to who I was, and what I wanted.

Remembering, however, that I stood here in the position of a captor, remembering, too, that since all these Spanish galleons had been under the protection of the French admiral (with also three Spanish ships of war, though 't is true *they* did not count for much), I replied in the French language, which, as I have before said, I had very well:

"I am an officer from the English fleet,

and am now in charge of this vessel. Open the door without delay."

"Are you an English officer?" the voice now said, in my own tongue, to which I — thinking that the tones were soft, gracious ones enough — replied:

"I am an English officer. Open the door at once."

Then I heard the bolt shot back, and entered the great cabin.

What kind of personage I had expected to find behind that door I scarcely now can say — though I do remember well enough that, judging by the gentle, musical voice which had replied to my summons, I should not have been over-surprised to find myself face to face with some Spanish woman — yet the person who appeared before me raised my curiosity when we now stood face to face, for, certainly, I had expected some one vastly different from him on whom I now gazed — perhaps a Spanish sailor; a woman, as I have mentioned, or some old don who had managed to get left behind when all the rest had fled.

Yet I saw none of these.

Instead, a youth, somewhat tall — I remember that his eyes were almost on a level with mine, and I am tall myself — also extremely handsome, while, to add to that handsomeness, his dress was rich, if not costly. But first for his appearance.

Those eyes were soft, dark ones, such as, I think, our poets call "liquid," and they looked out at me from an oval face, dark and olive in complexion, over which the black hair curled in mighty becoming waves, though it was not all visible, since on his head he wore a beaver cap, looped up at one side with a steel buckle, and with, in it, a deep crimson feather—a hat that added extremely to his boyish beauty. For that he was a boy of almost tender years was certain. Upon his upper lip there was that soft down which is not a moustache, but tells only where some day a moustache will be; his colouring, too—a deep, rich red beneath the olive skin—proclaimed extreme youthfulness. But, what was even more agreeable than all, was the bright, buoyant smile with which he looked at me—a smile which flashed from those dark, soft eyes and trembled on the full, red lips, yet seemed strangely out of place here in this captured vessel, and upon the face of a prisoner—for such, indeed, he was.

But now—even as we were saluting of each other, and while I noticed the easy grace with which this youth took off his beaver hat—I noticed also the handsome satin coat he wore, the embroidered, open-worked linen collar, and the pretty lace at his sleeves; perceived, also, that his breeches were lined with camlet and faced with white taffeta. I spoke to him, saying:

"Sir, I am afraid this is but a rough visit which I pay. Yet, since I find you aboard this galleon, you must know what brings me here; must know that it and all her consorts have fallen into our power — the power of England and Holland."

"In faith, I know it very well," the young man answered. "Heavens, what a cannonading you kept up! Yet — though perhaps you may deem me heartless if I say so! — I cannot aver that I am desperate sick at the knowledge that you have drubbed France and Spain this morning. *Carámba!* I am not too much in love with either, though you find me a passenger here."

"Monsieur is not then either French or Spanish?" I hazarded, while he unstrapped his blade from its *porte-epée* and flung it on the cabin locker as though it wearied him. "Perhaps English, to wit. And of the West Indies? A passenger taking this ship as a means whereby to reach his native land?"

He looked at me with those soft dark eyes — I know not even now why they brought up the thought of velvet to my mind — paused a moment then said:

"Monsieur, I do protest you are a wizard, a conjuror, a geomancer. In truth you have hit it. I am English, though not by birth — but subject to England."

"I should scarce have thought, indeed," I ventured to say, "that monsieur was of English blood."

"No?" with a slight intonation. "And why not? I flatter myself that I have the English very well."

"You have it perfectly," I replied, making a little bow, "but scarce the English look. Now a Spaniard — a Frenchman — I would have ventured to say, judging by your appearance, to ——"

Again that merry laugh rang out, and again that handsome youth told me I must be a wizard. "For," said he, "you have pinked me in the very spot. My mother was a Spaniard — my father a Frenchman. And we have lived so long in Jamaica that I speak English like an Englishman: You see?"

Then almost before I could answer that I did see and understand, this handsome youth — who seemed as volatile as a butterfly! — began to sing softly to himself:

> "And have you heard of a Spanish lady?
> How she wooed an Englishman?
> Garments gay and rich as may be,
> Decked with jewels, had she on."

While at the same time he picked up an instrument which I learned later was known as a viol d'amore, and began to produce sweet sounds from it.

Now, this youth won so much upon me, what with his appearance—and already I found myself wondering what the ladies must think of him!— and his light, merry nature, that, had other things been different, I could very well have passed the whole day with him in this main cabin, only there was duty to be done. By now I knew that the men would most like have reached the bullion chests and be ready for getting them out; wherefore, the moment he ceased his song, I said as courteously as may be:

"I have to leave you now, sir—there is work to be done in this ship by nightfall. Yet, since you say you are a British subject, we must take some care of you. Will you come with me to see one of the admirals, who will dispose of you as best may be? If you seek to reach England, doubtless they can put you in the way—give you a passage—or what do you propose doing?"

For answer he shrugged his shoulders indifferently, then said:

"England is my destination—yet there is no pressing hurry. I am on my road to seek some friends there, but I mind not if I tarry a little. One of these friends—oh! a dear old creature, a Saint, I think—I have been bent on finding for some years now. And I shall find him. Then—but no matter! A few more weeks in comparison with those years matter but little. I shall find him. Oh, yes. I have no fear."

I, too, shrugged my shoulders now—for this was, after all, no answer to my question; then I said:

"But how will you proceed? You can scarce stay here—this galleon will probably be sunk by the admiral directly she is unloaded. What will you do?"

He shrugged his shoulders with a look of extreme indifference, muttering something in Spanish, which I thought might be a proverb; then said: "Indeed, sir, I do not know. But this admiral of yours, what will he do with me—where take me if I go with you? I thought to ship at one time from Cadiz to England; then, later, when I learned we were coming in here, I thought to travel by land to some near port and find a vessel for the same place. Now I know not what to do."

Neither did I know what to suggest that he should do, except that I told him it was very certain he must see the admiral, who, without any doubt, I thought, would find him an opportunity of reaching England—would probably take him with the fleet.

"And," I went on, "this should be of some service to you, in the way of money, at least. 'T will be a good thing for you to be put on English ground at no cost to yourself. Also, you may have goods or specie in this ship, which can be saved for you. And then, too, you will be near those friends you speak of—that one, especially, who is a Saint—who will doubtless help and assist you."

Again I saw the bright, luminous smile come upon his features, as he answered:

"Ay! he would assist me, no doubt. Oh! yes. *Mon Dieu!* Yes! Beyond all doubt. And he will be so glad to see me. We have not met for some time. But, sir, I thank you very much for your concern about me. Only, as far as money goes, I am not needy. I have bills about me now, drawn on the old Bank of Castile, and also on some goldsmiths of London, as well as some gold pieces in my pocket. While as for the goods or specie you speak of—why, never fear! Neither this galleon nor any other has a pistole's worth of aught that belongs to me on board —the risk was too great with the seas swarming with English ships of war. No, sir, beyond the box which contains my necessaries, I stand to lose nothing."

"I rejoice to hear it," I said, "though doubtless, since you are a British subject, all that belonged to you would have been sacred. Yet, even as 't is, 't is better so." Then, seeing the bo'sun at the cabin door, pulling his long matted hair by form of salute, and, doubtless, wondering what kept me so long away from him and his men, I said: "Now I must leave you for a time. Yet it will not be long. I trust you have all you require to sustain you until we reach the ship I am attached to."

But even as I spoke, and without listening much to his answer, which was to the effect that a good meal had been eaten that morning before the battle began, and that, if necessary, he knew very well where to lay his hands on some food, a thought struck me which I wondered had not occurred to me before during my interview with him. Therefore, turning to him, I said:

"But how comes it that I find you here alone—or all alone but for the reverend monk whom I saw above? How is it that you and he did not desert the ship as the others must have done?"

"Oh! as for that," he replied, still with that sweet smile of his, and still with that bright, careless air which he had worn all through, and which caused him to appear superior to any of the melancholy as well as uncomfortable circumstances by which he was surrounded, "as for that, the explanation is simple enough." Then, speaking rapidly now, he went on:

"We saw your great ships break the boom; ha! *por Diós*, 't was grand, splendid. We saw your ships range themselves alongside the Frenchmen, saw them crash into them their balls, set them afire, destroy them. *Espléndido! Espléndido! Espléndido!*" he exclaimed, bursting into the Spanish in his excitement. "Poof! away went the *Bourbon*, topping over on her side, up went the fireship—we heard your shouts and cries, heard the great English seamen singing their songs. I tell you it was glorious. *Magnifico!* Only—these creatures here—the *canailles*—these *desperdicios*—these—*Diós!* I know not the word in English—thought not so. 'Great God!' screamed Don Trebuzia de Vera, our captain—a miserable pig, a coward. 'Great

God, they win again, these English dogs; curse them! they never lose, we are lost! lost! lost! And see,' he bellowed, 'the French admiral lands, he flees, deserts his ship, ha! sets it afire. Flee we, too, therefore. Flee! Away! To the boats, to the shore, to the mountains. Away! They come nearer. Away, all, or there will not be a whole throat amongst us.'"

"We knowed that was what would happen," chuckled the bo'sun, who still stood at the open door, his fierce face lit up with a huge grin of approval. "Go on, young sir. Tell us the tale."

And, scarce heeding him, the youth, who had recovered his breath, went on:

"They obeyed him—they fled. Into the water, up the rocks, off inland they went. They never cast a thought to us, to Padre Jaime and myself, the only two passengers in the ship. Not they—they cared no jot whether we were blown up, or shot, or sunk, no more than they thought of their ingots in the hold. Their wretched lives were all in all to them now."

"Therefore they fled and left you here!"

"They fled and left us here, setting fire first to the ship, and caring nothing if we were burnt in it or not. Though that could scarce have happened, I think, since it would have been easy enough for us to plunge into the water and get ashore. Also the reverend father above bade me take heart—though I needed no such counsel, having never lost mine—averred that your side had won, that the next thing would be the arrival of your boats to secure the plunder—which has fallen out as he said—and that then both he and I would be safe. Which also has come to pass," he concluded.

"The reverend father appears to be well versed in the arts of war, captures and so forth," I remarked, as now we made our way together to the waist of the ship, followed by the bo'sun. "A strange knowledge for one of his trade!"

"*Por Diós!*" the young fellow said, "'t is not so strange, neither, as you will say if ever you get him to speak about the strange places in which he has pursued his ministrations. Why, sir, he has assisted at the death of many a dying sinner of the kind we have in our parts, held cups of water to their burning lips, wiped the sweat of death from off their brows. Oh!" he said, stopping by one of the galleon's great quarter deck ports, in which the cowards who fled from the heavily armed ship had left a huge loaded brass cannon run out, which they had not had the spirit to fire; stopping there and laying a long, slim hand upon my arm — while I noticed that the nails were most beautifully shaped — "Oh! he has been in some strange places; seen strange things, the siege and plunder of Maracaibo, to wit, and many other places; seen blood run like water."

"The siege and plunder of Maracaibo!" I found myself repeating as we drew near the fore-hatches, which were now open. "The siege and plunder of Maracaibo!" Where had I heard such words as these before, or words like them? Where? where? On whose lips had I last heard the name of Maracaibo?

And, suddenly, I remembered that that wicked old ruffian, who had been fellow-passenger with me in *La Mouche Noire* had mentioned that place to the filthy black who was his servant — or his friend.

And — for what reason I know not, for there was no sequence whatsoever in such thoughts and recollections — I recalled his drunken and frenzied shouts to some man whom he called Grandmont; his questions about some youth nineteen years old, who was like to be by now grown up to be a devil like that dead Grandmont to whom he imagined he was speaking.

Which was, if you come to think of it, a strange sort of recollection, or memory, to be evoked simply through my hearing again the name of that tropic town of Maracaibo mentioned by this handsome young man.

CHAPTER XI.

FATHER JAIME.

Under the direction of the second bo'sun, the men who had all come into the ship with me had now gotten the battens off and had lifted the hatch hoods — for although it has taken some time to write down my meeting and interview with this young gentleman, it had not, in very fact, occupied more than twenty minutes — and I found them already beginning to bring up some large chests and boxes with strange marks upon them.

Also, I found standing close by the opening the monk whom the young man had called Father Jaime, he being engaged in peering down into the hold with what seemed to me a great air of interest, which was not, perhaps, very strange, seeing that the treasure below was now destined for a far different purpose from that for which it was originally intended.

He turned away, however, from this occupation on seeing us approach, and said quietly, in the rich, full voice which I had previously noticed, to the young man by my side:

"So, Señor Juan, you have found a friend, I see. You are fortunate. This way you may light on your road to England."

"And you, sir, what is your destination, may I ask?" I said, for I knew I should soon have to decide what to do with him. The grey-haired officer had given me, among other hurried instructions, one to the effect that anything which was brought up from below was to be instantly sent off to Sir George Rooke's flagship; and 'twas very easy to see that there was none too much specie in this ship—while I knew not what was to be done with the merchandise. Therefore, the time was now near at hand for me to return and report myself, taking with me my findings, while, also, I should have to take with me these two whom I had discovered left behind on board.

Father Jaime bowed graciously on my asking this question—indeed, he was a far more courteous and well bred man than I, perhaps in my ignorance, had ever supposed would have been found amongst his class—and replied: "I, sir, have to present myself at Lugo, where there is a monastery to which I am accredited." Then, with an agreeable smile, he continued:

"I trust I shall not be detained. Already I am two years behind my time—as is our young friend here, Señor Juan Belmonte, and——"

"Two years!" I exclaimed.

"In truth, 't is so," my young gentleman, whose name I now learned, replied. "Two years. These galleons should have sailed from Hispaniola that length of time ago, only so many things have happened. First there was the getting them properly laden, then the fear of filibusters and buccaneers——"

"That fear exists no longer, my son," the monk interrupted. "They are disbanded, broken up, gone, dispersed. There will be no more buccaneering now, the saints be praised."

He said: "the saints be praised"; yet had he not worn the holy garb he did, I should have almost thought that he said it with regret. Indeed, were it not for his shaven crown and face, he would not have ill-befitted the general idea I had formed of those gentry—what with his stalwart form, bold, fierce eyes and sun-browned visage.

"Ay, the saints be praised!" the young señor repeated after him, "the saints be praised. They were the curse of the Indies—I am old enough to remember that. Yet, now, all are gone, as you say, dispersed — broken up. Pointis has done that, and death and disease. Still, where are they? — those who are alive — I wonder."

"There are few alive now," the monk replied, "and those of no worth. Recall, my son, recall what we know happened in the Indies. Kidd is taken, Grogniet dead, Le Picard executed. Townley — a great man that! — I — I mean, a great villain — fell with forty wounds in his body; at Guayaquil nine brave — nine vagabonds — left dead; and more, many more."

"And the villain Gramont" — and now I started; was this whom he called Gramont the man that old vagabond Carstairs had spoken of — as I supposed — as Grandmont? — "forget not the greatest of them all, holy father. What of him?"

"He died at sea. Drowned," Father Jaime replied. Then added: "He was the boldest of them all."

"'T was never known for certain that he was so drowned," Belmonte said.

"'T was known for certain; is certain. I have spoken with those who saw his ship's boats floating near where he must have been cast away and lost. Fool that he was! Madman! Louis the King gave him his commission, made him Lieutenant du Roi.

Then, because the devil's fever was hot in his blood, he must make one more of his accursed cruises, and go filibustering thus, besieging towns, plundering and destroying once more. The fool! to do it 'neath the King's lilies — to ruin himself forever, when he was rich, rich — ah, heavens! how rich he was! 'Tis well for him that he was drowned — disappeared forever. Otherwise the wheel would have been his portion. And," he added after a pause, "righteously so. Righteously so!"

Stopping as he said those words, he saw that we were regarding him with interest — for, indeed, had this drowned buccaneer been a friend of his he could scarcely have spoken with more fervency — then added, impressively:

"My sons, I knew that man — that Gramont; and I — I pitied him. Knowing his fate, and much of his life, I pity him still."

Then he turned away and began telling of his beads as he strode up and down the deck. And I, remembering all I had overheard the man Carstairs say, determined that, if the chance arose, I would ask the reverend father if he had known this Carstairs, too; for I had sufficient curiosity in my composition to desire to learn something more about that hoary-headed old vagabond, though 't was not at all likely that I should ever set eyes on him again.

That chance was not now, however, since at this moment there came alongside the whole flotilla of boats, which had been despatched severally to the various galleons, they being at this time all collected together ere going back to the admiral, and needing only us to make them complete. Wherefore, giving orders to have all the chests and boxes which we had unearthed placed in our own boats, we stepped over the side, I motioning to the father and the señor to take their places by me.

"Your necessaries," I said, "can be fetched away later, when 't is decided how your respective journeys are to be brought to an end."

And now, ere I get on with what I have to tell, it is fitting that — to make an end of this siege of Vigo, which, indeed, reinstated later, in the opinion of the Parliament and their countrymen, all those who had failed at Cadiz — I set down what was the advantage to England of this taking of the galleons, though, in truth, that advantage was far more in the crushing blow it administered to the French sea service than in aught else; for it broke that service's power more than aught else had done since the time of La Hogue, ten years ago; and it crippled France so upon the waters that, though she still continued to fight us boldly whenever we met, she was able to do but very little harm in that way.

Of the fifteen great ships of war which the French admiral, Chateaurenault, commanded, five were burned up, some being set alight by themselves ere they fled, the others by us. Four others were run ashore and bulged. Five more, not so badly injured, were taken home by our fleet, and afterward did us good service against their old masters, these being *Le Prompte, L'Assure, Le Firme, Le Modère,* and *Le Triton;* while the remaining one, *Le Bourbon,* was captured, as I have said, by Vandergoes, and fell to the share of the Dutch. Then, of their frigates, we burnt two, and also a fireship other than the merchantman loaded with snuff. Also, we burnt and destroyed three Spanish men-of-war.

As to the galleons, eight of them were sunk by their owners, the others were divided between our Dutch friends and ourselves. And this is what we got for our share: A few ingots of gold, several bars of silver and some jewels—the principal thing of worth amongst these being a great crown of gold set with rubies; a gold crucifix enriched with many stones, seven hundred pounds' weight of silver bars, many cases of silver ore, and some enormous cases of plate. Also, there was much cochineal, tobacco, logwood, cocoa, snuff and sugar, some of which was saved and some was sunk to the bottom. And the gold and silver was afterward taken to our English mint and coined into five-pound pieces, crowns, half-crowns and shillings, each piece having "Vigo" stamped beneath the queen's head, thereby to distinguish it. Later on, and somewhat later, too—it was when I drew my share of the prize money, to which I became entitled as having taken part in that great fight—I observed that my pieces had that word upon them.

But alas! there should have been much more, only the galleons had lain twenty-five days within that harbour ere we got to them, and, during that time, they had landed much which had been sent on to Lugo, and, had it not been for that foolish Spanish punctilio, which would not allow anything to be done hastily, they would have gotten all of their goods and precious things ashore. Only, because they should have gone into Cadiz and discharged there, and had instead come to Vigo, much delay happened ere the order for their doing so was given. Which was very good for us.

Our loss, considering the fierce fight both sides made of it, was not considerable. Hopson, his ship, because she had borne the brunt of the encounter, did suffer the most, she having one hundred and fifteen of her sailors killed on the deck or drowned, with nine wounded; the *Barfleur* and the *Association* had each but two men killed; the *Mary* lost none; the *Kent* had her bo'sun wounded, while for ourselves, we had many wounded, but none that I know of killed. Of those who went ashore to attack the Fort of Redondella under his Grace of Ormond, none of much note were slain, but Colonel Pierce got a bad wound from a cannon shot fired by one of our own men-of-war, and some other colonels were also wounded.

'T was through a mighty mass of wreckage and floating spars, masts and yards, that we passed toward the *Royal Sovereign*, which lay back a bit and was nearest the mouth of the strait and beyond where that boom had been, and as we did so I saw my young gentleman, Señor Belmonte, turn somewhat pale as he observed the terrible traces which battles

—and more particularly sea battles—always leave behind. Indeed, the soft red flush leapt to his cheeks, and the full scarlet lips themselves looked more white than red as his eyes glanced down at the objects that went a-floating by on the water; and, perhaps, since he was so young, 't was not very strange that these sights should have sickened him. For there passed us dead men with half their heads blown off; others with a terrible grin of agony upon their faces; some with half their inwards dragging alongside them like cords—the waves all tinged a horrid reddish brown—while hats, wigs and other things floating by as the tide made, were but cruel sights for so young a man—and he, probably, no fighter —to see. And, after such a lusty encounter as this had been, one could not hope to witness anything much better.

As for the monk—on whom I could not but instinctively fix my eyes now and again, for (although I could not have told why) the man had fascinated me with the knowledge which he seemed to have once possessed of all those hideous filibusters and sea rovers who now, he said, were dead and gone and driven off the ocean—he seemed to regard these things as calmly and impassibly as though he sat in some lady's boudoir. His dark eyes, 't was true, flashed here and there and all around — now on a headless man, and now on the contorted features of another, but he paled not, nor did he express or give any sign of interest in aught until we ran alongside our noble *Royal Sovereign*, when he cast his eye approvingly over her.

"A great vessel," he said, "a mighty craft! Worthy to represent her great country"; then grasped the life line hanging down, as I motioned him to ascend her gangway, and went on board as calmly as though accustomed to going over the sides of ships every day of his life. From the main shrouds there hung a flag when we stepped on board, which I have since learned to know denoted that a council of war was being held in the ship; also there were many captains' gigs and some admirals' barges all about her, so that 't was plain enough to see, even without that flag, that a consultation was taking place on board. And scarce had I given my orders for the chests to be hauled in than the first lieutenant approached me and asked very courteously if I was not Lieutenant Crespin.

A moment later I was being ushered into the great main cabin, leaving my two companions on the deck for the present —

and in another instant was making my salutations to the grey-haired admiral, Sir George Rooke, who sat at the head of the table, and to his Grace, the Duke of Ormond — a brave, handsome soldier — who had come on board after taking of the Fort of Redondella.

And now I pass over the many flattering things said to me by those great officers seated there — since we had flown straight to Vigo after the *Pembroke* had picked up the fleet at sea, and had at once been occupied in our preparations for taking of the galleons, this was the first time we had met — over, also, the compliments paid me for the manner in which I had made my way from Holland to Cadiz and Lagos. Suffice it that both Sir George Rooke and the duke told me that my services would not be forgot, and that when I returned to my Lord Marlborough I should not go unaccompanied by their commendations. However, enough of this. And now I told my tale of the morning, and of the two persons I had found on board *La Sacra Familia* — told, too, that they were at this moment on board the *Royal Sovereign*, I having deemed it best to bring them along with me.

"Let us see them," said Rooke, and

straightway bade his flag lieutenant go bring them in.

But I think that, although I had told all assembled at this board what kind of persons these were whom I had discovered in the ship, all the admirals, generals and captains were astonished at their appearance when they stood before them; while so handsome a show of it did my young Señor Belmonte make, that, perhaps almost unknowing what he did, Admiral Hopson pushed a chair toward him and bade him be seated. And because such courtesy could not be shown to one of these visitors without the same being extended to the other, the monk was also accommodated with a chair in which he sat himself calmly, his eyes roving round all those officers assembled there.

"You were passengers in this galleon — the — the — *Sacra Familia?*" Sir George said, glancing at a paper in his hand, on which I supposed the names of all the captured ships were written down, "and as this officer tells me, are anxious to proceed to your destination. Will you inform me of what that destination is, so that we may assist you in your desire?"

"Mine," exclaimed Señor Juan—and as his sweet, soft voice uttered the words musically, all eyes were turned on him, "is England eventually; yet," and he smiled that gracious smile which I had seen before, "my passage was but paid to Spain — and I am in Spain. Beyond being permitted to go ashore here with my few necessaries, I know not that I need demand any of your politely proffered assistance."

Sir George shrugged his shoulders while he looked attentively at the handsome young man — who, I thought, to speak truth, received the civilities of his speech with somewhat too much the air of one accustomed to having homage and consideration paid to him — then he said quietly:

"That, of course, shall be done at once. There can be no obstacle to that. We only regret that the rigours of war have caused us to inconvenience any ordinary passenger. You have of course your papers."

"Yes, I have them here," and he produced from his breast a bundle, at which Sir George glanced lightly.

Then he turned to Father Jaime, who preserved still the look of calmness which had distinguished him all through. Yet I wondered, too, that he should have done so, for he had been subjected to even more scrutiny than Belmonte had been, perhaps because of the garb he wore; scrutiny that, in one instance at least, would have disquieted a less contained man, since Admiral Hopson, I noticed, had scarcely ever taken his eyes off him since he had entered the cabin, or, when he had taken them off, had instantly refixed them so upon his countenance that 't was very palpable to me that the man puzzled him. But what need to describe that look which all the world has often seen on the face of one who is endeavouring to recall to himself where, or whether, he has ever seen another before.

"And you, sir?" the admiral asked.

"My destination," the monk replied, his voice firm, full and sonorous as before, "is the Abbey of Lugo; and since 't is far nearer here than Cadiz, I can scarce regret finding myself at Vigo, instead of at the latter place."

And, even as he spoke, I saw Hopson give a slight start and look even more intently at him than before.

Then he bent forward toward Father Jaime, and said quietly: "Reverend sir, is it possible that we have ever met before? In the West Indies, to wit?"

CHAPTER XII.

WHAT DID THE ADMIRAL DISCOVER?

Not a month had elapsed ere I stood alone on the beach of Viana, which is in the province of Entre-Douro-é-Minho, in Portugal, and watched, with somewhat sad thoughts in my mind, the white foresail and mainsail of the *Pembroke's* jolly boat rising and falling on the waters as, gradually, it made its way out to sea to where, a league off, there lay the English fleet. The English fleet, and bound for England!

Vigo was freed of its enemies and captors; over night, at dark, the whole of the British forces had cleared out of the bay, and, this morning, Juan Belmonte and myself had been put ashore at this miserable Portuguese town, or rather village, lying some twenty miles south of the Spanish frontier.

Briefly, this was the reason why I found myself standing alone upon this beach watching that fast disappearing boat, while, walking up to the town, went Señor Juan to seek for lodgings for us for the night.

After that council was concluded on board the *Royal Sovereign*—and from which Father Jaime, Belmonte and myself had retired after our interview with the admirals—the conclusion had been arrived at that, the work being done here—namely, the French fleet in our power and the Spanish galleons destroyed—it would be impolitic as well as unnecessary for the English to remain any longer in the place. This decision was, however, come to totally against the desire of the Duke of Ormond, who himself was anxious to take possession of the town of Vigo, to lie there during the winter months, and, in the spring, to open again the campaign against France in that portion of Spain. Unfortunately, however, for this idea—which was in fact a mighty good one, and, if carried out, might have gone far toward crippling France even more than she was eventually crippled—it was impossible. There were no provisions whereby his army could be sustained for the winter, nor had Rooke a sufficiency in his ships to provide him with, and neither would the admiral consent to leave behind a portion of his fleet with which—should it come to that—the duke could escape in case of necessity.

"For," said he to Ormond, as I learnt,

"you have seen, my Lord Duke, the disaster which has followed on our enemies trusting themselves within this narrow and landlocked bay. Would your Grace, therefore, think it wise to follow their bad example and give them an opportunity which, doubt not, they would take as soon as possible, of retaliating upon us?"

And to this Ormond could but shrug his shoulders, being able to find no answer to such remark. Therefore, at last — for all was not decided on the instant, but only after many more councils and much further argument — it was resolved that the fleet should remain no longer, nor, of course, the land forces neither.

But while all these determinations were being come to, I had had more than one interview with Rooke and Ormond (both of whom had entertained and made much of, nor ceased ever their commendations of, me), since it was very necessary that a decision should be come to as to what was to be my future course. For my work was done, my connection with this fleet over; I had no more business there. It was time I got back to my own regiment. Only how to get there — that was the question!

"You will scarce find at any port, Spanish or Portuguese," said the admiral to me, "a vessel putting to sea now; the risk is too great. For, consider, we are all about, and none know what may be our next move — this one has frightened all this part of the world. Then that old dog, Benbow, lieth in wait farther up. While to make the seas still more dangerous, the French ships of war and the privateers are everywhere. In truth, all traffic on the water is at an end for a time."

"Tis not so on land, though, sir," I ventured to say, "with a good horse I would undertake——"

"What!" exclaimed Ormond, with a laugh, "not surely to make your way to Flanders by land! You would scarce try that."

"Ay! but I would, though, my Lord Duke," I said, laughing, too, at the look of amazement on his face. "In very truth, I would. I have thought it all over."

"'Tis impossible! You would never arrive."

"Your Grace, I think I should. Permit me to explain. We are here in Spain——"

"Ay," said Rooke, interposing, "and so we are. But, Mr. Crespin, you would never get ashore, or, getting there, would never escape out of Vigo. Remember, the town itself is not in our hands, and the moment we were gone you would be set upon, or, even though you should be unmolested while we remain here, you would be followed from Vigo and —— "

"Sir," I interrupted in my excitement, "this is my plan: There is a seaport hard by here, called Viana, and 't is in Portuguese territory—therefore neutral—yet inclining more to us than to France."

"Aye," said Rooke, "and will come over to us ere long. The king leans to our side the most, because we are strongest on the seas—this taking of the galleons will decide him."

"Meanwhile," I went on, "'t is neutral. Now, from there I can make my way to Spain——"

"There's the rub! When you are in Spain. And afterward, in France. What then?"

"In both countries I can be a Frenchman," and now I saw these two great officers look at me attentively. "I have the French tongue very well—well enough to pass through Spain as a Frenchman, while —when in France—I can pass as a Spaniard who knows the French."

"'S heart!" exclaimed Ormond, slapping of the table with his be-ringed hand, "but I would you were in one of my regiments. You have a brain as well as a stalwart form. You must go far; and shall, if my word is any good with Jack Churchill."

"My Lord Duke, you are most gracious. Yet may I not ask if the plan is a fair one? At least, remembering that, by sea, the way is closed."

Fair or not fair, at least I brought them to it—more especially since, even though they had most utterly disapproved of my proposed method, they could neither of them have opposed it. For I was the Earl of Marlborough's officer; nay, more, I was his own particular and private messenger; I had come under his orders, and was still under them. Moreover, his last words to me had been: "Do your duty; fulfil the task I charge you with; then make your way back to me as best you can." That was all, yet enough.

Therefore it was arranged without more demur, though Sir George Rooke, who was now growing old, shook his head somewhat gravely, even as he ceased endeavouring to turn me from what I had resolved on.

"For," said he, kindly, "I like it not. You are still young—some years off thirty, I should suppose—and you are a good soldier—too good to be spared to any crawling Spaniard's knife or to fall into any truculent Frenchman's hands. And I would have taken you to England and put in the first queen's ship for Holland, had you chosen. Still, as you will, you will. Only, be very careful."

"Sir!" I said, touched at his fatherly consideration. "Be sure I will. Yet I think I can take care of myself. I have a good sword and a strong arm, and—well, one bullet is much the same as another. If one finds me in Spain or France, 'twill be no worse than one in Flanders. And, perhaps, my bullet is not moulded yet!"

As for his Grace, he took a different tack, he being younger and more *débonnair* than the admiral.

"Oddsbobs," he said, "bullets are bullets, and may be a soldier's lot or not. But for you, Lieutenant, I fear a worse danger. You are a good-looking fellow enough, with your height and breadth, blue eyes and brown hair. Rather, therefore, beware of the Spanish girls, and keep out of their way—or, encountering them, give them no cause for jealousy! Oh! I know them, and—well, they are the devil! 'Tis they who wield the knife—as often as not against those whom they loved five minutes back."

And, looking at the duke—who was himself of great manly beauty—I could well enough believe he knew what he was talking of. For, if all reports were true—but this matters not.

The time had not, however, yet come, for some day or so, for me to set out, since 't was arranged that I should be put ashore by one of the *Pembroke's* boats when the fleet went out of the bay, and that then my last farewell would be made to those amongst whom I had now lived for some weeks. Meanwhile, Sir George asked me what had become of my young friend, the Spanish gentleman, whom he called my "captive."

Now, this young captive had had still another interview with him after that first one, Sir George having sent for him from the *Pembroke*, into which he had been temporarily received as a guest—since *La Sacra Familia* had been sunk by us after being dismantled of all in her of any worth—and he had once more renewed his offer of taking him to England. And it surprised me exceedingly—I being present at this interview—to observe the extraordinary courtesy and deference which he—who was more used to receive deference from his fellow-men than to accord it—

showed to the youth; for he took him very graciously by the hand when he entered the cabin, led him to a seat, and, when there, renewed once more that offer of which I have spoken.

Indeed, his politeness was so great that I began to wonder if, by any chance, the admiral knew of this young man being any one of extreme importance, to whom it might be worth his while, as the chief representative of England here, to pay court. Yet, so silly was that wonderment that I dismissed it instantly from my mind, deciding that it was pity for his youth and loneliness which so urged the other.

"If you would go with us," he said, sitting by Belmonte's side, and speaking in the soft, well bred tones which were special to him, "you should be very welcome, I assure you, sir; and I do not say this as a sailor speaking to one who has by chance fallen into his hands, so to put it, but as an old man to a — to a young one; for, sir, I have children myself, some young as you, some older; have sons and — and daughters, and I should be most grateful to all who would be kind to them."

Now, as he spoke thus there became visible in Señor Juan another trait of character which I had scarce looked to see, it proving him to be a youth of great susceptibility. For, as the admiral made his kindly speech, I saw the beautiful dark eyes of the young man fill with tears—'t was marvellous how handsome he appeared at this moment—and, a second later, he had seized the old man's hand and had clasped it to his breast and kissed it.

But, even as he performed this action, I also saw Sir George start a little, give, indeed, what was but the faintest of starts; yet beneath the bronze upon his manly face there rose a colour which, had he not been a sailor, and that a pretty old one, might have appeared to be a blush. But because he was so manly and so English himself—being always most courteous and well bred, though abhorring, as it seemed to me, all signs of emotion—I concluded that this foreign style of salutation did not commend itself over-much to him; yet he listened very courteously, deferentially almost, it appeared, to the words of gratitude which the youth was now pouring out—words of gratitude for his offer, yet combined also with an absolute refusal of that offer.

"Very well; since you will not, sir," he said, when the young man had finished, "there is no more to be done. Yet, take a word of warning from me, I beseech you.

You will find it hard to reach England in a better way than I have suggested to you. Both France and Spain must be overrun with troops of all kinds at this time and — if you fall into their hands with your papers about you, showing you are an English subject — it may go hard. Also" — and now he tapped the cabin deck with his red-heeled shoe and looked down at it for a moment — "also — you are extremely well favoured. That, too, may injure you should — should — but," he went on, and without concluding his last sentence, "you understand what I mean," and now he gazed at Señor Juan with clear, frank eyes; gazed straight into his own.

For the life of me I could not understand what he was driving at, even if the youth himself could; since how a man should be injured by his good looks, even though in a hostile country, I failed to conceive. Certain, however, it was that the other understood well enough Sir George's meaning — his next action showed plainly enough that he did.

For now the rich warm colouring left his soft downless cheeks, even the full lips became pale, and he lifted his long slim hand and thrust it through the clusters of curls that hung over his forehead, as though in some distress of mind; then said, a moment later, looking up now and returning the admiral's glance fearlessly, while speaking very low.

"Yes, I understand. Yet, Señor, have no fear."

But I noticed, all the same, that he lifted his other hand as though to deprecate Sir George saying another word, which gesture he too seemed quite to understand, since he gave a half bow very solemnly ere he turned away.

Later, after Señor Juan had departed, and when Admiral Hopson had come over to the *Royal Sovereign*, to prepare for another of those endless councils which took place daily, Sir George looked up at me from some papers he was perusing, and said: "You are in the *Pembroke*, Mr. Crespin. Where have they bestowed that young man?"

"He is very comfortable, sir," I replied. "They have given him a spare cabin in the after flat."

"And the officers? Do they make him welcome, treat him with courtesy?"

"Oh, yes, indeed. He is popular with them already, sings them sweet songs accompanied by that instrument of his; is a rare hand at tricks of all kinds with the pass-dice and cards, and so forth. They will miss him when he has gone."

"Humph! Does he say who or what he is — which island in the Indies he belongs to — who are his kith and kin?"

"He says not much, sir, on that score; except that he is well enough to do — is traveling more or less to kill time — cares very little where he goes to for the present, so that he sees the world. As for his home, he appears best acquainted with Jamaica."

"Ha!" said Sir George. "He says all that, does he? Yet, though 'tis not permissible to doubt those who stand more or less in the degree of guests, I somewhat suspect that young man of not being all he appears to be. There is some other reason for his voyage to Europe than that he gives; he comes not on mere pleasure only. I know that — some day if you ever meet him again you will very likely know it, too, Mr. Crespin."

"Perhaps," exclaimed Admiral Hopson — who was soon to become Sir John Hopson (with a good pension) for the gallant part he had played in the late fight — "he was a friend of that accursed monk, although he has not levanted as he did. And since you talk of meetings, why, i'fags, I would like to meet that gentleman once more."

.

"Levanted!" Sir George and I exclaimed together. "Is the monk set out?"

"Ay, he is," replied the other. "Went last night—the instant he could get his necessaries out of the galleon's hold. It was discourteous, too, since I had previously sent to crave a few words with him."

"'S faith," Sir George exclaimed with a laugh, "you are not turning Papist, old friend, are you? Didst want the monk to shrive or confess you, or receive you into his church?"

"Not I—no Papistical doings for me," the blunt old gentleman replied. "The church my mother had me baptised in, and under whose blessing I have been fighting all my life, is good enough for me to finish in. Still, had I a foolish woman's mind to change, 't would not be to that man I should go."

"Why!" exclaimed Sir George, "what know you of him? Yet—yet," and he spoke slowly, "you know the Indies, Tom —and the monks are not always what they might be. Did you chance to know him, since you sent to demand an interview?"

"I thought so," said the inscrutable old sea dog quietly, "wherefore I sent asking him for a meeting. Yet, as our beloved friends the French say, the cowl does not always make the monk. Hey? And, if 't is the man I think, 't was not always the cowl and gown that adorned his person—rather, instead, the belt and pistols, buff jerkin, scarlet sash, long serviceable rapier handy, and—have at you, ha! one, two and through you. Hey!"

And as he spoke he made a feint of lunging at his brother admiral with a quill that lay to his hand.

CHAPTER XIII.

"DANGERS WORSE THAN SHOT OR STEEL—OR DEATH."

Now I return to the beach at Viana, on which I stood after having quitted the fleet—yet still, ere I go on, I must put you in the way of knowing how it comes about that for companion I have Señor Juan Belmonte, who at this moment is making his way into what proved to be a very filthy town in search of lodgings for us for the night. And this is how it came about:

When it was decided finally that I should part from the British squadron on the day they cleared out—they intending to anchor over night outside of Vigo bay and to send forward some frigates scouting ere going on their way to England—I made mention to Belmonte that such was my intention. Also I asked him—I finding of him in his cabin, where he was reading a Spanish book of love verses—what he meant to do with himself, since, if he did not leave the ship when, or before, I did, he would be forced to accept Sir George's invitation to proceed to England with hin.

"Oh, my friend!" he said, with ever the soft, gentle smile upon his handsome features, "my friend and conqueror"—for so he had taken to terming me—"I want no terrible journey to England in these great fierce ships of war. Tell me, tell me, *amigo mio*, what you are going to do yourself. Your plans! Your plans!"

"My plans," I said, seeing no reason why I should not divulge them to him, since it was impossible he could do me any hurt, even if so inclined, which I thought not very likely, "are simple ones. I go ashore at Viana, find a horse—one will carry me part of the journey, then I can get another—and so, by God's will, get to the end, to my destination."

"But the destination. The destination. Where is it? Tell me that."

"The destination is Flanders, the seat of the present war. I am a soldier. My place is there."

"Aye, aye," he replied. "I know. You have told me. Your service is not with these ships nor their soldiers, but with others—a great army, far north."

"That is it," I said.

"And you will travel all that way—mean to travel—alone!"

"I must," I said, "if I intend to get there. There is no other way."

"Take me with you!" he exclaimed, suddenly, springing impetuously to his feet from the chair in which he sat. "Take me with you! I will be a good companion—amuse you, sing to you, wile away the long hours, stand by your side. If necessary," yet he said this a little slower, and with more hesitation, as I thought, "fight with you."

Now, putting all other objections which rose to my mind away for the moment, this last utterance of his did not recommend him very strongly to me. "Fight for me, indeed!" I thought. "A fine fighter this would be!—a youth who had turned pale at seeing a dead man or two floating by in the water after the battle, or at hearing the shriek of a wounded one as we rowed past him on our way to the *Royal Sovereign!*"

However, aloud I said:

"Señor Belmonte, I fear it cannot be as you desire. The road will be hard and rough, the journey long; there will be little opportunity for singing and jiggettings. Moreover, death will always be more or less in the air. If, in Spain or

France, I am discovered—nay, even suspected of being what I am, an English soldier—'t will be short shrift for me. I shall be deemed a spy, and shot, or hung to the nearest tree. Take, therefore, my counsel at once, and follow it. Go you to England in this ship, as the admiral invites you. That way you will be safe and easy."

"No, no, no," he answered. "I will not; I will not. I will go with you. I like you," he said, with a most friendly glance. "If—if you go alone—if we part here—we shall never meet again. That shall not be. I am resolved. And—and—only let me go, and I will be so good! I promise. Will not sing a note—will—see there!" and, like a petulant boy as he was, he seized his viol d'amore, which hung on a nail in the cabin, and dashed it to the floor, while, a moment later, he would have stamped his foot into it had I not stopped him. "Yes, I will break it all to pieces. Since it offends you, I will never strike another note on it, nor will I ever sing again—not in your hearing, at least—though I have known some who liked well enough to hear me play—and sing, too."

"Juan," I said, not knowing in the least why his impassioned grief moved me so much as to address him thus familiarly, which I had never done before, "it offends me not at all; instead, I have often listened gratefully to the music of your voice and viol. But now—now—on such a journey as I go it would be out of place, even if you were there, which you must not be."

"I must. I must. I must," he answered. "I will. You called me Juan just now—ah! you are my friend, or you would not speak thus. Oh!" he went on, and now he clutched my arm and gazed fervently into my face, "do not refuse. And see, think, Mervan," pronouncing my name thus, and in a tone that would have moved a marble heart, "I shall be no trouble to you. I can ride, oh! like a devil when I choose—I have ridden with the Mestizos and natives in the isles—and I can use a pistol or petronel, also a sword. See," and he whipped his rapier off the bed where it was a-lying, drew it from its sheath impetuously, as he did everything, and began making pass after pass through the open door of the cabin into the gangway. "I know what to do. Also, remember, I can speak Spanish when we are in Spain—pass for a Spaniard if 't is necessary—and—and—and——" he broke off, "if you will not take me with you, why, then, I will follow you; track you like a shadow, sleep like a dog outside the inn in which you lie warm and snug; ay! even though you beat me and drive me away for doing so."

Again and still again I resisted, yet 't was hard to do; for, though I had spoken against his singings and playings, and kept ever before my eyes the stern remembrance of my duty, which was to make my way straight to my goal and crash through all impediments, I could not but reflect that this bright, joyous lad by my side would help to cheer many a lonely hour and many a gloomy mile. Yet again I spoke against the project, putting such thoughts aside.

"Child," I said, "you do not know, do not understand. Our — my — path will be beset with dangers. *I* know what I am doing, what lies before me. Listen, Juan. 'T is more than like that I shall never reach Flanders, never ride with my old troops again, never more feel a comrade's hand clasped in mine; may perish by the way side, have my throat cut in some lonely inn, be shot in the back, taken as a spy. Yet 't is my duty. I am a soldier and a man; you are —— "

"Yes?" with an inward catching of the breath, a flash from the dark eyes.

"A boy; a lad; also, you say, well

enough to do, with a long and happy life before you, no call upon you to fling that life away. Juan, it must not be."

"It shall," he said, leaning forward toward me. "It shall; I swear it by my dead mother's memory. Boy! Lad, you say. So be it. Yet with the will and determination of a hundred men. To-morrow, Mervan, to-night, to-day, if I can get a boat to the great ship out there, I visit the admiral and ask him to put me ashore with you. And he will do it. Great as he is, in command over all you English here, I have a power within," and he struck his breast with his hands, "a power over him which will force him to do as I wish. Do you dare me—challenge me?"

"No," I answered quietly, though in truth somewhat amazed at his words, while still remembering the strange deference Sir George had shown all along to the youth. "I dare to say you may prevail—with him."

"Aye—with him!" and now he laughed a little, showing the small pearly white teeth, somewhat. "With him! I understand. But you mean not with you also. Yet, with you, too, I shall prevail. I will follow you till you give me leave to keep ever by your side. Remember, if I am not

Spanish, I have lived in Spain's dependencies. I can be very Spanish when I choose," and again he laughed, and again the white teeth glistened beneath the scarlet lips.

"If," I said, scarce knowing or understanding what power was influencing me, making me a puppet in this youth's hands — yet still a yielding one!— "the admiral gives his consent to put you ashore, then I——"

"Yes. Yes. Yes. Yes, Mervan?" he interposed quickly.

"Then I will not withhold mine. Come with me if you choose—remember, 't is at your own risk."

In a moment his whole face was transfigured with joy. Seeing that joy, I deemed myself almost a brute to have ever tried to drive him away from me, although I had endeavoured to do so as much for his own safety as my own. He laughed and muttered little pleased expressions in Spanish which I neither understood nor am capable of setting down here; almost I thought he would have flung his arms around my neck and embraced me. Indeed, it seemed as though he were about to do so, but, suddenly recollecting himself, desisted — perhaps because he knew that to us English such demonstrations were not palatable.

And now I have to tell how Sir George placed no obstruction in the way, allowing him to go ashore with me; yet, when he heard that we were to travel together the look upon his face was one of extreme gravity, almost of sternness. Also, he maintained a deep silence for a moment or two after I had told him such was to be the case, and sat with his eyes fixed on me as though he were endeavouring to read my very inmost thoughts. But at last he said quietly, and with even more than usual of that reserve which characterised him :

"You have found out nothing about this young man yet, Mr. Crespin, then?—know nothing more about him than you have known from the first? Um?"

"I know nothing more, sir."

Again he paused awhile, then spoke once more, with the slightest perceptible shrug of his shoulders as he did so:

"Very well. 'T. is your affair, not mine. You are not under my command, but that of the Earl of Marlborough. You must do as seems best to you. Yet have a care what you are about." Then he leant forward toward me, and said : "Mr. Crespin, you have done extremely well — have gained a high place in our esteem. When his Lordship reads what the Duke of Ormond and myself have to say about you, you will find your promotion very rapid, I think. Do not, I beseech of you — do not imperil it in any way; do not be led away into jeopardising the bright future, the brilliant career, that is before you. Run on no rock, avoid every shoal that may avert your successful course."

"Sir," said, "I am a soldier with many unknown dangers before me. This boy can add nothing to their number. Yet, sir, for your gracious consideration for me I am deeply grateful."

Still he regarded me, saying nothing for a moment or so, then spoke again:

"Dangers!" he said — "the dangers every honest soldier or sailor encounters in his calling are nothing; they are our portion; must be avoided, if may be; if not, must be accepted. And he who falls in the battle has naught to repine at — at least he falls honourably, leaves a clean memory behind."

"Sir!"

"But there are other dangers that are worse than shot, or steel — or death! Many a brave soldier and sailor has gone under from other causes than these. Mr.

Crespin, I say no more — have, perhaps, said too much, were it not that you have strangely interested me." Then, abruptly, he went on, and as though with the intention of forbidding any more remarks on that subject: "Captain Hardy shall be instructed to send you both ashore on the morning after we go out. Here are some papers from the duke and myself to the Earl of Marlborough. Be careful of them; they relate to you alone. I — we — hope they will assist you to go far."

I bowed and murmured my thanks, for which he observed there was no necessity whatever, then gave me his hand and said:

"Farewell, Mr. Crespin; we may not meet again. I wish you all you can desire for yourself. Farewell."

But he uttered no further word of warning of any kind, and so let me go away from him wondering blindly what it was he knew of this young man; wondering above all what it was against which he covertly put me on my guard.

Later on — though not for some time to come — I knew and understood.

* * * * * * * * * *

I found Juan — after the sails of the boat from the *Pembroke* had faded into little white specks upon the surface of the water, until they looked no bigger than the flash made by seagull's wing—found him outside the one and only inn of this small town, lolling against the doorpost—made dirty and greasy with the shoulders of countless Algarvian peasants—and amusing himself by trying to make a group of ragged children understand the pure Spanish he was speaking to them.

Then, as he saw me crossing the filthy street, he came over to meet me—never heeding the splashing of mud administered to the handsome long boots which he had now upon his legs, though he was dainty, too, in his ways—and began telling me of what arrangements he had already made for our journey.

"First, *mio amigo*," he said, joyously, "about the horses. Two are already in command. One, a big bony creature which is for you, Mervan, because you also are big and stalwart, and require something grand to carry you—while for me there is a jennet with, oh! such a fiery eye and a way of biting at everything near it. But have no fear! Once I am on its back, and *por Diós!* it will do as I want, not as it wants."

I laughed, then asked if these animals were to be our own.

"Oh, yes, our own," he said. "Our

very own. I have bought them — they are ours. And, if they break down — yours, I think, must surely do so — why, we will turn them loose into the nearest wood, and — buy some more."

"At this rate we shall spend some money ere we strike Flanders," I said.

"Ho! Ho! Money — who cares for money! I have plenty, enough for you and me, too. We will travel comfortably, *mon ami;* have the best of everything. Plenty of money, and — and, Mervan, do you know, if it was not for one of the most accursed villains who ever trod the face of the earth, I should be so rich that — that — oh! it is impossible to say. Mervan," catching at my arm with that boyish impetuosity of his which ever fascinated me; "you are English, therefore you know all the English, I suppose. In Jamaica and Hispaniola and all the other islands we know everybody. Mervan, who is, or where is, James Eaton?"

"James Eaton!" I exclaimed, with a laugh at his innocent supposition that we were all acquainted with each other in England as they are in the Indies; yet 'tis true that he could not know that our capital city alone had so vast and incredible a population as half a million souls! "James Eaton! Who and what is he? An officer? If so,

I might, perhaps, know, or get to know, something of him."

"An officer? Oh! yes, *por Diós!* he is an officer—has been once. But not such as you or those brave ones we have just parted from. An officer. *Corpo di Bacco!* A villain, *vagamundo*, Mervan—a *flibustier*—what the English call in the islands a damned pirate."

"Humph!" I said. "A friend of yours? Eh, Juan?"

"A friend of mine? Ho! Yes. *Mon Dieu!* He is a friend. Wait—when we are in England you shall see how much I love my friend. Oh, yes! You shall see. When I take him by his beard and thrust this through his black heart," and he touched the quillon of the sword by his side as he spoke.

"And is he the villain who has stolen your wealth?" I asked, as we entered now the door of the inn, I nearly falling backward from the horrible odours which greeted my nostrils when we did so.

"He is the villain. Oh! 'tis a story. Such a story. You shall hear. But not now—not now. Now we will eat and drink and be gay."

"But," I said, my curiosity much aroused, "if he has stolen your wealth how comes it you are rich, as you say? Have you two fortunes—two sources of wealth?"

"Yes," he replied, with his bright, sweet smile. "Two fortunes—the one he stole, the other—but no matter for fortunes now. I have enough and plenty for myself—and, Mervan, for you if you want it. Plenty."

"I, too, have enough for present wants," I said. "Quite enough."

"*Bueno. Bueno*," he said. "Then all is well. And now to eat, drink and be gay until to-morrow. Then away, away, away to Flanders—anywhere, so long as we are together. Joy to-day, work and travel to-morrow. But, Mervan," and once more he placed his hand supplicatingly on my arm. "Forgive. Forgive me. I—I have brought the viol d'amore."

CHAPTER XIV.

"IT IS WAR TIME! IF IT MUST BE, IT MUST."

We were English gentlemen furnished with passports to enable us to travel through Spain—which might not be difficult, since there were likely to be as many English troops in that country as there were French, while one-half of the inhabitants wavered in their espousals of either us and Austria or Louis and Philip.

That, at least, was what we *meant to give* out if any one in Portugal—and in Viana especially—should make it their business to ask us any questions, which, however, was not very likely to be the case; for, in this miserable hole—and miserable it was beyond all thought—there were none who could have any possible right to so ask us of our affairs, there being no consul of any country whatever in the place—and, for the rest, we were English. That was enough; we were English, come ashore from that great fleet whose deeds of the last few weeks had spread consternation for leagues around and on either side of Vigo,

ACROSS THE SALT SEAS. 191

and whose topmasts were now very plainly visible a mile or so out from the shore; topsails, too, which would be conspicuous enough to all in Viana for another day or so, until the scouts returned with their news; and before this fleet had disappeared we should be gone, too — on our road to Spain, to France, to Flanders.

That road was already decided on — we were poring over the chart now upstairs in the sleeping room Juan had secured for me, he having another one for himself on the opposite side of the corridor — poring over it by the light of an oil lamp and the flames cast by a bright cork-wood fire which we had caused to be lit, since 'twas already very cold, it being now November.

We had resolved, however, that the great high road to France would not be the very best, perhaps, for our purpose — the road which, passing through Portugal into Spain at Miranda and Tuy, runs through Valladolid and Burgos up to Bayonne and France, for these towns were in the kingdoms of Leon and Castile, and here all were, we learnt, for Philip and France; but we knew also that with other parts of Spain it was no so. Away on the eastern shores, Catalonia and Valencia had declared for Charles of Austria and the allies. Nearer to where we were, namely, in Galicia, above Portugal, they wavered. Yet 't was said now that they inclined toward us, perhaps because Vigo is in Galicia and, therefore, they had had a taste of how we could be either good friend or fateful foe. Certainly we had shown we could well be the latter!

"Yes," I said to Juan, my finger on the chart; "this way will be our road. Across the frontier where the Minho divides the two countries, then up its banks to Lugo, and so through the Asturias to Biscay and Bayonne. That is our way, and, after all, 't is not much farther than t' other. And safer, too. If Galicia leans to us, so may the Asturians. If not, we shall be no worse off than if we traversed Leon, Castile and Navarre."

"*Vogue la galère!*" cried the boy, who generally varied his exclamations from Spanish to French and French to English — whichever came uppermost — "I care nothing. We shall be together, *mio amigo;* that's enough for me."

"Together for a time," I put in; "for a time. Remember, once we reach Flanders — if we ever do — which is more than doubtful — my service claims me. 'T is war there, hard knocks and buffets for me — for you the first sloop or vessel of any sort that will run you over to the English coast."

"Oh, la, la!" said Juan, "'t is not come yet. We have a month, at least, together, and perhaps even then we will not part. This great soldier, this fierce captain you speak of, this English lord who contends with France — perhaps he will let me fight too. Give me — what is it you call it? — a pair of colours. Then we could fight side by side, Mervan, could we not?"

I nodded and muttered: "Perhaps," though in truth I thought nothing was more unlikely. In some way I had come to have none too great an opinion of the youth's courage or capacity for fighting, remembering how he had paled, nay, almost shuddered, at the sight of those poor dead ones floating in Vigo harbour; while for the "pair of colours"—well, there was plenty of interest being made on all sides by those of influence in England to obtain such things for their own kith and kin. There would be mighty little chance for this young stripling to be received into any regiment. Therefore I went on with our plans, saying, as I still glanced at the chart:

"That must be the road. And from Lugo across the mountains to Baos, then to

Elcampo, and so to Bilbao up to Bayonne. That is the way."

"To Lugo," he repeated, meditatively. "To Lugo. Humph! To Lugo. That is the way they went, you know—Chateaurenault and his captains—when they fled from you."

Now I started when he said this, for I had, indeed, forgotten the slight rumour I had heard to that effect—forgotten it amidst all the excitement of the stirring times that had followed the battle and the taking of the galleons. Yet now the fact was recalled to my mind, I did not let it alter my determination, and after a moment's reflection, I said :

"Still it matters not. They will not have gone that way for the same reason that we shall go it. On their road to France! Chateaurenault will not stay there, but rather push on to Paris to give an account of his defeat—make the best excuses he can to his master. Nor will he come back—an he does, he will find nothing here. His ships are sunk or being carried to England, and 't is so with the galleons that are not themselves at the bottom of the ocean. 'T is very well. To-morrow we set out for Lugo, take the first step on our road."

And on the morrow we did set out—

amidst, perhaps, as disagreeable circumstances as could be the case.

For when we rose early the snow was falling in thick flakes; also 'twas driven into our faces by a stiff northeasterly wind which brought it down from the Cantabrian mountains, and soon our breasts were covered with a layer of it which we had much ado to prevent from freezing on them, and could only accomplish by frequent buffets. Yet we were not cold, neither, since our horses were still able to trot beneath it — for as yet it lay not upon the roads, and we could thus keep ourselves warm. Yet, withal, we made some ten leagues that day — the animals under us proving far better than might with reason have been expected, judging by their lean and sorry appearance — and arrived ere nightfall at a small village — yet walled and fortified, because it lies close on to the Spanish frontier—called Valenza. And here we rested for the night, finding, however, at first great difficulty in being permitted to get into it, and, next, an equal trouble in obtaining lodgings in the one inn of the place.

Also we learnt that it behooved us to be very careful when we set out next day, or we might find it impossible to enter Spain, which now lay close at hand, and separated only by the Minho from this place; or, being in, might find it hard to go forward.

"For," said the host, a filthy, unkempt creature who looked as though he were more accustomed to attending to cattle in their sheds than to human beings, but who by great good fortune was able to speak broken French, "at Tuy, where you must pass into Spain, they are rigourous now as to papers, letting none enter who are not properly provided. *Basto!* 't is not a week ago that one went forward who was passed through with difficulty. And a Spaniard, too, though from the Indies."

"From the Indies!" exclaimed Juan, with impetuosity. "From the Indies! Why, so am I and — and this señor," looking at me, "both from the Indies. Therefore, we can pass also, I should suppose."

"Oh, for that," answered the man, "I know not. Yet this old man went through, somehow. He had come up from the south — from Cadiz, as I think, or Cartagena, or the Siérras — in a great coach and four, travelled as a prince, had good provisions with him, and ho! — he gave me to taste of it! — some strong waters that made me feel like a prince, too, though the good God knows I am none!" and he cast his eyes round the filthy room into which we had been shown. "Also, he had his papers all regular; also," and here he gave a glance at us of unspeakable cunning, "he was generous and open-handed. That spared him much trouble."

"Perhaps 't will spare us, too!" again exclaimed Juan. "We can also be generous and open-handed."

"It will do much. Yet the papers! The papers! Have you the papers?"

Now, we had no papers whatsoever that would stand us in such stead; therefore, when we were alone together in the room which was to be ours, and in which there were two miserable, dirty-looking beds, side by side, covered with sheepskins for coverlets — and perhaps for blankets, too! — we fell to discussing what must be done; for it was at once plain and easy to see that at Tuy we should never get through. I had no papers nor passports whatever, while Juan bore about him only those which proved that he was a subject of England.

"Yet," said he, "they knew not that on board *La Sacra Familia*, and, because I could speak Spanish as well as they, deemed me a Spaniard. I wonder if I could get through that way."

"*You* might, possibly," I replied. "I am sure I never should. The Spanish which I know is scarce good enough for that."

"'T is true," he said, reflectively—"true enough. Yet, you have the French. See, Mervan, here is an idea. I am a Spaniard and you are a Frenchman, for the moment. Both countries are sworn friends now as regards their government, if not their people. Why should not we be travelling together as natives of those lands?"

"An we were," I answered, "we should not be without passports. Remember, we come to them from Portugal; therefore, to have gotten into Portugal as either Spanish man or Frenchman, we should have wanted papers; and we have none. Consequently, the first question asked us will be, How got we into Portugal? Then what reply shall we make? That we came from the English fleet, which has just destroyed their galleons? That will scarce do, Juan, for our purpose, I think."

Acknowledging such to be the case, Juan sat himself down on the dirty bed and began to ponder.

"At least we will not be whipped," he muttered, "and at the outset, too. Mervan, we must find another road somehow, or, better still—there must be some part of the frontier which runs the northern length of this miserable land, and which is unguarded. Can we not get across without any road? Up one side of a mountain and down another, and so — into Spain!"

"'T is that I have thought of. Yet there are the horses—also a river to cross. And, as luck will have it, the mountains hereabouts are none too high nor dense with woods, nor do they run from east to west, but rather south and north. Such as there are, you can see from this window," and I pointed in the swift, on-coming darkness of the November evening to where they could be seen across the river, their summits low, and over them a rusty rime-blurred moon rising.

Then I went on:

"Juan, we must tempt the landlord with some of that *largesse* which the old man who came in the coach seems to have distributed so lavishly—only, he has bestowed it on the Spanish side—ours must begin here. Come, let us go and see what can be done with him."

"But what to do?" the boy said, looking at me with his strange eyes full of intelligence and perhaps anxiety.

"This: there must be some way of traversing the river when there is no town on either side—if the worst came to the worst we could swim it on our horses at night."

"On such a night as this!" exclaimed Juan, shuddering and glancing out through the uncurtained window at the flakes of snow which still fell. "It would be death," he whispered, shuddering again.

"You are easily appalled," I said, speaking coldly to him for the first time since our acquaintance. "Yet, remember, I warned you of what you might expect in such an expedition as this. You would have done better to accept the admiral's offer. A cabin in the *Pembroke* would have been a lady's withdrawing room in contrast to what we may have to encounter."

"Forgive me. Forgive," he hastened to say pleadingly. "Indeed, indeed, Mervan, I am bold and no coward — but, remember, I am of the tropic south, and 't is the cold of the river that appalls me—not fear for my life. Like many of our clime, I can sooner face death than discomfort."

"There will be enough facing of both ere we have done—that is, if we ever get farther than here," I said, almost contemptuously.

"So be it," he exclaimed, springing to his feet and evidently bitterly hurt by my tone. Indeed, 't was very evident he was, since the tears stood in his eyes. "So be it. We face it! Now," and he rapped the table between us as though to emphasise his words, "continue your plans, make your suggestions, bid me swim rivers, cross mountains, plunge into icy streams or burning houses, and see if I flinch or draw back again. Only—only," and his voice sank to its usual soft tones, "do not be angry with me."

That it was impossible to be angry with him long I felt, nor, for some unexplained reason, could I despise him for his evident objection to discomfort—the discomfort which would arise from so trifling a thing —to me, a cuirassier—as swimming one's horse across a river on a winter night. And, as my contempt, such as it was, vanished at once at his plea to me not to be angry with him, I exclaimed:

"At worst it shall be made as light for you as may be, since you are only a boy after all! And if that worst comes," I continued, in a good natured, bantering way, which caused the tears to disappear and the smiles to return, which brought back to my mind a song my good old father used to sing about "Sunshine after Rain"—"if that worst comes, why, I will swim the river with you on my back, and your jennet shall swim by my horse's side. Now, for the landlord!"

We found that unclean personage a-sitting over a fair good fire, which roared cheerfully up a vast open chimney from the stone floor upon which the logs were, with, by his side, a woman who was blind, as we saw very quickly when she turned eyes on us which were naught but white balls with no pupils to them. And, because we at once perceived that there was no power of sight in those dreadful orbs, I made no more to do, but, slipping of my finger into my waistcoat pocket, pulled out two great gold doubloons—worth more than our guineas —and held them up before him. Then I said in French, and speaking low, because I knew not whether that stricken one might understand or not:

"See, this will pay our addition and more. Now listen. You may equally as well have them as the *guarda frontéra* at Tuy. Will you?"

He nodded, grasping the pieces—I noticed that he kept them from clinking against each other, perhaps because he wanted not his wife to know that he had gotten them—then put each into a different pocket, and said: "She understands not the French. Speak."

"We have no papers. Listen; we are English! We must cross into Spain. Tell us some other road; put us in the way, and — see — to-morrow morning, these are for you also."

And I took forth two more of the golden coins.

He looked at us a moment, then said: "You — hate — Spain?"

Again I nodded.

"So all of us here at Valenza," he went on. "A fierce, cruel neighbor, would trample on us because we are weak. Will seize us yet an England helps not. Crush them — and France — the world's plague! Listen!"

Then, as we bent our heads, he went on:

"From here there is a bye-road leads to the river bank; it crosses by a wooden bridge into Spain, a league this side of Melagasso. I will put you in the way in the morning. Once over that bridge, there is a road cut from the rock that mounts two hundred paces. There at the summit is the *guarda frontéra*. Two men are there, an old and a young one. Kill them, and you are through, leaving no trace behind. Afterward, there is no sign of life for three leagues."

"Kill them!" I exclaimed. "Must that be done?"

"Ay — or silence them. But — killing

is best. And — and — the cliff is high, the river runs deep beneath. Cast them in, and you are safe."

"They may see us passing the bridge — kill *us* ere we can mount the road."

"Do it in the night," the fellow whispered. "In the night, when all is dark. And 't will be almost nightfall ere you are there. Do it then."

"There is no other way, no other entrance to Spain?"

"None — without papers."

"Good. It is war time! If it must be, it must."

CHAPTER XV.

"DRAW SWORDS!"

Another night had come—'t was already dark—and Juan and I sat on our horses in the cork wood, at the end of which we could hear the Minho swirling along beneath the ramshackle bridge that divided Portugal from Spain. And, as good fortune would have it, there was on this, the Portuguese side, no *guarda frontéra* whatever. Perhaps that poor, impoverished land thought there was naught to guard from ingress, also that nothing would be brought from Spain to them. The traffic set all the other way!

Because there was no need for us to be too soon where we were now; indeed, because 't was not well that we should be here ere nightfall, the landlord had not awakened me until nine in the morning. And then, on his doing so, I perceived that the other sheepskin-clad bed by my side had not been occupied at all. Wherefore I started up in some considerable fright, calling out to him through the door to know where was my friend, the young señor, whom I had left warming himself at the great fire below over night, and saying that he would follow me to bed ere long.

"Oh! he is below," he replied. "Has passed the night in front of the fire wrapped in his cloak, saying that 't was there alone he could keep himself from death by the cold. He bids me tell you all is well for your journey, the horses fresh; also there is a good meal awaiting you"; whereon I performed my ablutions, hurried on my garments and rapidly made my way to the public room below.

"Juan," I said, "you should have warned me of your intention of remaining below. This is not good campaigning, nor comradeship. Had I awakened in the night and found you missing, I should have descended to seek for you, fearing that danger had come to you, and 't is not well for travellers to be aroused unnecessarily from their beds on winter nights. Also we should keep always together. Soldiers — and you have to be one now! — on dangerous service should not separate."

"Forgive," he said, as, it seemed, he was always saying to me, and uttering the words in his accustomed soft, pleading voice. "Forgive. But — oh! Mervan!"

pausing a moment as though seeking for some excuse for having deserted me for the night—"oh! Mervan! that bed was so —so filthy and untempting. And the room so cold, when without fire. And it was so warm here. I could not force myself to leave this room.

Remembering what he had said about those who came from the tropics dreading cold and discomfort even more than death, I thought I understood how he should have preferred sleeping here to doing so above. Therefore, I merely said:

"There might be worse beds than that you would not use—may be worse for us ere long. Still, no matter. You slept warm here as I did upstairs. Yet 't is well I did not waken. Now let us see for breakfast and our departure," and giving a glance at the landlord, who was bringing in a sort of thick soup in which I saw many dried raisins floating, also some eggs and coarse black bread, as well as some chocolate which smelt mighty good and diffused a pleasing aroma through the room, I tapped my waistcoat pocket to remind him of the other doubloons that were in it. And he nodded understandingly.

The journey to where we now stood this evening was as uneventful as though we had been traveling in safety in our own England. The road into which the man had put us in the morning led first of all through countless villages — I have since heard that in all Europe there is no land so thickly sown with villages as this poor one of Portugal — then trailed off into a dense chestnut-fringed track that was no longer a road at all.

And now we knew that we were close unto the spot where our first adventure on the journey, that we hoped might at last bring us to Flanders, must of necessity take place. We were but half an hour's ride from the crazy bridge the man had spoken of as connecting his country with Spain — the bridge on the other side of which was the rocky path, with, at the top of it, the hut in which we should find two Spanish *guardas frontéras* armed to the teeth and prepared to bar the way to all who could not show their right to pass.

Yet we were resolved to pass — or leave our bodies there.

"There is," the landlord had said, "a holy stone at the spot where the path leading to the bridge enters the cork wood. You cannot mistake it. Upon that stone is graven the Figure, beneath it an arrow pointing the way to Melagasso. Your path

ACROSS THE SALT SEAS. 209

lies to the left and thus to the bridge. God keep you."

We left that stone as he had directed, with one swift glance upward at those blessed features—I noticing Juan crossed himself devoutly—slowly over fallen leaves that lay sodden on the earth beneath their mantle of snow, and over dried branches blown to the earth, our horses trod. And so for a quarter of an hour we pursued our way, while still the night came on swifter and swifter until, at last, we could scarce see each other's forms beneath the thick foliage above our heads.

Yet we heard now that swirling, rushing river—heard its murmur as it swept past its banks, and its deep swish as it rolled over what was doubtless some great boulder stone out in the stream—heard, too, its hum as it glided by the supports of the bridge that we knew was before us. Also, we saw above our heads a light gleaming—a light that we knew must come from the frontiermen's house.

And we had to steal up to where that light twinkled brightly, in what was now the clear, frosty air, since the snow had ceased —indeed, had not fallen all day—and all was clear overhead; to steal up, and then, if might be, make our hasty rush past on our horses' backs, or stay to cross steel and exchange ball with those who barred our way.

"Forward to the bridge!" I whispered to Juan, fearing that even from where we were my voice might be borne on the clear night air up to that height. "Loosen, also, your blade in its sheath! And your pistols, too — are they well primed?"

"Yes," he whispered back, his voice soft and low as a woman's when she murmurs acknowledgment of her love. "Yes."

"You do not fear?"

"I fear nothing — we are together," and, as he spoke, I felt the long, slim, gloved hand touch mine.

A moment later we had left the shadow of the wood; we stood above the sloping bank of the river rushing by; another moment and our horses' feet would be upon the wooden bridge — its creaking quite apparent to our ears as the stream swept under it.

"'T is God's mercy," I whispered again to him, "that the river is so brawling; otherwise the horses' hoofs upon these boards would be heard as plain as a musket's roar. Ha! I had forgotten!"

"Forgotten what, Mervan?" the gentle

voice of Juan whispered back. "Forgotten what?"

"If they should neigh! If there should be any of their kind up there!" and as I spoke, as the thought came to me, I felt as though I myself feared.

"Pray God they do not; yet, if they do, it must be borne." And now I noticed his voice was as firm as though he had experienced a hundred such risks as this we were running. Then he added: "The Indians muffle theirs with their serapes when they draw near a foe. Shall we do that?"

"No," I answered, "'tis too late. Let's on. Yet, remember, at the slowest pace. Thus their hoofs will fall lighter." And again I exclaimed: "Thank God, the river drowns their clatter!"

Yet, a moment later, and I had cause for further rejoicing. From above where that light twinkled there came a sound of singing — a rich, full voice a-trolling of a song, with another voice joining in.

Or was there more than one voice joining in? If so, we might have more than the old man and the young one, of whom the landlord had spoken, to encounter. Almost directly Juan confirmed my dread.

"There are half a dozen there," he said,

very calmly. "I know enough of music to recognise that. What to do now?"

"To go on," I answered. "See, we are across the bridge—there is the road—in another moment we shall be ascending the path. Praise heaven, we can ride abreast."

And in that other moment we were riding abreast slowly up that path, the snow that lay on it deadening now the sound of the horses' hoofs, while the voices within helped also to silence them.

"I know the song," Juan whispered—and I marvelled at his calmness—his! the youth's who had been so nervous when there was naught to fear, yet who now, when danger was close upon him, seemed to fear nothing—"have sung it myself. 'T is 'The Cid's Wedding.'"

"'T will not be songs about weddings that they will be engaged on," I said, "if any come out of that hut during the next ten minutes; but rather screeches of death—from us or them. Have your sword ready, Juan, also your pistols."

"They are ready," he said. "Yet what to do? Suppose any come forth ere we are past the door, over the frontier. Am I to ride straight through them—are we to do so?"

"Ay. Sit well down in your saddle,

give your nag his head, and — if any man impedes your way, stand up in your stirrups, cut down straight at him, or, if yours is not a cutting sword, thrust straight at the breast of — Ha!"

My exclamation — still under my breath, since my caution did not desert me — was caused by what now met our eyes, namely, the opening of some door giving on to the road in front of where the frontier cabin stood; the gleaming forth into that road of a stream of light, and then the coming out from the hut and the mingling of some four or five figures of men in the glare.

Now, when this happened, we had progressed up the hillside road two-thirds of the way, so that we were not more than seventy paces, if as much, from where those people were; yet, as I calculated, even at this nearness to them, we might still, if all went well, escape discovery. For we were under the shelter of the shelving rock which reared itself to our left hands, and not out in the middle of the road, which was here somewhat broad; and, therefore, to the darkness of the night was added the still deeper darkness of the rock's obscurity. And, I reflected, 't was scarce likely any would be coming our way from this party, which was evidently breaking up, since the Portuguese and Spaniards did not, I thought, fraternise very much. 'T was not very probable any would be returning our way. Consequently, I deemed that we were safe, or almost so; that, soon, some of those in the road would take themselves off, and would leave behind in the hut none but the old man and the young man of whom the landlord had spoken. Nay, more, a glance down the road in the direction of where we were would, in the darkness of the night. reveal nothing of our whereabouts. And I conveyed as much to Juan by a pressure of my hand, yet leaning forward, too, over to his side and whispering:

"All the same, be ready. It may come to a rush. If one of our horses neighs or shakes itself — so much as paws the earth — if a bridle jangles — we are discovered."

And a glance from those bright eyes — I protest, I saw them glisten in the darkness of the starlit night! — told me that he had heard and understood. Told me, also, that he was ready. After that — after those whispered words of mine, that responsive glance of his — we sat as still as statues on our steeds, hardly allowing our breath to issue from our lungs — watching — watching those figures.

"God! would they never separate? Would not some depart and the others retire into the cabin and shut the door against the cold wintry night? Offer us the opportunity to make one turn of the wrist on our reins, give one pressure of our knees to the animals' flanks and dash up the remains of the ascent and past the hut ere those within could rush out and send a bullet after us from fusil, gun or musketoon?

At last they gave signs of parting — we heard the *buenas noches* and the *adiós* issuing from those Spanish throats; we saw two of the men — their forms blurred and magnified in the outstreaming rays of the lamp —clasp each other's hands; we knew that they were saying farewell to one another. And then — curse the buffoon! — and then, when they had even parted and two had turned toward the door to re-enter, and the others had taken their first steps upon the road forward — then, I say, one of these latter turned back, made signs to all the others, and, when he had fixed their attention, began to dance and caper about in the road, imitating for the benefit of his friends, as I supposed, some dance or dancer he had lately seen.

From the lips of my doubtless high-strung companion there came a long-drawn breath; almost I could have sworn I heard the soft murmur of a smothered Spanish oath; and then once more those whom we watched parted from each other — the buffoonery was over, the imitation, if it was such, finished. Again, with laughs and jokes, they broke up and separated.

"Our chance is at hand, at last!" I whispered.

Was it?

The others — those going away — had disappeared round a bend of both rock and road; the two left behind were retiring into their house when, suddenly, the last one stopped, paused a moment, put up his hand to his head as though endeavouring to recall something, then put out his other hand, seemed to grasp a lantern from inside the door, and, slowly, began a moment later to descend the road where we sat our steeds.

And now we were discovered beyond all doubt; in a moment or so he would perceive us; another, and he would challenge us; would shout back to his comrade in the hut — perhaps call loud enough to attract the attention of his departing friends. We should be shot down, our horses probably hamstrung, we brought to earth, prisoners or dead.

"Swords out!" I said to Juan, "and advance. Quick, put your horse to the canter at once; ride past him—over him if need be."

A moment later and we had flashed by the astonished man, the jennet that bore Juan springing up the hill like a cat, my own bony but muscular steed alongside; behind us we heard his roars; an instant after the ping of a bullet whistled by my ears, fired at us by the other one in the hut as we advanced; another moment and he was out in the road, endeavouring to swing a wooden gate, that hung on hinges attached to the cabin, across the road. Also, which was worst of all, we heard answering calls from the men who had gone on ahead—tramplings and shouts—we knew that they were coming back to help.

But we were at the gate now, and still it was not shut, there wanted yet another yard or so ere its catch would meet the socket post, and, shifting my reins into my sword hand, I seized its top bar, endeavouring to bear it back by the combined weight of my horse and myself upon the man striving to shut it.

Then I heard the fellow at the gate call

out something of which I understood no word, heard Juan give a reply with—who would have believed it of him at this moment—a mocking laugh; heard the word, *Inglese;* knew intuitively that he had told them who and what we were, and had defied them.

And also, as I divined all this, I saw that the other men had returned, had reached the gate and were lending their assistance to aid in its being barred against us.

It was war time, as I had said before; I took heart of grace in remembering this, and I set to work to hew my way, even though I killed all who opposed me, toward the distant goal I sought. One brawny Spaniard who, even as he lent his whole weight to the gate, drew forth a huge pistol, I cut down over those bars, he falling all a-heap in the road; another I ran through the shoulder; and I saw the steel of Juan's lighter sword gleam like a streak of lightning betwixt the upper and the second bar; I heard the third man who had come back give a yell of pain as it reached him, while a pistol he had just fired fell to the ground — he falling a moment later on top of it.

And now there was but the original man left at the gate, and still it was not shut! Wherefore I brought the whole strength

ACROSS THE SALT SEAS. 219

and power of my body to force it back so that there should be room for us to pass.

Yet, even as I did so, I had to desist, for from behind, I heard Juan shout:

"Mervan, Mervan, help me!" and on looking round I saw that the jennet was riderless. Saw also, that he was down, that the man who had begun to descend the hill was wrestling with him on the ground, and that, as they struggled together, both were rolling over toward the lower part of the precipice or rock side, which hung perpendicularly above the swift flowing river.

CHAPTER XVI.

THE FIRST FIGHT.

In a moment I, too, was off my horse — had tied it and the jennet's reins together — and had flung myself on the man — a big, brawny fellow who had one arm around Juan's body while, with his disengaged hand, he felt for a knife in his girdle.

Even as I did so I saw that they were both perilously near the edge of the rock which hung over the river, that in a few more moments both must have gone over it — over and down, crashing through bushes and shrubs until they fell into that rapid stream below, or were hurled on to the timbers of the crazy bridge, with, probably, their bones broken all to pieces.

Yet, small as was the space left in which a third man might intervene, be sure I lost no time in doing so, in flinging myself upon that muscular Spaniard and in tearing him off his prey. Seizing him by the collar of his jacket, one hand around his throat, I dragged him from the boy — for I was as muscular as he, and, maybe, younger, too—

wrenched him to his feet and sent him reeling back into the road.

"Catch the horses," I said to Juan, "quick. And mount yourself. Be ready. Once I have disposed of this fellow there remains none but the one at the gate."

And, although the lad tottered as he rose to his feet, he did as I bade him, and, securing the animals, which had but backed a few paces down the road, got into his saddle again. Then he said — though faintly: "I will go forward and dispose of the remaining man."

Yet there was still this one to be disposed of — and I understood at a glance that I had no easy task before me ere I could do so.

He was a fellow of great bulk — this I could observe in the light of a watery half moon that now peeped up over the bend of the rock by where the cabin stood; also he was well armed. In his hand he held now a long cavalry sword, which he had drawn from its steel scabbard with a clash even as he staggered back against the rock; with his other hand he fumbled at the silken sash around his waist, in which was the knife he had endeavoured to draw against Juan.

In God's mercy, he had no pistol!

He muttered some hoarse words — to me they conveyed little — yet no words were needed. I knew as well as though he had spoken my own tongue that one of three things must happen now: That great inch-deep blade either buried in my heart or my head cleft open with it, or my straight English weapon through and through him!

Then we set to it.

As animals which are bereft of speech fight, so we fought now — only more warily. For they fly at each other's throats, in a moment are locked in each other's grasp, their fangs deep in the other's flesh. It was not so with us. We had not to come too close, but rather to guard and feint, to avoid each other till the moment, the one critical and supreme moment, came. Thus we began.

At first, perhaps, because of the deadly weight of his blade — better for cut than thrust — he aimed twice at my head, and tried again a third time, then jumped back with another of his — to me — unintelligible hoarse and raucous exclamations; for, at that attempt, I had quickly — ay! and easily, too — parried the blow, had disengaged my weapon, and, with a rapid thrust, had nearly struck home — had missed the inside of his ribs by an inch only. Then knew that the next time I should not fail.

"Curse you," I muttered, "if I could speak your *patois*, I'd tell you that you are doomed." While to myself I said: "He is a clumsy fool, and — he is mine."

We had turned in these passadoes, as I drove him back; so, too, I had edged him round. Now, 'twas I who had the rock behind me, 'twas he who had the declivity of the lower precipice behind him.

And he knew it as well as I — saw in a moment all that this meant, and — endeavoured to turn again.

Yet he never had the chance. Trust me for that! — as my recollection of the daily lessons in the fence school at Hounslow, which for a year Dutch William's best *ferrailleurs* had taught me ere my father got my guidon for me.

He never had the chance! Yet he strove hard for it, too; proved that Spain made no bad choice when she sent him to this frontier post; strove hard to beat me round again, to bring my back in the position his was — to the lip of the plateau — and failed.

If I could have spoken to him in his *patois* — for 'twas scarce Spanish — if I could have made him understand, if he would have discontinued his contest with me, I would have spared him, and willingly; would have bidden him let me go in peace, and be saved himself. For he was a brave man; too good a one for the doom that must now be his. Yet he forced me to it, forced me to go on, ceased not for one instant his swinging blows and thrusts, forced me to parry and thrust in turn for my own salvation — to drive him back step by step to the brink of the precipice behind him. And, now, it was not five paces behind him.

His was the danger — I wondered if he knew it — yet mine the horror. Above the clashing of our swords I heard now the dull, hoarse roaring of the river below, heard its angry swish as it struck past the timbers of the bridge below — in my desire to save him I told him madly in my best Spanish to desist — to save himself. Also, I think, he saw upon my face some look of horror at the fate that must be his, some beads of sweat, perhaps, upon it, too — I know I felt them there — saw them, and — God help him! — misunderstood them. Misunderstood, and thought my look of horror, my sweat, were for my own safety.

With a leap, a roar, he came at me again like a tiger springing at its prey, his blows raining upon my sword; almost I thought that even now he would have borne me to

ACROSS THE SALT SEAS. 225

the earth, have conquered. And I thrust blindly, too, in desperation, knew that my blade was through his arm, saw him jump back, stagger—and disappear!

And up from below where he had last stood there came a scream of awful fear and terror, the branches and the bushes crashed, there was a thud upon the water a hundred feet below—and then nothing more but the swirl of the river and its hoarse murmur as it swept along.

It had not taken much time in the doing. A moment later I was running up the road to where the gate stood, swung back now so that the road was clear. And Juan was sitting on his horse, a pistol in his hand, and in the road, standing beneath him, his hands by his side, stood the last remaining man, dreading to move, palsied with fright, and speechless.

"What shall we do with him?" the youth asked, turning on me a face in which there was now left no vestige of that brilliant colour it had once borne. "What? Kill him?" and his eyes flashed ominously, so that I knew the lust for blood was awakened.

"Nay," I said. "Nay. There is no need for that. Bind him and lock him up here in his hut. That will do very well.

Also, he is old. What of these others?" and I turned to those who lay in the road.

As I looked at them, it seemed that none were hurt to death—for which I was thankful enough, since a soldier needs but to disable his enemy, and seeks not to take life needlessly. The one whom I had first cut down seemed to have but a scalp wound—doubtless the thick, coarse hat of felt he wore had turned my blade; he whom I had run through the shoulder had but a flesh wound, which would trouble him for some weeks at most; while the fellow whom Juan had pinked had got an ugly gash in the neck.

"We will put them all in here together," I said, pointing to their hut, "then leave them. Doubtless they will be relieved in some hours. Yet the longer ere it happens the better. We must press on and on till we are well clear of this part of the world. There will be a hue and cry."

After saying which, I proceeded to drag the wounded men in—one of them was able to enter the place unaided, though not without many melancholy groans and ejaculations—and then motioned to the old man to follow.

But now, obeying me even as I so pointed to the door, he cast an imploring glance at

ACROSS THE SALT SEAS. 227

Juan, and then muttered something to him, the boy answering him with a laugh. And on my demanding to know what he had said, my companion replied:

"He saw you take up the lamp. Therefore he asked if you were going to burn them all when they were locked in the hut."

"Humph!" I said. "It has not quite come to that."

Time was, however, precious now, therefore it was useless for us to remain here any longer, or to waste any more of it; whereon, again taking up the lamp, I carried it out into the road. Then I removed the key from where it hung by the side of the door, and, going out, locked them all inside.

"Now," I said, "they can remain there till some one comes by to set them free. Yet, if that some one comes across from Portugal, and our late landlord speaks truth, they will be in no hurry to do that friendly office for them." After which I blew out the lamp, and, walking to the edge of the under precipice, hurled both it and the key down into the river beneath.

For some time after we had set out upon our journey again we rode in silence, Juan being as much occupied, I supposed, with his thoughts as I with mine. And, indeed, my own were none of the pleasantest; above all I regretted that that brave man with whom I had fought had gone to his doom. For, although killing was my trade, and although I had already taken part in several skirmishes and fights, I had none too great a liking for having been obliged to slay him. Yet I consoled myself with the reflection that it was his life or mine, and with that I had to be content. But also there were other things that troubled me, amongst them being what I feared would prove certain, namely, that there would be that hue and cry after us of which I had spoken for some time at least, and until we had left the frontier far behind. Nor, since Lugo was but a short distance from this place, would it be possible for us to stop there even for so much as a night's rest. We must go on and on till we had outstripped all chance of being recognised as the two men who had forced themselves into a hostile country in the manner we had done.

But now, breaking in on these reflections, I heard Juan's soft voice speaking to me, murmuring words of admiration and affection.

"Mervan," he said, "if I liked you before—ay! from the very moment you stood outside the cabin door of *La Sacra Familia* and bade me unlock it, and when the first sound of your voice told me I had naught to fear—I love you now. My life upon it! you are a brave man, such as I delight in seeing."

I laughed a little at this compliment, yet soberly, too, for this was no time for mirth—also, I recognised clearly enough that every step the animals beneath us took brought us nearer to other dangers, by the side of which our recent adventure was but child's play—then answered:

"And what of yourself, Juan? You have done pretty well, too, I'm thinking; go on like this, and you will be fitted to ride stirrup to stirrup with the most grim old blades of Marlborough's armies when we get to Flanders—if we ever do! I thought you nervous, to speak solemn truth; now I am glad to have you by my side."

Yet," said the boy, his face radiant with delight, as I saw when he turned it on me under the rays of the moon, "I was deathly sick with fear all the time. Oh! my God!" he cried suddenly, "what should I have done, what become of me, if you had been struck down?" Then added, anxiously, a moment later. "You are not wounded?"

"Not a scratch. And you?"

"Nor I, either. Yet I was so faint as I

guarded that old man by the gate, that I doubted if I could sit the horse much longer; I should have fallen to earth, I do verily believe, had you not joined me when you did."

"Poor lad," I said, "poor lad. You have chosen but a rough road, a dangerous companion. You should have gone to England in the *Pembroke*, with the fleet. You would have been half way there by now, and in safety."

"Never!" he said. "Never!" And, as if to give emphasis to his words, he turned round in his saddle toward me, placing his left hand on the cantle as though to obtain a steady glance of my face, and continued.

"I told you we were friends, sworn friends and true. Also, that to be together was all that I asked. Mervan, our friendship is rivetted, bound, now; nothing but death or disaster shall part us — nothing; till at least, this journey is concluded. Then — then — if you choose to turn me off you may; but not before. You have not yet learnt, do not know yet, what a Spanish — a — a man reared amongst Spaniards feels when he swears eternal friendship."

After which he regained his position and rode on, looking straight between his horse's ears. But once I heard him mutter to himself, though still not so low, either, but what I heard it very well:

"Friendship. *Diòs!*"

And this warm, fervent youth, this creature full of emotion and glowing friendship, was him against whom the admiral had expressed some distaste when he learned that I proposed to ride in his company; had doubted if that companionship might not be of evil influence over my fortunes during the journey. If he knew nothing, what did it all mean? I asked myself. Above all (and this I had pondered on again and again, though without being able to arrive at any answer to the riddle), why warn me against one whom he, when brought into contact with that one himself, had treated with such scrupulous deference?

Even as I thought again upon these things I resolved that as our acquaintance, our friendship and comradeship ripened, I would ask Juan who and what he was.

For at present I knew no more than I have written down—that he was young and handsome, and was well to do. But beneath all, was there some mystery attached to him? Some mystery which the older and more far seeing eyes of Sir George had been able to pry into and discover, while mine were still blinded to it?

We were passing now through a wild and desolate region, a portion of the western extremity of northern Spain, in which we met no sign of human life or human habitation, hardly, indeed, any sign of animal life. Also we had struck a chain of mountains densely clothed with cork and chestnut woods, the trees of which were bare of leaves, and through the branches of which the wind moaned cheerlessly. On our left these mountains, after an interval of barren moorland, rose precipitously; to our right the Minho rolled sullenly along, the road we traversed lying between it and the moor. So desolate, indeed, was all around us now that we might have been two travellers from another world journeying through this, a forgotten or undiscovered one; no light either far or near twinkled from hut or cottage, neither bark of dog nor low of cattle reached our ears; all was desolate, silent and deserted.

Yet, even as the road lifted so that we knew we were ascending those mountains step by step, we observed signs which, added to the well kept state of the road itself, told us it was not an altogether unused one. For though the snow lay hard and caked upon it, we could observe where it had taken the impression of cart wheels and of animals' hoofs, could perceive by this that it was sometimes traversed.

And, presently, we observed something else, something that told us plainly enough that we were now in the direct way for Lugo, observed that there branched into the road we were travelling an even broader one than it — causing, too, our own road to broaden out itself as it ran further north; a road in the middle of which was a huge stone column or pedestal, with arms also of stone upon it, pointing different ways, and with, carved on them, words and figures.

And of these arms one pointed west and bore upon it the words: To Vigo; another pointed north with, on it, the words: To Lugo.

And seeing all this by the aid of a tinder box and lantern which we carried amongst our necessaries — seeing it, too, by craning our necks and standing up in our stirrups — we knew that we had now struck the route along which those must have come who had fled from Vigo after the taking of the galleons.

CHAPTER XVII.

MY GOD! WHO IS HE?

All that night we rode, yet slowly, too, for the sake of the horses, and in the morning—which broke bright, clear and frosty, the sun sparkling and shining gaily amongst the leafless branches and trees of the forests through which we passed—reached a little town, or village, about half way 'twixt the frontier and Lugo, a place called Chantada, and not far from another town named Orense, which, because it had a large population—as we gathered from a sight of its roofs and spires, all a-shining in the morning sun, as we could see very well from the mountains as we passed along them—we avoided. Also, we avoided it because it lay not so much upon our direct route, by some three or four leagues, as Chantada itself.

"Now, come what may," said I to Juan, as we drew near this place, "and even though we should be pursued from the border—which is not very like—we must stop here for some hours. We require rest ourselves; as for the beasts, they must have it; otherwise they will have to be left behind and others found. And that would be a pity — they are better than might have been looked for!" As, indeed, they were, especially considering the haphazard manner in which we had come by them, both having kept on untiring on the road, while, as for the jennet which Juan bestrode, it was, possibly because of his light weight, as fresh as on the hour we set out.

Then, turning to him, I said, even as I noticed that he showed no signs of fatigue — at which I marvelled somewhat! — and that his handsome face was as bright and full of colour as it had ever been:

"You must be a-weary, Juan? Three or four hours' sleep will do you a world of good. And you shall have it, my lad, even though I sit at your door with a drawn sword in my hand to prevent interruption."

As usual, he smiled that gracious, winsome smile upon me — a smile which was always forthcoming in response to any simple little kindness I evidenced to him — and said:

"I could ride on for hours thus — feel no fatigue. Maybe 't is the brightness of the morning that heartens me so; perhaps the crisp coolness of these mountains—Heavens! how different 't is from aught we know of in the Indies!—that makes me insensible to it! Yet, Mervan," and he gave me a glance from his eyes, under the dark and now dishevelled curls that hung almost over them, "there is one thing I long to do now. Mervan, do not refuse. I have earned the right!"

"What is it, child?" I asked, wondering what strange request he might be about to prefer.

"Let me sing and play a little. 'T will do no harm, and—and—you know—the viol is here," and he touched lightly the valise strapped in front of his saddle.

"Sing, if you will," I said, yet casting a glance around and ahead of me to see if there were any about whose curiosity might be attracted by the music—though in sober truth it would not much have mattered had there been. In such a land as this—though I scarce knew it then!—for a traveller to pass along on his way singing for cheerfulness and for solace was no strange thing, but rather, instead, the custom. "Sing, if you wish—I shall be glad enough to hear a merry note or so. For audience, however, there will be no other."

"I want none," he replied, "if you are

content." And by now, having got out the little viol d'amore, he struck a few notes upon it and began to sing.

At first his song was, as I understood and as he told me afterward, a love-ballad addressed by a youth to his mistress; the words — as he uttered them — soft and luscious as the trill of the nightingale on summer night. And his marvellous beauty added also to the effect it had on me, made me wonder how many dark, tropic beauties in the lands he came from had already lost their hearts to him. Nay, wondered so much that, as the last sweet tones of both his voice and viol died upon the crisp morning air, I asked him a question to that effect.

"Ho! Ho!" he laughed, yet softly as he had just now sung. "None! None! None! In the Indies I am nothing; all are as dark as I except when they are golden — fair — and — and — Mervan, *mon ami*, no woman has ever said a word of love to me."

"Humph!" I said, doubting. "Nor you, perhaps, a word of love to them."

"Nor I a word of love to them. Never, never. *Le grand jamais!*"

"Nor ever loved?" with a tone of doubt so strong in my voice now that he could not fail to understand it.

"Nor ever loved," he repeated. "Yes

—yes—I love now. Now!" Then, impetuously, as he ever spoke—like a torrent let loose from mountain side—he went on:

"Love! Love! Love! With heart and soul, and brain on fire. Love! so that for the creature I adore—have learnt to worship, I would—ah! what would I not do? Cast my body beneath that creature, plunge through fire or water—Oh!" he exclaimed, breaking off as suddenly as he had begun, "Oh! I am a fool! A fool! A fool!"

"But, surely," I said, "surely, with such as you are, that love does not go unrequited. If you have spoken to the object of this passion, told of this love you say you bear—and are believed—it must be returned. Such love as yours would not be simulated, must therefore be appreciated."

"Simulated!" he exclaimed. "Simulated. It cannot be simulated, not assumed like a mountebank's robe ere he plays a part. Any one can paint a flame, any tawdry daubster of an inn signboard, but not even Murillo himself could paint the heat. And my love is heat—not—not flame."

"And the lady? The lady?" I asked almost impatiently. "Surely she does—she must—return this love."

Volatile as he was, and, changing his mood again in a moment, he looked slyly at me under the dark locks, twanged the viol again and burst into another song, different from the one he had but recently finished, the song which I had previously known him to sing:

"Oh! have you heard of a Spanish lady,
How she wooed an Englishman?——"

"I am an Englishman now, you know, Mervan," interrupting the song. Then going on:

"Garments gay and rich as may be,
Decked with jewels, she had on."

"Did she woo you, then?" I asked, as he paused a moment.

For answer he sang again:

"As his prisoner fast he kept her,
In his hands her life did lie;
Cupid's bands did tie them faster
By the twinkling of an eye——"

He stopped abruptly and pointed ahead of him with the little viol, then wrapped it up again in his valise and said:

"See, *amigo*, there is the village—what was its name cut on the pedestal? Now what are we? Eh? And whence come we if any questions are asked?"

"You are a young Spanish gentleman," I said, repeating a lesson I had hitherto in our ride tutored him in, "from Vigo. I am a Frenchman. We are on our way to Bayonne to join the French forces. Also, we neither of us know English."

"*Bon, pas un mot*," he replied, catching me up brightly. "*Et nous parlons Anglais comme une vache parle Espagnol. N'est-ce pas, mon ami?*"

"*C'est ça. En avant*," I replied, and with a laugh we each touched our horses with the heel and cantered down into the village of Chantada.

'T was a poor place enough for any travellers to see, consisting of a long, but very wide street, with a fountain in the midst of a wide open square, around which there lay a number of grunting swine — lean and repulsive — and also some score or so of geese, all basking in the morning sun.

Yet next in importance to the church, which was on one side of this *plaza*, was that which we most sought for, an inn, and, perhaps because of the road being one of importance 'twixt both Portugal and Vigo to France, it was a large, substantial-looking house, long, and with many rooms on either side the great porte, as well as in the two stories beneath its sloping and serrated Spanish roof; also, it looked prosperous — a huge gilt coronet hung out over the unpaved street. For name it had painted along all its front, the words "Taverna Duquesa Santa Ana."

Under the great archway we rode in, seeing that in a vast courtyard there stood a travelling coach on which, although there were no horses attached to it, some baggage was still left piled up beneath some skins; hearing also the stamping of several horses in their stables.

"Ask," said I to Juan, speaking in French — as agreed between us, there was to be no more English spoken unless we were certain no ears could overhear us — "ask if we can be accommodated for some hours, say, until night. Then we must resume our journey. Ask that."

Obedient to my behest, the youth turned to a man who came out from the door giving entrance to the inn itself and, in Spanish, made his demand, whereupon the fellow, after bowing politely, said:

"There is ample accommodation for — for more — alas! — than travel these roads."

Then, because I addressed a word or so in French to him, he continued in that language, which, however, he had exceedingly badly:

"Messieurs will stay here till night, then push on to Lugo? *Bon*, they will be there by morning. So! So! Yes, in verity, they can have a good meal. There are geese, fowls, meat, also some wine of excellence. Messieurs may refresh themselves in all ways."

Our horses put in the stable, therefore, we sat down half an hour later in a vast *sala* — in which a great banquet might have been given with ease — to a dish of veal, a fowl, and an *olla-podrida*, all of which would have been good enough had they not been flavoured so much with garlic that — to my taste, at least — all pleasure was destroyed; also we had some most excellent chocolate and some good spirituous liquor to follow — at which latter Juan turned a wry face. Then ordering another meal to be ready ere we set out — with strict injunctions that the flavouring should on this occasion be omitted — we betook ourselves to the rooms above, where we were to get a few hours' rest.

Yet, as we passed along the whitewashed corridor, the windows of which gave on to the stable yard, the travelling coach standing there caught our eyes, and I said to the host:

"You have at least some one else here besides us. Some great personage, I should suppose, by his equipage," and I directed my glance to where the great carriage was.

"Ho!" said the man with the true Spanish shrug of the shoulder, which is even more emphatic than the French one, more suggestive, as it seems to me; "a personage of wealth, I should say, but no grandee — of Spain, at least."

"Of what land, then?" I asked. "And why a personage of wealth, yet no grandee?"

"Oh! well, for that," the man said, with again the inimitable shrug, "his deportment, his conduct is not that which our nobility permit themselves. Though I know not — perhaps it may be so — he is a nobleman of — well — possibly, England. He drinks heavily — name of a dog! but he drinks like a fiend, *un enragé* — cognac, cognac, cognac — also he sings all the night, sometimes so that even the fowls and the dogs are awakened, also all our house. Yet he pays well — very well!"

"Doubtless," I replied, quietly, "an English nobleman. Such is their custom, according to the ideas of other nations. Well, let us to rest," whereon Juan and I turned each into a room which the landlord indicated, and, so far as I was concerned, I slept calmly and peacefully until awakened by him at three of the afternoon.

Now, when I descended to where our other repast was prepared for us, which would probably be the last one of a substantial nature which we should be likely to get ere reaching Lugo, I found Juan there walking up and down the great *sala*, his sword swishing about against his left leg as he turned backward and forward petulantly. Also, I could see that something had ruffled his usually sweet disposition — that his colour was a little higher than in general, and that the soft velvet-looking eyes were sparkling angrily.

"Why, what is it?" I asked, even as the landlord brought in the first cover, "what is it, my boy? You are ruffled."

"Be very sure I am!" he exclaimed, speaking rapidly, and of course in French, so that the man heard and understood all he said. "I have been insulted——"

"Insulted!"

"At least rebuffed, and rudely, too; and by, of all men, a filthy blackamoor — a — a — *por Diós!* — a slave! Oh! that I had him in the Indies! He would insult no white one again, I tell you!" and he fingered the hilt of his weapon and stamped his shapely foot on the uncarpeted floor till his spurs jangled.

"Come," I said, "you can afford to despise the creature. How did it happen?"

"Happen! Happen!" Juan replied, still angry. "How?"

"Monsieur saw the black man preparing the luggage on the great coach," the landlord said, as he removed the dish-cover from a course of pork and raisins, "and asked which way his master went. And the fellow was surly, rude — said that was their business, not the affair of strangers. Also, they sought no companions, if — if the young señor meant that——"

"Who never offered our company," Juan broke in again. "Curse him! I wish I had him in the Indies!" he repeated.

"Come," I said again, "come. This is beneath you, Juan — to be angry with a slave! As well be vexed with a dog that yaps and snaps at you when you go to pat it. Sit down and eat your meal. We have a long ride before us."

Perhaps he saw some sense in my suggestion, for he flung himself into a chair and began to eat; and meanwhile the host, who was still hovering about, handing us now a dish of mutton dressed with oysters and pistachio nuts, and now some stewed pomegranates, chattered away at one side, telling us that the negro's master was not well—that he had been drinking again; but yet he was determined to set out at once.

"Though," said he, "but an hour before the caballeros rode in he had resolved to stay until to-morrow. I know not why he has changed his mind so swiftly. Oh! —the drink, the drink, the drink!" and he wagged his head.

That the dissolute man whom the landlord considered to be, in consequence, an English nobleman, was about to depart there could be no possibility of doubt. From where we sat at table, and because curtains to the windows seemed to be things of which those who kept the inn had never thought, we could see out into the courtyard quite plainly. Saw first the horses brought out—four of them—and harnessed to the huge, lumbering vehicle —the nobleman would have proved himself a kinder-hearted man if he had used six!—saw their cloths taken off their backs by the postillion, and observed the latter make ready to mount the near side leader. Also we saw the *facchinos* on ladders strapping tight the baggage which had been brought down and hoisted on top, then heard the landlord, who had now left serving us to attend to his parting guest, give orders that the noble traveller should be in-

ACROSS THE SALT SEAS. 247

formed that all was ready for his departure. Upon which we quitted our seats at the table and walked over to the window, Juan's curiosity much excited at the chance of seeing this drunken English *milor*, as he called him. We had not long to wait. For presently we heard a considerable trampling on the stairs and some mumbled words — to my surprise the deep, guttural tones seemed familiar! — and then we saw a wrapped figure carried out between two of the *facchinos* and lifted up into the carriage.

And behind that figure walked a negro, his head also enveloped in a rich red shawl — as though the black creature feared the cold night air, forsooth!

But, even as they lifted the debauched man into his carriage, the wrappings about his face became disturbed and fell back on his shoulders, so that I could see his face — and I started as I did so. Started even more, too, when, a second later, I heard Juan exclaim in a subdued voice:

"My God, who is he? Almost I could swear——"

While in my excitement I interrupted him, saying:

"That an English nobleman! That! —

Why, 'tis the drunken old ruffian who came from Rotterdam with me in the ship."

"And his name? His name?" Juan asked, breathlessly. "His name?"

"John Carstairs."

Even as I spoke the postillion cracked his whip, and the great carriage rolled out of the courtyard, the lamps twinkling and illuminating our faces as it passed before the window. Showed, too, as they flashed on Juan's face, that he was once more deathly pale and all his rich colouring vanished — as I had seen it vanish more than once before.

CHAPTER XVIII.

BETRAYED.

"His name is Carstairs? Humph!" Juan said to me when the last sound of the wheels had died away, and we no longer heard the rumbling of the great Berlin upon the stones of the roughly paved street outside. "Carstairs!"

"That is the name under which he was entered as a passenger in the papers of *La Mouche Noire,*" I answered. Then continued, looking at the boy as a thought came to my mind. "Why! have you ever seen him before, Juan, or have you any reason to suppose it is anything else than Carstairs?"

For the thought that had come to me, the recollection which had suddenly sprung to my mind, was the memory of the words Captain Tandy had used when first we discussed the old man. "'T is no more his name than 't is mine or yours."

Also I recalled that he had said, after meditation, that he was more like to have been one Cuddiford than anybody else.

And now it seemed as though this stripling who had become my companion, this boy whose years scarce numbered eighteen, also knew something of him—disbelieved that his name was Carstairs.

"Do you think," I went on, "that it is something else? Cuddiford, say?"

"Nay," he replied. "Nay. Not that. Not that. I have heard of Cuddiford, though. I think he was brought to London and tried. But—but—oh!" he exclaimed, breaking off, "it cannot be!"

"What cannot be?"

"If," he said, speaking very slowly, very gravely now, "if it were not eight years since I last set eyes on him, when I was quite a child; if he had a beard down over his chest instead of being close shaven, I should say, Mervan, that this was the ruffian I have come to England to seek; the villain who robbed me of the fortune my father left me — the scoundrel, James Eaton."

"James Eaton!" I exclaimed. "The man you asked me about; thought I might be like to know?"

"The same."

"Had he, this Eaton, been a buccaneer? for I make no doubt that man has." I said. "The captain of *La Mouche Noire* thought so—and—and—his ravings and deliriums seemed to point that way."

"I know not," Juan said. "Eaton was a villain—yet—yet—I can scarce suppose my father would have trusted him with a fortune if he had known him to be such as that."

"Who was your father, Juan?"

"I—I," he answered, looking at me with those clear starry eyes—eyes into which none could gaze without marvelling at their beauty—"I do not know."

"You do not know!—yet you know he bequeathed a fortune to' you and left it in the man Eaton's hands."

"Mervan," he said, speaking quickly, "you must be made acquainted with my history—I will tell it you. To-night, when we ride forth again; but not now. See, our horses are ready, they are bringing them from the stables. When we are on the road I will tell you my story. 'T will not take long. Come, let us pay the bill, and away."

"I will pay the bill," I said; "later we can regulate our accounts. And as you say, we had best be on the road. For if that old man has seen me, or if his black servant has done so—it—it—may be serious."

"Serious!" he repeated. "Serious!

For *you*, my friend?" And as he spoke there was in his voice so tender an evidence that he thought nothing of any danger which could threaten him, but only of what might befall me, that I felt sure, now and henceforth, of the noble, unselfish heart he possessed. "Oh! not serious for you."

"Ay," I replied. "Ay. Precious serious! Remember, he knows I went ashore in Lagos bay, that I sailed in the English fleet to Vigo. What will happen, think you, if he warns them at Lugo that such a one as I—an Englishman—who assisted at the taking of the galleons, is on the road 'twixt here and there? "

"My God!" the boy exclaimed, thrusting his hand through the curls clustering over his eyes—as he always did when in the least excited. "It might mean——"

"Death," I said, "sharp and swift; without trial or time for shrift; without——"

"But—whether he be Eaton—or—Carstairs—he is English himself."

"Ay, and so he is." I answered, "But be sure he has papers—also he can speak Spanish well, will doubtless pass for a Spaniard. Also, unless I am much mistook, had a cargo in one of those galleons—for what else has he followed up here? For what—but the hopes of getting back some of the saved spoil which has been brought to Lugo? That alone would give him the semblance of being Spanish — would earn him sympathy. Meanwhile, what should I be deemed? A spy! And I should die the spy's death."

"What then to do next?" Juan asked, with a helpless, piteous look.

"There is but one thing for *me* to do," I replied. "One thing alone. As I told you ere we set out from Viana, my task is to ride on straight, unerringly, to my goal — on to Flanders, through every obstacle, every barrier; to crash through them, if heaven permits, as Hopson crashed through that boom at Vigo — to reach Lord Marlborough or to fall by the wayside. That is my duty, and I mean to do it."

"Mervan! Mervan!" he almost moaned.

"'T is that," I went on. "But — think not I say it unkindly, with lack of friendship or in forgetfulness of our new found *camaraderie* — for you the need does not exist."

"What!"

"Hear me, I say, Juan. I speak but for your safety. For you there is no duty calling; the risk does not exist. You are free — a traveller at your ease."

"Silence!" he cried — his rich, musical

voice ringing clear through the vast *sala* in the midst of which we now stood once more; and as he spoke he raised his hand with a gesture of command. "Silence, I say! By the body of my dead and unknown father, you do not know Juan Belmonte. What! Set out with you and turn back at the first sign of danger, and that a danger to you alone! Oh!" he exclaimed, changing his tone again, emotional as ever. "Oh! Mervan, Mervan."

"I spoke but for your sake," I said, sorry and grieved to see I had wounded him. "For that alone."

"Then speak no more, never again in such a strain. I said I would never quit your side till Flanders is reached; no need to repeat those words. Where you go I go — unless you drive me from your side."

And now it was my turn to exclaim against him, to cry: "Juan! you think I should do that!" Yet even as I spoke, I could not but add: "The danger to you as well as me may be terrible."

"No more," he said. "No more. We ride together until the end comes — for one or both of us. Now, let us call the reckoning and begone. The horses are there," and he strode to the window and made a sign to the stable-man to be ready for us.

ACROSS THE SALT SEAS. 255

Yet ere the landlord came, he spoke to me again.

"Remember," he said, "that beyond our *camaraderie*, of which you have spoken — ay! 'tis that and more, far more — beyond all this, I do believe the old man whose face I saw as the great lamps shone full on it is James Eaton. I have come to Europe, to this cold quarter of the world, to find him. Do you think with him not half a league ahead that I will be turned from the trail? Never! I follow that man to Lugo — since his beard is gone I cannot pluck him by that, but I can take his throat in my hands, thrust this through his evil heart," and he rapped the quillon of his sword sharply as he spoke. Then added: "As I will. As I will."

"You do not think he has recognised you, too? Seen you, though unseen himself, while we have been in this house, passing through these passages and corridors? as I doubt not either he saw me, or that negro of his."

He thought a moment after I said this, then suddenly emerged from his meditation and laughed a bright, ringing laugh, such as I had learnt to love the hearing of.

"Nay," he replied. "Nay," and still he laughed. "He has not — could not recognise me. No! No! No! When I present myself to him he — will — he will be astonished."

And once more he laughed.

What a strange creature it was, I thought. As brave as a young lion; as emotional and variable as a woman.

In answer to our pealing at the bell, to our calls also, the landlord came in at last, not hurrying himself at all, as it seemed to us, to bring the bill. Indeed, we had observed him, as we looked forth from the window, engaged in a conversation with two of the townspeople — shrouded in the long cloaks which Spaniards wear — their heads as close together as if they were concocting a crime, though, doubtless, talking of nothing more important than the weather.

"The bill," I said, "the bill. Quick. Our horses await us, and we have far to ride."

"Ay," he replied. "Ay," and flinging down a filthy piece of paper on the table, added: "There is the bill"; and he stood drumming his fingers on the table while I felt for the coins with which to pay it. Yet, even as I did so, I noticed that the fellow's manner was quite changed from what it had been hitherto. His obsequiousness of the morning had turned to morose surliness, which he took no trouble to conceal. And, wondering if Juan, who was standing by, fastening his spur strap, had observed the same thing, I glanced at him and saw his eyes fixed on the man.

"There are two pistoles," I said, flinging them on the table. "They will more than pay our addition; give the rest to the servants."

"Ay!" he replied. "Ay!" but with no added word of thanks.

"Is 't not enough?" Juan asked.

"It is enough." Then he turned to me and said: "You are riding to Lugo to-night?"

"That is our road," I replied, feeling my temper mount at the man's changed manner. "What of it? Does that route displeasure you, pray?"

"Ho!" he grunted; "for that, it makes no matter to me." Then added: "The horses are there," in so insolent a tone that I had a difficulty in restraining myself from kicking or striking him. But I remembered that, before all else, our safety had to be consulted, and that naught should be done to cause delay to our progress; wherefore, I swallowed my ire as best I might.

Yet, as we rode out of the courtyard,

I saw at once that Juan's own thoughts tended exactly in the same direction as mine, since he said to me:

"That fellow has been told something by the old man — doubtless, that you are English — that we both are. *Por Diós!* Suppose he has informed him that you were in the English fleet!"

"I have no doubt that the man has been told so," I replied. "But no matter. If it were not for you I should not care a jot."

Then once more I saw the dark eyes turned on me, and wished that I had held my tongue — at least as regarded the latter part of my speech.

It seemed as if the town had gone to bed already. The great square was deserted — except that the geese and pigs were still in it, huddled together around the fountain, and severally cackled and grunted as we trotted by them; down the long street, as we rode, we saw no signs of any one being outside the doors.

Yet, as we neared the extremity of both the town and the street, and came to where the latter ended off into a country road stretching along a dreary-looking plain, over which the moon had risen, we saw that such was not precisely the case. At the end of the street, that which was the

ACROSS THE SALT SEAS. 259

last building was a little, low, whitewashed chapel; above its black door there was a figure in a little niche, with, burning in front of it, a candle in a miserable red-glassed lantern; and, feeble as were the rays cast forth from this poor, yet sacred, lamp, they were sufficient to show us three men on horseback, all sitting their steeds as rigidly as statues.

Judging by their long black cloaks and the tips of steel scabbards which protruded beneath them, and which were plainly enough to be seen, even in that dim, cloudy light, I imagined these men to be the town gendarmerie — though doubtless they had some other name to denominate them — and supposed this was a comfortable position which they probably selected nightly. Also, the position was at both an exit and an entrance to the place, therefore a natural one.

"A fine night, gentlemen," one remarked, and next I heard him say something to Juan, which he replied to; in both of their remarks the name of Lugo being quite distinct to my ears. But, beyond this, nothing else passed, and, a few moments later, we were riding at a smart trot across the dreary, moor-like plain.

"They asked," Juan said, in answer to

my question, "if our destination was Lugo. That was all."

"So I thought I heard," I said. And added: "Until we were past them I felt not at all sure they might not be on the lookout for us. Might, perhaps, intend to stop us. If Carstairs, or Eaton, or whatever his name is, blew upon me to the landlord, he would be as like to do it to the authorities also. However, we are in the open now, and all is well so far."

By this time the moon was well up, and we could see the country along which we were riding; could perceive that 't was indeed a vast open plain, with, however, as it seemed to me, a forest or wood ahead of us, into which the road we were on trended at last. Could see, too, the snow lying white all around, as far as the moor stretched, and looking beneath the moonbeams like some dead sea across which no ship was trying to find its way.

"A mournful spot," I said to Juan, as, half an hour later, we had almost reached the entrance to the great forest, which we had observed drawing nearer to us at every stride our beasts took; "'t is well we made a full meal ere we set out. We are not very like to come across another ere we reach Lugo."

ACROSS THE SALT SEAS. 261

I spoke as much to hearten up my companion as for any other reason, since I feared that, in spite of his bravery and firm-fixed determination to never leave my side, he must be very much alarmed at the thoughts of what might happen to us ere we had gone many more leagues.

But, remarking that he made no answer to my idle words, I glanced round at him and perceived that his head was turned half way back toward whence we had come, and that upon his face was a look of intense eagerness — the look of one who listens attentively for some sound.

"What is it, Juan?" I asked.

"Horses' hoofs on the road behind us," he said, "and coming swiftly, too. Hark! do you not hear?"

And even as he spoke I did hear them. Heard also something else to which my soldier's ears had made me very well accustomed: The clank of steel-scabbarded swords against horses' flanks.

"It is the men we passed by the chapel," I said, "following us now. Yet, if 't is us they seek, why not stop us ere we left the town? They could do as much against us there as here."

"They were but three then," the lad answered, calmly as though he were counting guineas into his palm instead of the hoof-beats of those on-coming horses; "now there are more — half a dozen, I should say. If 't is us they follow, they have waited to be reinforced."

And I felt sure that he had guessed right, since the very thought which he expressed had already risen in my own mind.

CHAPTER XIX.

THE SECOND FIGHT.

We had entered the forest five minutes later, and be very sure, we wasted no more time in waiting for those behind to come up, since, if 't was us they followed, we might as well be in its shadow as in the open. For if we were outnumbered the trees themselves would afford us some shelter, make a palisade from behind which we might get a shot at them if 't was too hot for a hand-to-hand encounter. At any rate, I had sufficient military knowledge to know that 't is best to fight against unequal odds with a base, or retreat, to fall back on, than to be without one.

Yet as we rode into this forest I loosened my blade in its sheath, and felt with my thumb to see that the priming of my pistols was ready; also bade Juan do the same; likewise to keep behind me as much as might be.

"For," said I, "if they mean attack I will give them no chance of beginning it. The first hostile word, and I force my horse between them, cutting right and left, and do you the same, following behind me. Thereby you may chance to take off those whom I miss."

And I laughed—a little grimly, perhaps—as I spoke, for I thought that if there were, indeed, six men behind us, my journey toward Flanders was already as good as come to an end. Yet, all the same, I laughed, for, strange though it may seem to those who have never known the delights of crossed steel, a fight against odds had ever an exhilarating effect upon me; which was, perhaps, as it should be with a knight of the blade.

Juan, however, did not laugh at all, though he told me he would follow my orders to the utmost, and, indeed, was so silent that I asked him if his nerves were firm. To which he replied that I should see when the moment came.

And now upon the crisp night air we heard the clang of those on-coming hoofs ringing nearer and nearer; a rough or deadened kind of sound told us the iron shoes were on the fallen leaves which covered all the track from where the wood began; the scabbards of the riders flapped noisily now against spur and horses' flanks; bridles jangled very near.

Then they were close upon us — five of them! — and a voice called out:

"Halt, there! You are Englishmen — one a sailor and a spy passing through the land."

"You lie!" rang out Juan's voice, in answer. "We are not Englishmen."

That his reply in fluent Spanish — the Spanish, too, of a gentleman, and not of a common night patrol — astonished them, I could see. The leader, he who had spoken, glanced round at his four comrades, and, an instant after, spoke again:

"Who are you, then, and why does not the big man answer?"

"He speaks French. I am Spanish. Molest us not."

"Molest! *Cuerpo di Baco!* We are informed you are English. Produce your papers!"

"We have none. They are lost."

"Ho! ho! ho!" the leader replied. "Very well, very well. 'T is as I thought. That man is English; he is denounced this night. As for you, the accursed English have many possessions wherein our tongue is spoken. We understand."

And he gave, as I supposed, some order, since all advanced their animals a few paces nearer, while, as they did so, Juan whispered to me in the French: "Be ready, but do nothing yet."

"You will return to Chantada with us," the spokesman said, sitting his horse quietly enough, yet with the blade of his drawn sword glistening in the moonbeams as it lay across the creature's neck—as, I observed, did the blades of all the others. "That finishes our affair. For the rest you will answer to the Regidór."

"We shall not return. Our way lies on."

"So be it. Then we must take you," and, as he spoke, I saw a movement of his knee—of all their knees—that told me they meant to seize us.

And I knew that the time had come.

"At them!" cried Juan at the same moment. "Advance, Mervan!"

A touch to the curb, and my beast fell back—'t was a good animal, that! had, I believe, been a charger in its day, so well it seemed to know its work—then a free rein and another touch of the heel, and I was amongst them, my sword darting like lightning around. Also, at my rear, came the jennet's head; near me there flashed the steel of Juan's lighter weapon; and in a moment we had crashed through them— they fell away on either side of us like waves from a ship's forefoot!—fell away for a moment, though closing again in an instant.

"Return and charge!" I cried to Juan, still in French. "At them again! See, one has got his quietus already!" As, indeed, he had, for the great fellow was hanging over his horse's neck, in a limp and listless fashion, which showed that he was done for. But now those four closed together as we went at them, Juan stirrup to stirrup with me in this second charge, and our tactics had to be changed. We could no longer burst through them, so that it was a hand-to-hand fight now; they had pistols in their holsters, but no chance to use them; they could not spare a hand to find those holsters—could not risk our swords through their unguarded breasts; wherefore we set to work, blade to blade.

We should have won, I do believe. Already I had thrust through and through one man's arm—as luck would have it, 'twas not the sword arm—already they backed before our rain of blows and cuts and thrusts, when, by untoward fate, my horse stumbled on the frosty road and came down; came down upon his haunches, slipping me from the saddle over the cantle and so to the earth; then regained its hind legs once more and dashed out from the fray.

And now our position was mighty perilous. Above I saw Juan on the jennet fencing well with two of the men; over me were the two others cutting down at my head, though, since by God's mercy I had retained my weapon, their blows were up to now unavailing. Yet I knew this could not be for long — nor last — wherefore I cried:

"Save yourself, Juan, save yourself; disengage and flee."

Under my own blade, under those two others that beat upon it so that I wondered it shivered not in my hand, I saw the boy manfully holding his own — once, too, I saw him rip up the jerkin of one of his opponents, and heard the latter give a yell of pain — then, "Great God!" I thought, "what has happened now?"

For there was a fifth man upon the scene. A man, tall and stalwart, mounted on a great, big boned, black horse, who had suddenly sprung from out a chestnut copse by the side of the track; a man in whose hands there gleamed a sword that a second later was laced and entwined with those attacking Juan; a man who hurled oaths in Spanish and French at them — I heard *carambas* and *por Diós's* and other words — which sounded like the rolling of some great cathedral organ as they came from his deep throat—*tonneres, ventre-bleus* and *carrognes* I heard.

Heavens! who was this man who beat back those others as a giant might push back a handful of children; whose sword — even as with one hand he grasped Juan round the waist — went through an adversary's neck so that he fell groaning upon me, his blood spurting as if from a spigot? Who was he who laughed loud and long as, with one accord, all those still alive turned and fled back upon the road they had come? Fled, leaving us, thanks be to God and this new arrival, the victors of the fray.

He sat his horse calmly now, looking after their retreating figures, his great sombrero slouched across his face, wiping his blade upon the coal-black creature's mane; then, as their figures disappeared from our view, he said in French:

"Warmer work this, Señor Belmonte, than twanging viols and singing love songs, *n'est-ce pas?*" and from his throat there came again that laugh.

Glancing up, I saw that which caused me to start, even as I heard Juan say: "You! You here! And in this garb!"— saw that which made me wonder if I had gone demented. For this man who had so suddenly come to our rescue, this *fine lame* whose thrusts had won the fray for us, was none other than the monk I had seen on board *La Sacra Familia*, the holy man known there as Father Jaime.

And swiftly as I gazed up at him there came to my recollection old Admiral Hopson's suspicions as to having seen him before, also the imitation pass he had made across the table with the quill at his brother-admiral, and his words:

"'T was not always the cowl and gown that adorned his person — rather instead the belt and pistols — the long, serviceable rapier, handy."

What did it mean?

Ere he answered either Juan's startled enquiries or my stare of amazement, which he must very well have seen in the moon's rays as I regarded him, he cantered off after my horse, which was standing quietly in the forest side by side with that other animal on whose neck the first wounded man had fallen — he was now lying dead upon the ground! — and brought both back to where we were, leading them by their reins.

"You will want your horse, monsieur," he said, "to continue your journey. *Bon Dieu!* you both made a good fight of it, though they would have beaten you had I not come up at the moment."

"Believe us, we both thank you more than words can express," I said, while Juan sat his jennet, still breathing heavily from his exertions, yet peering with all the power of those bright eyes at the man before him, "but your appearance is so different from what it was when last we met that—that I am lost in amazement. You were, sir, a holy monk then."

"*Cucullus non facit monachum,*" he replied, in what I recognised to be very good Latin, then added, with a laugh: "In journeying through dangerous places we are not always what we seem to be. To wit: Monsieur was either an English soldier or sailor when I saw him last—an enemy to Spain and France—hating both, as I should suppose. Yet now he is a private gentleman, and, I imagine, desires nothing less than that his real position should be known."

"But you—you," Juan interposed, "you were monk from the first moment I set eyes on you, from the hour when we left Hispaniola. Are you not one?"

"My boy," he said, and as he spoke he touched Juan on the sleeve as they both sat their horses side by side—I being also mounted again by this time—"my boy, I replied to your companion just now with a proverb. I answer you with another: 'Look not a gift horse in the mouth.' I have saved your life, at least, if not this gentleman's. And——"

But Juan stammering forth some words of regret for the curiosity he had shown, he stopped him with still another touch on the sleeve, and said:

"Briefly, let me tell this: I had reasons to be in Spain, to quit the Indies and accompany the galleons, get a passage by some means. It suited me to come disguised as a monk; there was no other way. For, rightly or wrongly, both Spain and France are my enemies; in my own proper character I could never have reached here. Being here, I am still in danger if discovered; to avoid that discovery I have now doffed the monkish garb, so that all traces of me are lost. Enough, however; I am on my road to Lugo. Does your way lie the same road?"

We both answered that it did, whereon he said, speaking quickly and, as I noticed, in the tone of one who seemed very well used to issuing orders, as well as accustomed to deciding for himself and others:

"So be it. Let us ride together—and at once. Every moment we tarry here

ACROSS THE SALT SEAS. 273

makes our position more dangerous. Those men will no sooner have returned to Chantada than every available soldier will be sent forward to arrest us, even though we be in Lugo itself. You will be recognised without doubt if you stay an instant in the town. Your one chance is to get into it and out again as soon as may be.

"And you?" I asked, as now we put spurs to our horses and dashed along the forest track. "And you? If any of those who were in this affray return with the soldiers you speak of, it will be hard for you, too, to escape recognition. Your form cannot be disguised."

"It will be disguised again," he answered very quietly, "when I have once more resumed the monk's garb. I have it here," and he tapped the great valise strapped on his horse's back. "It has not been worn since I got ashore at Vigo, and that's far behind this by many leagues. There are none here like to recognise me."

"You stay, then, in Lugo?"

"I must stay. I have affairs."

He said this so decidedly that we neither of us ventured to ask him any more questions, though, a moment or two afterward, he volunteered to us the statement that, if another horse he had previously bought when he landed at Vigo had not broken down, he would long ere this have been in Lugo. Only the finding of a fresh animal — the one he now bestrode — had taken him some time, and thereby caused him to be late on his road, which, as we said gratefully enough, was fortunate for us.

"Ay," he replied, "it was; and also that I was breathing my animal in the forest at the time those others overtook you. But, *nom d'un chou!* I have been a fighter in my day myself, and, since I could not see two men set upon by five, my old instincts were aroused; though," he added, with extreme *sang froid*, "had it been an even fray, I might have left you to it."

And now it seemed to both Juan and myself as though this man's assistance to us necessitated us showing some confidence in him; wherefore, very briefly, we gave him some description of why we were travelling together, and of how, because Juan had naught else of much importance to do at the outset of his arrival in Europe, he had elected to be my companion as far as Flanders.

"Humph!" he exclaimed at this, "he is a young knight errant, as I told him oft enough in the galleon, when he talked some rhodomontade about being on his way to

ACROSS THE SALT SEAS. 275

Europe to seek out and punish a villain who had wronged him. Well, sir, even if he finds not the man, he is likely enough to meet with sufficient adventures in your company ere he reaches Flanders."

"He thinks he has found him already," I said quietly, in reply.

"What!" and he turned his great eyes on both of us. "Found him. Here in Spain!" and he laughed incredulously.

"He thinks nothing of the kind," Juan cried hotly, roused more, I thought, by that scornful laugh than by my doubting words. "He is sure of it!"

And then he told the whole story of our having seen the old man's coach in the inn, of the black's insolent reply, of his departure at night, and of the little doubt there could be that he it was who had betrayed us to the people of Chantada; also he added:

"But I have him. Have him fast. He is but a league or so ahead of us, must stop some hours, at least, in Lugo. And then — then, James Eaton, look to yourself!"

As he uttered those words the black horse which the other bestrode plunged forward, pricked, as I thought, by some unintentional movement of the rider's spur, while that rider turned round in his saddle and gazed at Juan, his face, as it seemed to me, livid beneath the moonlight.

"Who? What name is that on your lips?"

"The name of a damned villain. The name of James Eaton."

"James Eaton. James Eaton — what is he to you, then? What evil has he done to you?"

"What evil?" Juan replied, with a bitter laugh. "What evil? and what is he to me? Only this: He was left guardian to me by my dead father, and — and — he ill-treated and robbed me. No more than that!"

"You! You! You!" this mysterious man said, his hand raised to his eyebrows, his dark, piercing eyes gleaming beneath that hand — upon his face a look I could not fathom. "You!"

CHAPTER XX.

"THE COWL DOES NOT ALWAYS MAKE THE MONK."

We were drawing very near to Lugo now, as the wintry morning gave signs of breaking; already the great spurs and cañons of the mountains that flanked the east side of the river Minho began to shape themselves into something tangible and distinct from the dull clouds at their summits, and their peaks and crags to stand out clearly. Also, we noticed that villages were scattered about at the base of these mountains; observed lights twinkling in the windows of cottages, and passed a bridge which spanned the river and carried on a road that led from that east side to the western one; a road with, on it, a great pedestal of rock, serving, as others which we had passed had served us, as milestones and finger-posts; a road leading, as we learnt, from another Viana, different from the one in Portugal at which Juan and I had landed from the English fleet.

We were drawing very near.

For the last two or three hours we had ridden almost in silence, knee to knee, all wrapped in our long cloaks, and with nothing breaking in upon that silence but, sometimes, the hoot of an owl from out the beeches and tamarisks which fringed the road, and sometimes the scream of an eagle far up in the mountains, roused, perhaps, from his eyrie by the clang of our animals' hoofs upon the hard-bound, frosty earth.

Yet some words had been spoken, too, ere we lapsed into this silence; for, as our friend and deliverer had exclaimed, "You! You!" on hearing that James Eaton had robbed Juan of whatever might have been left in his care by the lad's dead father, Juan himself had quickly exclaimed:

"Is he known also to you, then?"

"He was once, long ago — ay, long ago!" Then he paused, as though unwilling to tell more, though, a moment later, he said:

"And now you think he is ahead of us? — that we shall find him in Lugo?"

"Without doubt," Juan and I answered, both speaking together, while the former went on:

"He must halt for some time in Lugo, if only to get a change of horses."

" 'T is my belief," I struck in, "he will

do more than that. Judging from what I learnt of him in the ship which brought us both from Holland, Lugo is his destination, the end of his journey."

"Wherefore?" the man who had been "Father Jaime" asked.

"Because," I replied, "he was on his way to Cadiz, where, he thought, as all did, that the galleons were going in. And he told me in a frenzy, when he learnt that the English fleet was about in those waters, that he had a fortune on board two of the galleons. Be sure, therefore, he would follow them up to Vigo as soon as he could, after being put ashore at Lagos and learning that much of the treasure had been set ashore and then forwarded on to Lugo——"

"Would follow them here?" the other said. "Ha! Well, then, we shall surely meet," and he laughed a little, very quietly, to himself. "Must meet! And I—I shall have something to say to James Eaton—shall recall myself to him. He will be pleased to see me!" and again he laughed —though this time the laughter sounded grimly.

"I also shall have something to say to him," exclaimed Juan. "To——"

"Recall yourself to him also," the other broke in.

"Perhaps," the boy replied, "perhaps. We shall see, though it may not be just at first."

"At first," said the other, taking him up, "let me present myself. I assure you 't will be best. Let me put in my claim to his attention. Then you can follow suit."

"And I," I exclaimed, speaking now. "I, too, have something to settle with Mr. James Eaton, if that be his name. I owe it to him that my journey to Flanders has been interrupted by that scene upon the road, owe it to him that I ran a very fair chance of never continuing that journey further than a couple of leagues this side of Chantada.

I believe, too, that it was he who drew the attention of a French ship of war to the vessel which was carrying me and my intelligence to Cadiz, as then supposed."

"How?" asked the ex-monk, "and why?"

"The reason wherefore," I replied, "might be because he suspected my mission in some way. The manner in which he let the French ship know of our whereabouts was probably by leaving open the dead light of his cabin when he lay drinking, while all the others were closed so as to avoid her. Oh! be sure," I continued, "when you two have done with him I shall have an account also to make."

"We are three avengers," the other replied, with still that grim laugh of his. "James Eaton will have other things to think of besides getting back his treasure at Lugo, if it is there; for, when Señor Belmonte and myself and you have finished with him — sir," he said, breaking off and regarding me, "I do not know your name, how to designate you. What may it be?"

"My name," I replied, "is Mervyn Crespin. May I ask by what we are to address you? At present, at least, you do not style yourself 'Father Jaime,' I apprehend."

"Nay," he said. "Nay — not until I don the cowl again. But, see, none of us, I should suppose, are desirous of travelling through this hostile country, entering this town of Lugo, which may bristle with dangers to all of us, under our right names. Therefore — though even thus 'tis not desirous that these names should be spoken more often than needs — I will be Señor Jaime. There are Jaimes for second names, as well as first."

"And," exclaimed Juan, entering at once into the spirit of the matter, "there are

Juans for second names as well as first, also. Therefore I will be Señor Juan."

"And I," I said, "since I pretend to speak no Spanish, but am supposed to be a Frenchman, will be Monsieur Crespin. That is a French name, as well as English. There are scores of Crespins in Maine and Anjou — 'tis from there we came originally. 'T will do very well."

So, this understanding arrived at, we rode on afterward in that silence which I have told you of.

But now it was full day, cold, crisp and bright, with the sun topping the mountains to our left and sending down fair, warm beams athwart the river, which served to put some life into us, as well as a little extra heat besides that which the motion of our horses and the glow of their bodies had hitherto afforded us.

Also, we had left the forest now and entered a great plain which rolled away to the west of those mountains, and of the river which brawled and splashed at their base; a plain that in summer was, doubtless, covered with all the rich vegetation for which the north of Spain is famed, but that now stretched bare as the palm of a hand, and recalled to my mind the fair Weald of Kent when winter's icy grip is on it. Yet 't was well covered with villages, some close together, some a league or two leagues apart, and, under where the last spurs of the Cantabrian mountains swept round directly to the west, we saw rise before us the high walls of a town, with above them an incredible amount of towers — we making out between twenty and thirty of these as each stride of our animals brought us nearer to them.

"That," said Señor Jaime — as he was now to be called — though God only knew what his right name was! — while our eyes regarded it from still afar, "must be Lugo. Now let us decide for our plan of action. And, first, as to getting into it."

"Do you make your entry," I asked, "as a gentleman travelling through the land, or as priest — monk?"

"As monk!" he replied. "So best! I have other affairs here, besides the desire of meeting my old friend, Eaton. Now, observe, this is what I propose: You shall go first together — you will have no difficulty in getting in, seeing that there is no frontier to cross. Nor will you be asked for papers, since, once in, you will not get out again unless you appear satisfactory to those who are there."

"We must get out again after a short

rest, after a few hours," I replied. "I make no manner of doubt that by now we are followed from Chantada—if those who are behind us reach Lugo ere we have quitted it, we shall be stopped beyond all doubt."

Señor Jaime paused a moment ere he answered; pondering, doubtless, on this being the case. Then, speaking slowly, he said:

"If—if—'t were possible that you," looking at me, "and you," regarding Juan, "could also enter the town disguised; could appear as something vastly different from what you are, you would be safe; we would remain together. And—and—that would please me. We must not part, having met as we have done," and his eyes rested particularly upon Juan as he spoke, so that I felt sure he would far less willingly part with him than with me; that it was of this bright, handsome boy he was thinking most.

"I," exclaimed Juan, "would, above all other things but one—that one the not parting company with Mervan, my friend!"—how softly he murmured those words, "my friend!"—"stay here. For I am resolved to bring to bar that villain, James Eaton. But how—how to do it? How to enter the town disguised? We do not travel with masks and vizards, nor could we assume them an we did. Also, how to change our appearance sufficiently to be unrecognised by any of those behind?"

"For him," said Señor Jaime, addressing Juan, but looking at me, "'t is easy enough. I can help him to change himself in a moment. I have here," and he tapped the great valise strapped on to his horse's back, "a second monk's gown, of another order than the one I wore—that was a Carmelite's and, as you know, brown; the second is a Dominican's, and white. The object which brings me to Europe—later you shall know it—if it prospers, forced me to provide myself with more than one disguise."

Then after pausing a moment, perhaps to judge of the effect of this announcement on us, he went on: "Well, Monsieur Crespin! What do you say? Will you be a monk and stay with Juan till he has seen his beloved friend, James Eaton, or will you insist on his abandoning his interview with that personage and riding post-haste to Flanders? Only remember, if he and you do so, or if you do this alone, the chance is also missed of your having a reckoning with that old man also."

Now I was sorely posed by this suggestion of his — sorely. For, firstly, there was something bitterly distasteful to me, a soldier and, I hoped, a brave one, in masquerading in any such guise as this suggested. Also, I knew that it ill became me to tarry on my journey back for any cause whatever, let alone a new formed friendship for Juan Belmonte. My place was with the Cuirassiers, and with them I ought to be — both the earls having hinted that there would be some hard fighting ere long — while, as for revenging myself on the villain whose name now seemed for a certainty to be Eaton, well! that might easily be left to Señor Jaime and Juan. If they did not between them very effectually confound that hoary-headed scoundrel, I should be much astonished.

On the other hand, there were many things that made for my disguising myself ere I entered Lugo, and, rapidly enough as I sat my horse deliberating, those things ran through my mind. To begin with, it would be full of Spanish and French soldiers and sailors, the runaways from Vigo, who, undoubtedly, would have followed the bulk of the treasure which had been removed from the galleons and transported here; and it was possible that there might be some who would recognise me, since I had played a pretty prominent part in the attack. It might, therefore, be best that — little as this disguising of myself was to my taste — I should do as Señor Jaime suggested.

Yet, all the same — and in the next moment — I decided that I would not do this thing; for, besides that it was too repugnant to me, I knew that it would be useless. And, knowing this, I said so, in spite of the pleading, pitiful glances which Juan cast at me — glances which plainly enough implored me to adopt the monk's dress, and thereby be enabled to stay in Lugo until vengeance was wrought upon James Eaton.

"No," I said, turning to Señor Jaime, who sat quietly on my horse awaiting my answer, while I studiously avoided Juan's gaze. "No, I will not do it. I am a soldier, and as a soldier — at least as a man, and not a monk — I will get through Spain and France. Besides, the disguise would be useless."

"Wherefore?"

"In reply to that," I said, "let me ask you a question: What do you intend to do with your horse? Monks do not ride, as a rule — in Flanders I never saw one on horseback; also, your boots and great steel spurs beneath the gown would betray you."

Now, he seemed very fairly posed at this, and for a moment bent his head over his animal's mane, as though lost in thought. Then suddenly he burst out into one of his deep, sonorous laughs, and exclaimed:

"Body of St. Iago! I never thought of that. Though, for the boots, it matters not; I have the monkish sandals with me. And —and — perhaps the horse can be smuggled into the town somehow, and with it the boots! Ha! I must think!"

And again he became buried in thought; yet, a moment later, he spoke once more:

"If you enter Lugo as you are," he said, "you will be taken for a certainty. There are — there must be — many coming after us from behind, from Chantada — they will describe you. Remember, you were not only seen under the moon's rays during the fight in the wood, but in the town previously. And, if you are taken, there is no hope for you! Eaton has told that you are English — fought against the galleons at Vigo. God! it means the garrote for both of you. You understand what that is? An upright post, a hasp of iron around your neck and it, a wheel to screw that hasp tight to the post — with your neck between them! — and — and —

your eyeballs out of your head—your tongue half a foot long. That is what awaits you if you are taken."

"I will never be taken," I said, between my teeth, "to suffer that. Bah! If I cannot, if we cannot, get out of the town again on the other side, have I not this, and this?" and I touched my pistol holsters. "They will be in my belt then."

After saying which I turned to Juan to ask him if he agreed with me, and saw that Señor Jaime's ghastly description of the garrote had made him as pale as death.

"What think you, comrade?" I asked. "Is it not best that you and I forego our vengeance on this man, Eaton, and push on as fast as may be, leaving him to our friend here, who also seems to have a reckoning to make—who appears, also, one who can extort it? Or will you disguise yourself and stay behind?"

"Nay. Nay," he answered. "Where you go, I go. And—God knows I am no poltroon—yet—yet—I could not suffer that. I have seen it in the Indies—oh!" and he put his hands to his eyes, letting his reins fall. "Not that, not that!"

"Will you push on with me, then, foregoing your vengeance?"

"Yes. Yes, since my vengeance risks

such death as that. But," turning to the other, "you proposed a disguise for me. Was I to be a monk, too?"

"Nay," he said. "Nay. But you are a brave, handsome lad—I thought that in some way we might have transformed you into a woman. You would make a presentable one."

"A woman!" he echoed, looking mighty hot and raging at the suggestion. "A woman!—I, who have fought by Mervan's side! Never. Also," he added, after somewhat of a pause, "it is not as a woman that I intend to meet James Eaton, if at all; but as a man demanding swift justice. A woman would be like to get none of that from him."

CHAPTER XXI.

A NARROW ESCAPE.

That evening—or rather afternoon, when already the wintry night was at hand—Juan and I were in Lugo and once more making preparations to continue our journey—to go on west now, through the Asturias, Santander and Biscay, as our chart showed us, toward St. Sebastian and Bayonne, which would bring us into France. But also we hoped that, after we had passed by the former of these provinces, on reaching the sea, which we should then do, our journey by land might be at an end; that we might find, by great good fortune, at some seaside town a vessel, either English or Dutch, which would take us north to where we desired to go.

But, alas! 't is useless to write down all the plans we concocted in the dirty parlour of the inn we had rested in—an inn dignified by the name of the "Pósada del Gran Grifon," since 't was not to be our lot to make that journey, nor to set out upon it.

Let me not, however, anticipate, but

write down all that now befell us; also let me now begin to tell of the strange marvels that I was destined to behold the unravelling of, as also the dangers which from this period encompassed me.

We were alone, had entered Lugo alone, Señor Jaime having bidden us ride ahead of him and leave him to find his way into the town by himself.

"And," he said, "be very sure I shall do it. Fear not for me. Only, if I come not by the time four o'clock has struck, believe that either I have fallen into the hands of the enemy or that, for some reason, I have not been able to get face to face with Eaton. Therefore, ride on without me. Remember my disguise will save *me*. You have both refused to be disguised. By consequence, look to yourselves. We shall meet again. I know your road."

And now four o'clock had struck from the cathedral hard by, and he had not come. Yet, why not? we asked each other. A peasant whom we had met on the road when but a league between us and Lugo had mentioned this inn as one where good accommodation for man and beast could be obtained, and ere we parted from Jaime we had determined that it should be our meeting place.

And still he had not come. And it was four o'clock and past.

"We must go," I said to Juan, "we must go. 'T is courting frightful danger to remain here. Already I have observed half a dozen French and Spanish sailors pass this window, whom I saw on board some of the ships and galleons; also some officers. If I meet them face to face, and they remember me, as I do them, there will be——"

"What?" asked Juan, his face full of terror.

"Well — no Mervyn Crespin a few hours hence! that's all."

"Oh, come, come, come," he exclaimed, catching at my arm. "For God's sake, come! Why, why did we ever enter this town! 'T was madness. We should have remembered they had fled hither."

"There is no other high road to France and Flanders," I said, "that justifies the risk. Yet, Juan, remember, even now it is not too late for you to part from me, if you choose. Your coming on here means nothing. *You* did not fight against the galleons; therefore you are in no danger——"

"Silence!" he said again, as he had said once before. "Silence! I will hear no word about leaving you."

Then suddenly he came away from the window, at which he had been standing, and crossed the room to me.

"Look," he said. "Look from out that window into the street; then say if it is not too late for us to part — if my danger is not as great as yours. Look, I say!"

Glancing first at him, in wonderment at his exclamation, and what the meaning of it might be, yet with some sort of understanding mounting to my brain also, I stepped across to the dirty, unwashed window and looked out into the street.

And then I understood.

Through the dim light cast on the now darkened street by oil lamps, swung across it at intervals, and also by the candles burning in *relicários*, set into the walls, as well as by the feeble glare which emerged from curtainless and unshuttered windows, I saw a band of men slowly passing, their drawn swords in their hands, or with musketoons upon their shoulders.

And ahead of all this body, which was composed of perhaps a dozen, there marched two of those with whom we had fought on the road between Chantada and this place — the leader who had addressed us, and another. As they passed along they gazed at each man whom they encountered; halting opposite our window, they looked at an inn which faced ours directly, a little place on which was painted the name, "Pósada Buena Ventura."

"Open the window a crack," I said to Juan—doing so myself, however, as I spoke—"and let us listen. Hear what they say. Softly," and following my words we placed our ears to the inch-wide orifice.

And then we heard every word as it fell from their lips.

"That house opposite," the leader said, is the last to be examined except this and another"—while Juan whispered: "I cannot catch its name—It sounds like the San Cristobal. Yes. Yes. 'Tis that. Ha! And, see, they enter the house opposite. Yet some remain in the street." And we both peered from behind the side of the window at them as they stood there in the road, a crowd of urchins gathered round.

"We are trapped," I said, "trapped. We can never get out. The horses are in the stables behind—also, the gates are shut."

"God!" exclaimed Juan, suddenly, even as I spoke, "they have finished there already—are coming here. Another five minutes and they will be in this room."

"What shall we do?" he wailed a moment later.

"Escape while there is time — from this room, at least. Loosen your sword in its sheath — follow me," and I drew him back from the window.

"But where? Where to go to?"

"Out of the house, at least. Come. The stairs lead down to the back part of the house; there is the yard and the stables — also a garden. I observed it when the horses were put up. Come. There is a wall at the end of the garden which separates it from another. If we can get over that we can at least escape into the town. By God's grace, there may be some way out of it besides the gates. And we have the cloak of night to help us."

All the time I was speaking I had been drawing Juan toward the door; also I had seen that my papers and money were bestowed about me safely — I doubted if we should ever see our valises again! — or, for the matter of that, our horses. It would be heaven's providence now if we ever got out of this town alive, and even that I deemed unlikely. And at this crisis that was all we had to hope for, if so much.

"Lift your *porte epée* by the hand," I

whispered. "If the scabbard clanks on the stairs we are undone. Follow me."

In another instant we were outside the door of the room. For precaution and as a possible means of gaining time I drew the key from the inside of the lock, then placed it in the keyhole outside, made a turn and, again withdrawing it, dropped it into my pocket. This would take up some moments, while they clamoured without, bidding us open. It would take some few more to break down the door, which they would very probably do. They might be precious moments to us.

It was quite dark outside in the corridor, but at the farther end there glimmered a faint light from an oil lamp set upon a bracket, though its rays scarcely reached here, namely, to the head of the deep oak stairs opposite where the door of the room we had just quitted was. But from below, which was a stone-flagged passage running from the front of the house to the back, there was another light—thank God, 't was nearer the street than the exit to the yard!

We descended seven steps, then the stairs turned sharply from a small landing —we ourselves did not dare, however, to turn them.

For below, in that cold stone corridor,

we heard and recognised the voice of the man who had challenged us in the forest ere the fight began, a night ago.

"Here, are they?" we heard him say. "Here — so the birds are caught. The one, big, stalwart, brown — that is the English *demonio* — the other, younger, dark, handsome, might play the lover in one of Véga's spectacles. Ha! And the third who joined in the murder — an elder one, swart and grimy, black as the devil himself — is he here, too?"

"Nay," said the woman, whose voice told us she was the landlady, "there are but two, the bronzed one and the youth. You will not hurt him! Nay! Nay! *Diós!* he is young and beautiful."

"Have no fear. *We* will not hurt either, if they do not resist. If they do, we shall cut them down. But—otherwise—no! no!" and he laughed a fierce, hard laugh. "Oh, no. There are others to hurt them — the governor, the Regidórs, the judges. Ho! They will hurt them through the garrote — or — or — the flames. The brasero! The wheel! Now lead up to them. Where is the room they harbour in?"

"I will fetch another lamp," the woman said. "This one is fixed. Wait." And we heard her clatter down the corridor on her Spanish pattens. Yet she paused, too, a moment, and turned back, saying:

"Spare him — the young one. Heavens! his lips and eyes are enough to madden an older woman than I am."

"Quick, then, quick," the other answered. "They sleep in the prison tonight, and our supper waits at the gatehouse. Quick."

"Shall we dash through them?" Juan whispered; and now I noticed that, as before in the hour of danger, his voice was firm and steady. "One might escape even though the other is taken." And I heard him mutter, in even lower tones: "Pray God it is you."

"No," I said. "No. We go together. Together escape or — die."

Then, even as I spoke, I saw what I had not observed before, owing to the dim light in which all was surrounded; saw that opposite to us on the landing — where the stairs turned — there was a door. Closed tight into its frame, 't was true, yet leading doubtless into some room opening off the stairs which led up to the other one we had quitted.

I was near enough to put my foot out quietly and touch it with my toe and — God be praised! — it yielded, opened inward.

"Into it," I said in Juan's ear, "into it. They will pass it as they go up to where we have come from. When they have done so we may creep down. In!"

A moment later we had entered that room, had quitted the stairs—and the woman had come back and rejoined the men, was leading them up those very stairs, across the very spot where a few instants before we had been standing.

Yet our hearts leapt to our mouths—mine did, I know!—when we who were standing on the other side of the door heard him stop outside it, and, striking the panel with his finger—the rap of his nail upon it was clearly perceptible to our eager ears—say to the woman:

"Is this the room—are they here?"

The woman gave a low laugh in answer; then she said:

"Nay. Nay. 'T is mine. 'By the saints! what should they do there! That handsome *Inglés*, devil though he be!—or that lovely boy? Heavens, no!" and again she laughed, and added: "Come. They are here. Up these stairs."

Even as we heard their heavy, spurred feet clatter on those stairs we were seeking for some mode of escape, and that at once.

Alas! 't was not to be out of the door

again and down into the stone passage, as we had thought.

For one glance through a great crack, and we saw, by peering down below, that these Spanish alguazils had some method in their proceedings. They had left two of their number behind; they stood in the passage waiting for what might happen above; waiting, perhaps, to hew down the two fugitives whom those others were seeking for, should they rush down; waiting for us. There was no way there!

Then, for the room — what did that offer?

It was as dark as a vault — we could distinguish nothing — not even where the bed was — at first. Yet, later, in a few moments — while we heard, above, the rapping of sword hilts upon the door of the chamber we had just quitted — while we heard, too, the leader shouting: "Open. Open — *Bandidos! Assassinatóres! Espias!* or we will blow the lock off"—we saw at the end of the room a dull murky glimmer, a light that was a light simply in contrast to the denser gloom around — knew there was a window at that end.

Was that our way out?

Swiftly we went toward it — tore aside a curtain drawn across a bar — the noise the rings made as they ran seemed enough to alarm those men above, must have done so but for the infernal din they themselves were making—opened the lattice window—and, heaven help us!—found outside an iron, interlaced grate that would have effectually barred the exit of aught bigger than a cat!

We were trapped! Caught! It seemed as if naught could save us now!

"Lock the door," I whispered to Juan. "They will come here next. The moment they find we are not in the other room!—ha! they know it now, or will directly."

For as I spoke there rang the report of a musketoon through the empty passages of the house. They were blowing the lock off!

Desperately, madly, exerting a force that even I had never yet realized myself as possessing, I seized the cross-bars of that iron grating; I pushed them outward, praying to God for one moment—only one moment—of Samson's strength. And—could do nothing! Nothing, at first. Yet—as still I strained and pushed, as I drew back my arms to thrust more strongly even than before—it seemed as if the framework, as if the whole thing, yielded, as if it were becoming loosened in its stone or brick setting. Inspired by this, I pushed still more, threw the whole weight of my big body into one last despairing effort—and succeeded! The grate was loosened, torn out of the frame; with a clatter of falling chips and small *débris* it fell into the yard ten feet below.

My prayer was heard!

"Quick, Juan," I said, "quick, come. Out of the window, give me your hands. I will lower you. 'T is nothing."

From Juan there came in answer a cry, almost a scream of terror.

"Save me! Save me!" he shrieked, "there is another man in the room!" and as he so cried, I heard a thump upon the floor—a thump such as one makes who leaps swiftly from a bed—a rush across that floor. Also a muttered curse in Spanish, a tempest of words, a huge form hurled against mine, two great muscular hands at my throat.

In a moment, however, my own hands were out, too, my thumbs pressing through a coarse beard upon a windpipe. "Curse you," I said in Spanish, as I felt that grasp on me relax. "Curse you, you are doomed," and drawing back, I struck out with my full force to the front of me.

Struck out, to feel my clenched fist

stopped by a hairy face—the thud was terrible even to my ears!—to hear a bitter moan and, a moment later, a fall—dull and like a dead weight!—upon the floor.

"Come, Juan, come," I cried. "Come."

CHAPTER XXII.

WHO? GRAMONT?

As he scrambled through the window — as I let him down by his hands, so that, with the length of his arm and mine together, his feet were not more than a yard from the ground — I heard those others outside the door. Heard also the woman shriek:

"There is none in here, I tell you — pigs, idiots! If they have escaped, 'tis to the street or to the roof. Search those rooms first. This is my chamber. *Diòs!* Are you men to enter thus a woman's apartment!"

"So be it," the leader said. "We will. But, remember, if we find them not we will search this room. Remember!" and we heard him and the others striding off to some other part of the house.

By this time I was myself half out of the window. From the creature I had felled to the floor there came no sound; but from the door outside I heard the woman whisper:

"Renato, come forth. Quick, I say! If

they find you here you are lost. You will be taken—sent to the colonies. Come forth!"

Then I waited to hear no more, understanding clearly enough that the woman had herself been sheltering in her own room some malefactor, probably some lover. And, doubtless, he had thought we were seeking for him, had found him in that darkened room—that we were the alguazils. His presence was explained.

Taking Juan by the hand, I passed rapidly by the stables as we went away from the street and up into the garden beyond—a small place, neglected and dirty, in which I had noticed, when we arrived, numbers of enormous turnips growing—vegetables much used in the country.

Then, a moment later, we were close by a low, whitewashed wall—'t was not so high as my head—over which I helped Juan, following instantly myself.

"Heaven knows," I said, "where we are now, except that we have left the inn behind. This may be the garden of some great *residéncia*, or of another inn. Well, we must get through somehow into the street beyond."

"And afterward?" Juan asked, his face

close to mine, as though trying to see me in the dark of the night. "Afterward?"

"God knows what—afterward! We shall never get out of the gates, 'tis certain. There are five—all are doubtless warned by now. Pity 'tis we did not follow our friend's suggestion and disguise ourselves. That way, we might have been safe. I as a monk, you as a woman, we should never have been recognised."

"'Tis too late," said Juan. "Too late now. We must go on; on to the end. Yet I wonder where that friend, Jaime, is. Perhaps taken, his disguise seen through."

We had reached the house to which this garden belonged by now—a different one from the neglected thing we had lately left, well cared for, and with great tubs of oleanders and orange trees placed about it at regular intervals, as we could now see by the rising moon, which was peeping over the chimney tops and casting its rays along a broad path which we had followed; were close up to the house, a great white one, with this, its garden side, full of windows covered with *persianas*, or jalousies, and from some of them lights streaming.

"'Tis an inn, for sure," I said, "and full of—hark! whose voice is that?"

Yet there was no need to ask; 'twas a

voice not easily forgotten which was speaking now; the voice of the man, Señor, or "Father," Jaime."

"Ay," we heard in those rich, sonorous tones, "alive, and here to call you to account."

And following this we heard another voice, supplicating, wailing, screaming, almost: "No! No! No! Mercy! Pardon!"

Beneath the moon's increasing rays we gazed into each other's eyes, then quickly, together — as if reading each other's thoughts also — we moved toward where those sounds proceeded from.

Toward a room in the angle of the great white house, with a door opening on to the garden in which we stood — 't was open now, though half across it hung a heavy curtain of some thick material. It was easy enough to guess how 't was that curtain was thrown half back and the door stood open.

That way Jaime had come upon his prey.

Standing behind that door, behind that heavy half-fallen curtain, this was what we saw: The man Jaime, with in his hand a drawn sword — doubtless he had hidden it beneath his monk's gown since he returned to the assumption of the latter.

In front of Jaime, upon his knees, his

hands clasped, his white hair streaming behind him, was the man whose name I had deemed to be Carstairs, or Cuddiford, but which Juan had averred was in truth James Eaton.

"Alive!" Jaime went on. "Alive. Villain, answer for your treachery ere I slay you. Where is my wealth—my child's wealth. Where is my daughter?"

As he spoke I heard a gasp, a moan beside me, felt a trembling. And, looking down, I saw Juan staring into the room, his eyes distended as though he was fascinated.

"My child," Jaime went on. "My child. Where is she?"

"I—I—do not know," the old man muttered—hissed in a whisper. "I do—not know. She left me—years ago. Yet—I loved her."

"Liar. I have heard of you in the Indies. You stole the wealth I left in your hands for her—you drove her forth. Answer. Is she dead?"

"I lost all in trade," Eaton moaned again, "all, all. I thought to double it—you were dead—they said so—would never come back. I—I——"

"Look," whispered Juan in my ear. "Look behind you."

At his words I turned, and then I knew that we were lost, indeed. Lost forever.

The men from Chantada, accompanied by those of Lugo, were in this garden—had followed us over the wall, had found out our way of escape.

We were doomed! The garrote—the stake—were very near now.

They saw us at once, in an instant—doubtless our forms stood out clearly enough in the beams of the lamp as they poured forth into the garden—and made straight for us, their swords drawn, the unbrowned barrels of their musketoons and pistols gleaming in the moonlight. And the leader shouted, as he ran slightly ahead of the others: "You cannot escape again. Move and we fire on you!"

Yet we heeded him not, but with a bound leapt into the room where those two were—leapt in while I cried: "Jaime, we are undone. Assist us again."

Then swift as lightning I shut the door to, let fall the curtain and drew my sword. "I will never yield to them," I said. "Juan and I escape or die here together."

"Together!" Juan echoed, drawing also his weapon forth.

There was but time to see a still more frightened glance on Eaton's face than before—if added terror could come into a man's eyes more than had been when those eyes had glinted up at Jaime as he stood over him, it came now as Juan sprang to my side, his hat fallen off and his hair dishevelled—while those men were at the door giving on to the garden. And in an instant it was burst open by them—'t was but a poor frail thing!—they were in the room.

"Yield!" the leader cried, "yield, or you die here at once!"

But now Jaime was by our side; three blades were flashing in their faces; we were driving them back, assisted also by a fourth—the negro servant of Eaton, who had sprung into the room from another door. Yet that assistance lasted but a second. Doubtless the unhappy wretch preferred it, thinking it was his master who was in danger! A pistol was fired by some one, and I saw him reel back, falling heavily on the floor, dead, with a bullet between his eyes. And, as he did so, from Eaton there came a scream, while he flung himself over the creature's body.

With those others pistols were now the order of the day, fired ineffectually at first, while still I and the leader fought hand-to-hand around the room. And I had him safe. I knew if I was not cut down from behind that he was mine. My blade was under and over his guard. I prepared for the last lunge, when — curses on the luck! — a bullet took me in the right forearm; there ran through that arm, up to my shoulder, a feeling of numbness, a burning twinge; my sword fell with a clang to the floor.

And in another moment two of them had sprung on and secured me; two others had grasped Juan, and disarmed him, too.

And now there was none on our side to oppose himself to them but Jaime.

"Shoot him down! Kill him!" the leader cried. Then added: "You fool, there is naught against you, yet, if you court fate, receive it."

But, great fighter as he was, what could he do against all those? One hung upon his sword arm, another clasped a leg, a third was dragging at his neck from behind, a fourth holding his monkish gown.

In another moment he, too, was disarmed. We were beaten — prisoners! The lives of all of us were at an end. None could doubt that!

The leader drew a long breath, then turned to where, at the open door of the passage, were gathered the landlord, as I supposed; several *facchinos* and some trembling women servants, white to the lips, and said:

"Observe, all you. I take these men— these *asasinos* within your house. I denounce these two," and he indicated Juan and me, "the one as an English spy and a man who fought against us at Vigo, this other one, this boy, as his comrade and accomplice. Bear witness to my words, also to their deeds of blood."

From that crowd in the passage there came murmurs and revilings in reply: "You should have slain them here," some said; "Better the garrote or the flames in the *plaza da mercado*," said others.

"As for this monk, this false monk— for such I know him now to be—easy enough to recognise him as one of the brigands we fought with the other night— had he not joined in this fray he had been safe. We sought him not. Now, also, the flames or the garrote for him." Then, breaking off, he exclaimed: "Who is this —and that black slave lying dead there?" and he pointed to Eaton and the other. "Who are they?"

"A gentleman and his servant staying in this, my house," the landlord said, speaking for the first time, "doubtless assaulted by the *vagabundos*. Oh! 't is terrible."

"Off with these three," the leader said. "To the prison in the ramparts to-night — the judge to-morrow."

And as he gave his orders his men and the men of Lugo with him formed round us, prepared to obey.

But, now, for the first time Eaton spoke, approaching the leader fawningly, speaking in a soft voice.

"Señor," he said, "ere you take them away, a word. "This one," looking at me, "you knew already — at Chantada; I have told you who and what he is. For the boy it matters not. He is but a follower."

Yet as he spoke I noticed he carefully avoided Juan's eyes, fixed full blaze on him as they flamed from out of his now white, marble face.

"These, I say, you know," he went on. But for this other one — this pretended monk, this brigand of the night — you do not know him; nor who he is and what has been. Let me tell you."

"Viper," Jaime murmured. "Villain. Thief! Yet," he continued, "I stoop not to ask your silence. Speak. Tell all. But, James Eaton, beware. Caged tigers sometimes break their bars and get free."

"Yours will never be broken," the leader said, looking at the same time with a wondering glance from one to the other.

"'T is true. 'T is very true," Eaton went on, his voice oily, treacherous as before. "Yet since you might break yours, I give this gentleman a double reason for binding you faster. Sir," turning to him whom he so addressed, "this monk, this brigand as he appears, would be an innocent man were he that alone, in comparison with what he really is."

"Who in the name of all the fiends is he, then? Answer quick."

"A murderer," the old man hissed now, raising his voice, "not four-fold, but four thousand-fold. See," and he pointed his fingers at Jaime, "see in him the man who sacked Maracaibo, Guayaquil, Campeachy; the man who has burnt men and women alive in their houses like pigs in a stye, sunk countless Spanish and French ships, plundered, murdered, ravished — the arch-villain of the Caribbean Sea — not dead, but alive, and trapped at last. The buccaneer, filibuster, pirate — Gramont!"

Amidst their voices — their shouts and cries — for all in Spain had known that awful name, though its owner had long been deemed dead and lost at sea — I heard a cry

— it was a scream — from Juan; I saw him reel as he stood by my left side, then staggered heavily against me, supported from falling to the floor only by my unwounded arm around him.

He had fainted.

And, as I held up the drooping form, I learnt the secret hidden from me for so many days. I knew now what it was that Sir George Rooke had earlier learnt. I penetrated the disguise of Juan Belmonte.

CHAPTER XXIII.

SENTENCED TO DEATH.

I lay within a darkened cell in the prison which formed part of the ramparts of Lugo. Lay there, a man doomed to death; sentenced to be burnt at the stake, as a spy taken in a country at war with my own. To be burnt at the stake on some Sunday morning, because that day was always a day of festival, because all Lugo would be there to witness, because from all the country round the peasants would come in to see the Englishman expire in the flames.

Doomed to death!

Yet not alone. By my side—his right hand nailed to an upright plank! (so the sentence had run) to which our bodies were to be fastened by chains—was to stand that other man, Gramont—the pirate and buccaneer who, as Eaton had testified, had been called the Shark of the Indies.

I had been tried first by the Alcáide of Lugo and the principal Regidór, assisted by the Bishop of the province, an extremely old man—and had been soon disposed of.

Evidence was forthcoming — there was plenty of it in Lugo in the shape of French sea-captains and sailors from the Spanish galleons — that I had fought with the English at Vigo; also, that I had slain men betwixt the border and here. And, again, there was the evidence of Eaton that I had travelled from Rotterdam as the undoubted bearer of the news that the galleons were approaching Spain.

Also, not content with all this, I was on my way through the land, gleaning evidence of all that was taking place within it, so as to furnish, as none could otherwise suppose, information to my countrymen when I should reach them.

No need for my trial to be spun out; one alone of all these facts was enough to condemn me, and, after a whispered conference between the Alcáide, the Regidór and the Bishop, the latter delivered the above sentence, his voice almost inaudible because of his great age, yet strong enough for the purpose — powerful enough to reach my ears and those of the small crowd within the court house; that was sufficient.

So I knew my fate, and knew, too, that it was useless to say aught, to utter one word. I had lost the game; the stakes would have to be paid in full.

Then began the unravelling of the history of him who stood beside me—swarthy, contemptuous—his eyes glancing around that court, alighting at one moment on the withered form and cadaverous face of the Bishop, at another on the figure of the Regidór, a moment later on the Alcáide, a younger, well favoured man, whom I guessed a soldier in the past or present.

Gramont's condemnation was assured by the part he had played on that night when he assisted us on the road 'twixt Chantada and Lugo. That alone would have forfeited his life amidst these Spaniards; yet, perhaps from curiosity, perhaps because even they doubted whether so summary an execution, and one so horrible, was merited by that night's work, they decided to hear the denouncement of Eaton, the story of Gramont's past life. They bade the former speak, tell all.

And what a story it was he told!

Sitting in a chair near the Bishop, looking nearly as old as that old man himself, he poured out horror after horror; branded the man by my side as one too steeped in cruelty to be allowed to live another hour, if what he said was, indeed, true.

Told how this man had ravaged all the Spanish main — had besieged Martinique, Nombre de Diós, Campeachy, and scores of other places, shedding blood like water everywhere — had sunk and plundered ships; burnt them and the men in them — burnt them alive; gave instances, too, of cruelty extreme.

"I have known him to tie dead and living together and fling them to the sharks," he said — "dead and living *Spaniards!* Also hang them to the bowsprit by a cord round their waists, a knife placed in one hand, so that, while freedom was theirs if they chose to sever the rope, a worse death awaited them when they fell into the water — a death from sharks, from alligators! Oh, sir, oh, reverend prelate," he continued, stretching out his hands toward the old, almost blind man, "I have seen worse than this. Once he and his followers besieged a monastery full of holy fathers, governed by a bishop saintly as yourself; and they defended it vigorously, bravely — would have driven this tiger back but for one thing."

"What?" asked the younger of the judges, the Alcáide. And I noticed that now, as all through this testifying of Eaton, that Alcáide seemed less disposed to accept his evidence than the others were. Later on I knew the reason that so urged him.

"What?" he said.

"Some of the priests had already fallen into his hands and the hands of his crew. Then they it was whom he forced to advance first against the monastery — to fire the brass cannon they had brought with them against their brethren; forced them to do so, so that those brethren should not know them, should shoot them down first.

"Also," said the Alcáide, "it might have been to prevent their firing at all. In open war a great commander would, perhaps, have availed himself of such a cunning ruse."

Then I knew for sure this man had been, or was, a soldier.

More, much more, was told by Eaton — 't is best I set down nothing further — then the end came. The sentence was passed; he, too, was doomed to die, by my side, on the Sunday that should later be appointed.

"Break off," the Bishop said. "Justice will be done." Whereupon he glanced down at his papers — I wondering that he could see them with those purblind eyes — while, pausing in his attempt to rise, he said:

"Yet there was another. The youth"—and here I pricked up my ears, for of Juan I had heard nothing since taken to the prison in the ramparts—"the youth who fought by the side of this man—this spy—this *Inglés*. How comes it he is not before us?"

For a moment, as it seemed to me, the Alcáide hesitated, then he said:

"He is not well. He was hurt in the *mêlée;* he cannot be brought before us for some days. Later, if necessary, he can be tried."

Although I had drawn as far away from Gramont as I could since I had learned his true nature and character and the bloodshed of which he had been guilty, I could not prevent myself from letting my eyes fall on him now; and I saw that for the first time there was a look of eagerness in his eyes, that he was watching the younger of those judges, watching as though filled with an intensity of feeling as to what might next be said.

"If necessary, Capitan Morales," the Regidór said, speaking now for almost the first time, "if necessary! By all reports he is as bad as his elder comrades. A wild cat, all say. Why should it not be necessary?"

"He is very young," the Alcáide replied,

undoubtedly confused, "very young; also he — he — is not well. I should do wrong to produce him before you in the state he is. As governor I must use my discretion," and he made a feint of being engaged with the papers before him.

Then I felt sure that he, too, knew Juan's secret, as I now did.

And I wondered to what advantage he might put that secret on behalf of Juan. Wondered while I felt glad at the thought which had now risen to my mind — the thought that, at last, Juan might be saved from our doom.

Again the Bishop said at this time — doubtless his worn old frame was fatigued by the morning's work:

"Let us rise. There is no more to be done, since — since — this youth cannot yet be brought before us," and once more he placed his white, shrunken hands upon the desk in front of him to obtain the necessary aid to quitting his seat.

But now the governor, whose name was Morales, made a motion of dissent, accompanying it, however, by soft, respectful words.

"Nay, most reverend father, nay," he said, "not yet, if you will graciously permit that we continue our examination farther," while as he spoke the Bishop sank back again with a wearied look of assent. "I am not satisfied."

"Not satisfied," the old man whispered, while the Regidór also echoed his words, though in far louder tones. "What is it you are not satisfied with, Capitan Morales?"

"With that man's testimony," he exclaimed, pointing his finger over his desk at Eaton. "In no manner of way satisfied," and as he spoke it almost seemed—I should have believed it to be so in any other country but Spain, a land of notorious injustice and love of cruelty for the sake of cruelty —as if the crowd in the court somewhat agreed with him. Also, even as he spoke, a voice shouted from the midst of those forming it:

"Ay! How knows he all this? Ask him that."

Glancing my eyes in the direction whence those words came, they fell upon a man of rude though picturesque appearance, whose voice I thought it was; a fellow bearded and bronzed, with, in his ears, great rings of gold; a man whom, I scarce know why, I instantly deemed a sailor. Perhaps, one of the many who had fled from the galleons or the French ships of war.

"I am about to ask him that!" exclaimed Morales, though he cast an angry glance toward the crowd. "It is his answer to that which I require."

Then all eyes were instantly directed toward Eaton, one pair flaming like burning coals from beneath their bushy brows —the eyes of Gramont.

Looking myself at him, noticing the ashy colour of his face as he heard that unknown voice uprise amidst the people gathered in the court—as also he heard in reply the words of Morales—noticing, too, the quivering of his white lips and the look as of a hunted rat that came into his eyes—I found myself wondering if he had not thought of how his denunciation of the man by my side was his own accusation also.

"I ask you," went on Morales, "how you know all these things. None but an eye-witness, a participator, could have told as much!"

Upon that muttering and gesticulating crowd, upon the shaggy, black-bearded Asturians and Biscayans—some of them rude mountaineers from the Gaviara and some even ruder sailors from the wild and tempest-beaten shores of Galicia—upon the swarthy Spanish women with knives in their girdles and babes at their bare breasts, there fell a hush as all listened for his answer—a hush, broken only by his own halting attempt to find an answer that should be believed—gain credence not only with the judges, but the people.

"I have—heard—it said—heard it told," he whispered, in quavering tones. "'T was common talk in all the Indies—his name hated—dreaded. Used as a means to fright the timid—to——"

He paused. For, like a storm that howls across the seas, sweeping all before it in its course, another voice, a deeper, fuller, more sonorous one, swept through that court and drowned his; the voice of the lost man by my side.

"Hear me, you judges," he cried, confronting all—standing there with his manacled hands in front of him, yet his form erect, his glance contemptuous, his eyes fire. "Hear me. Let me tell all. I have the right—the last on earth granted to one such as I—for one who sees and reads his doom in all your faces. Give me your leave to speak."

"Speak!" the Bishop murmured, his

tones almost inaudible. "Speak—yet hope nothing."

"Hope!" Gramont said. "Hope! What should I hope? Nothing! in truth. No more than I fear aught. I am the man this one charges me with being—am Gramont. That is enough. Gramont, the filibuster—one of a hundred of your countrymen, of Frenchmen, of Englishmen. But," and he glanced proudly around the court, "the leader of them all, of almost all. Yet, if I am guilty, who is there in the Indies that is innocent? Was Morgan, the English bulldog?—yet his king made him deputy-governor of his fairest isle. Was Basco, Lolonois—is Pointis? Answer me that. And, you of Spain, you, one of her bishops, you, one of her soldiers," and he glanced at each of them, "how often has one of you blessed the ships that sailed from your shores laden with men of my calling—how often have men of your trade," again he glanced at Morales, "belonged to mine? Yet now I, a Frenchman, a comrade in arms of you Spanish, am judged by the words of such as that"—and this time his eyes fell on Eaton.

Also all in the court looked at him again.

"Now," went on Gramont, "hear who and what he is—hear, too, how he knows all that I have done. He was my servant — my ship's steward once — then rose through lust of cruelty to be my mate and second in command. And he it was who first whispered that the captured monks and priests, as he terms them, should be sent against the monastery at Essequibo. Only — he has forgotten, his memory fails — they were not monks and priests — but *nuns.*"

"No, no, no!" shrieked Eaton, as a tumult indescribable arose within the court, while now the mountaineers and seamen howled, "burn him and let the other go," and the fierce dark-eyed women clutched their babes closer to their breasts, fingering the hilts of the knives in their girdles at the same time.

"Nuns! Holy nuns!" the Bishop gasped. "Great God!"

"Ay! Holy nuns. And hear one more word from me; it is the truth, though it avails me nothing. I was not at Essequibo then, was far away, was, in truth, at Cape Blanco. And he — he — James Eaton, was the man."

There rose more tumult and more uproar — it seemed as though all the men in the court would force the barrier that separated them from the judges and from

Eaton and us, the prisoners — would slay that villain, that monstrous wretch, upon the spot. But at a look from the Alcáide some of the alguazils and men-at-arms by that barrier, thrust and pushed them back, and made a line between them and the body of the court.

"Again listen," Gramont went on, when some silence had at last been obtained. "It is my last word. I was not there — was gone — the band was broken up, dispersed. From Spain had come an order from your king that those who desisted were to be pardoned; from Louis of France came the same news by Pointis. And I was one who so desisted, took service under Louis, was made his lieutenant. Also I was on my way to France when I was cast away. Cast away, after leaving my child, my wealth, in that man's hands for safe keeping. He drove the one from him with curses and cruelty, he stole the other. And — hear more — those galleons coming to Cadiz were bringing that stolen wealth to him — because I knew that it was so I came in them to Spain, hoping by my disguise to meet him, to wrench it back from him, to call him to account for his treatment of my girl."

On the court there had come a hush — as the calm comes after the storm; hardly any spoke now — yet all, from Bishop downward, regarded Eaton, trembling, shivering there.

And once more in that hush, Gramont's voice uprose again.

"For myself I care not. Do with me what you will. But, remember, I denounce him, that man there, as pirate and buccaneer ten times more bloodthirsty and cruel than any other who ever ravaged the Indies; I denounce him, the denouncer, as thief, filibuster and spy. Do with me what you will — only take heed. Spare him not. And if you seek corroboration of my word, demand it of him who is my fellow-prisoner, demand the truth from Juan Belmonte."

CHAPTER XXIV.

MY LOVE! MY LOVE!

The days passed as I lay in my dungeon in the ramparts, and each morning when the jailer — who, I soon learned, was deaf and dumb — came with a loaf of bread and jar of water, I braced myself to receive the tidings that it was my last on earth.

Yet a week went by and I had not been summoned to the plank and flames — I began, as I lost count of time — as I forgot the days of the week themselves — to wonder if, after all, the sentence was one that they did not dare to carry out. And, remembering that in Spain nothing could be done without reference to the powers at Madrid, I mused upon whether, if they did so dare, the sanction for the execution of Gramont and myself must be first obtained ere the execution could take place; also I mused on many other things, be sure, besides my own impending fate, a fate which, I thought, would never be known to any of my countrymen, which would be enveloped forever in a darkness nothing could lift. I thought of

Juan and of the secret which that wild, impulsive nature had concealed from me for so many days — wondered what would be the end of that career; thought, too, of Gramont, the man whose blood-guiltiness had been so great, yet who, as he stood by my side a doomed man, had seemed almost a hero by reason of his indifference to, his scorn of, his fate.

The dungeon, as I have termed it, though in fact it was more like a cell, was in and at the uppermost part of the ramparts of Lugo — noted for being the most strongly walled and fortified town in all Spain — was, indeed, a room in the great wall which sloped down perpendicularly to the Minho beneath; a wall, smooth and absolutely upright, or vertical, on which a sparrow could scarcely have found a crevice in which to lodge or perch, rising from eighty to a hundred feet from the base of the rock on which it was built and through which the river rushed. This I had seen as we had passed under it on the other side of the Minho when we approached the town; could see, indeed, in the daytime as I glanced down on to the river beneath through the heavily grated and barred window which admitted light to my prison; also I could observe the country outside and the mountains beyond, while I

ACROSS THE SALT SEAS. 333

heard at night the swirl of the river as it sped by those rocks below.

Because there was no chance of escape for any creature immured within this cell, since none could force away those grates and bars, even had he possessed that strength of Samson, for which I had once prayed; because, also, had I been able to do so, there was nothing but the jagged rocks beneath, or the swift river, into which to cast myself, I was not chained nor manacled; was at liberty, instead, to move about as I chose; to peer idly out all day at the freedom of the open country beyond, which would never again be mine, or to cast myself upon the pallet on the floor and sleep and dream away the hours that intervened between now and my day of doom. Nay, I was at liberty, had I so chosen, to strangle myself with my bedding, or, for the matter of that, my belt or cravat, or end my life in any manner I might desire. Perhaps, though I knew not that it was so, it might be hoped such would be the end. It might save trouble and after consequences.

None came near me all the day or night, except that mute jailer, of whom I have spoken, when he brought me my bread and water every morning, and it was, therefore, with a strange feeling of surprise—with a plucking at my heart, and a fear, which I despised myself for, that my last hour was come—that one night, as I lay in the dark, I heard footsteps on the stones of the passage outside the cell door—footsteps that stopped close by that door, some of them heavy, the others light. I heard, too, the clash of keys together, the grating of one in the huge lock, a moment later.

"Remember," I whispered to myself. "Remember, you are a man—a soldier. Be brave."

Then slowly the door opened, and a figure came in, bearing a light in its hand, while, a second later, the door was closed and locked again from the outside; the heavy footsteps were heard by me retreating down the passage.

The figure was that of "Juan" Belmonte.

"You here?" I said, springing up, and then I advanced toward it, my hands outstretched, while my companion of so many days sprang to my arms, lay in them, sobbing as though with a broken heart.

"Do not weep, do not weep," I said, and, as I spoke, my lips touched that white brow —no whiter now than all the rest of the face, "do not weep. What is, is, and must be borne."

"My love, my love!" those other lips —whose rich crimson I had once marvelled at so much—sobbed forth now, "my love, how can I help but weep? Oh, Mervan, I have learnt to love you so, to worship you, for your strength and courage! And now to see you thus—thus! My God!"

"Be brave still," I said; would have added "Juan"; only, not knowing, I paused.

"What shall I call you?" I asked.

"Juana."

"Do they—the judges—know?"

"The Alcáide knows: 'T is through that knowledge I am here."

"Why," I whispered, my arms about her as she clung to me, "why was this disguise assumed, these dangers run? Oh! Juana, since I learnt what you were in truth I have shuddered, sweated at the memories of your risks. What reason had you for coming to Europe as a man? and with such beauty, too! 'T is marvellous it was never seen through."

"They would not give passage to women in the galleons," she answered. "Therefore I came as I did; also I knew I might better find Eaton—confront him, in a garb, another sex, which would prevent him from recognising the little child he had treated so evilly." Then, suddenly, with a wail, she exclaimed: "Oh, my God! Mervan, I have not come to talk of this, but to be with you for our last hour; one hour before we die. The Alcáide has granted me that—and one other thing—on conditions;" and I felt her shudder in my arms.

"Before we die," I repeated stupidly, saying most of her words over again. "Granted you this and one other thing—and on conditions. What conditions? Tell me all; make me to understand. *We* die? Not you! They cannot slay you."

From some neighbouring church a deep-toned bell was pealing solemnly as I spoke. Far down below, by the river banks, I heard the splash of some fishermen's boats as they went by to their night work—always, until my eyes close for the last time, I shall remember those sounds accompanying her words in answer to mine—shall hear them in my ears—her words: "I can slay myself."

"Juana!"

"Must slay myself," she went on, "there is no other way. Can I live without you—or, living, fullfil hose conditions?" and, even as she said this, our lips met.

"But," I asked, my voice hoarse with

grief and misery, "what are they, and wherefore granted?"

"He gives me one life — his — my father's! My God! *he* my father! — he will not give me yours because he thinks you are my lover — and — and the condition is that on the night when he is set free, I fly from Lugo with him, Morales, to Portugal. He will be safe there, he says. 'T is rumoured the king has joined England."

"And you accept the terms?" I asked, bitterly, knowing that I loved this girl as fondly as she loved me. Had loved her since I discovered her sex as she reeled into my arms on that night. "You accept?"

"I accept. Nay!" she exclaimed, "do not thrust me from you — you cannot doubt my love, my adoration. Else why am I here a prisoner in Lugo — why, except because I could not quit your side, could not tear myself from you?"

"How then accept?"

"Listen. I must save him. God! — he is my father — to my eternal shame! Yet — yet, being so, his soul must not go to seek its Maker yet — 't is too deeply drenched with crime, he must have time — time to live — to repent — to wash away his sins. Oh! Mervan, you are my love, my love, my first and only love—will be my last—yet—I must save him."

"At what a cost! Your own perdition!"

"No, no. Listen. Morales leaves here the day before my unhappy father is given his chance of escape—the door of his cell will be set open for him at night; none will bar his exit by a back way—I, too, shall be gone. Morales will take me with him in my own proper garb, that of a woman. Then—then—because I shall not believe in my father's freedom until I am sure of it, know it, he will join us at the frontier—not the one which we passed, but where the road crosses to Braganza at a place called Carvallos—and——"

"You will keep your word!"

"Yes. To myself—not him. My father will be safe—Morales unable to do more against him—I—I shall be dead. Once I am assured all is well with him I shall end my life. There will be nothing more to live for."

"Suppose," I whispered, "suppose—it might be!—that I should escape, and, doing so, find you dead! Oh, Juana, how would it be with me then? How could I live?"

"Ah, my love," she said, whispering, too, "can you not believe I have thought of that—believe that if all hope of your escaping was not gone I should not have decided thus? But, Mervan, you are a brave man, have faced death too often to fear to do so once again for the last time. Mervan, my love, my life — there is no hope. None. He has told me — he — Morales — that the morning after all are gone but you, you will surely be put to death. My own, my sweet, there is no hope."

"If I could escape first——"

"It is impossible. Impossible. Oh! I have begged him on my knees again and again to give you the same chance as he gives my father — have told him that, since he ruins himself to set free the one, it would cost him no more to let both go—yet, yet — he will not."

"Why not?"

"I have said. And he makes but a single answer. One is my father — the other my lover. Laughs, too, and says he does not jeopardise his own body—ruin for certain his own life in his own land — to fling that lover back into my arms."

"Still, if he knows that until a few days ago I deemed you a boy——"

"Knows it!" she exclaimed. "Oh, my God! have I not told him so a hundred times — sworn that we were but strangers thrown together scarce a month past; had never met before. And to all my vows and protestations he replies: 'Knowing you now to be a woman—as I have myself by chance discovered—he must love you as I do. I will not save him to steal you from me.'"

"Yet, with this refusal on his lips, you yield—or appear to yield."

"My father! My father!" she cried, flinging her arms madly around my neck. "My father! My father! For his sake I must yield. Oh, my love, my love, my love —I must."

* * * * * * * * * *

I cannot write down—in absolute truth, cannot recall—our last sad parting, our frenzied words, our fond embraces. Suffice it that I say we tore ourselves apart at the sound of the mute's footsteps—that Juana was borne away almost insensible.

For that we should never meet again in this world we recognised—we were parted forever. I had found and won—although till lately unknown to myself!—the most fond and loving heart that had ever yielded itself up to a man—found it only as I stood upon the brink of my grave.

Yet if there were anything that could reconcile me to my loss of her it would be that grave, I knew; that—or the casting of my ashes to the wind after my body was consumed by the *brasero*—would bring the oblivion I desired. And, since she, too, meant to die the moment her father was safe, neither would be left to mourn the other. At least the oblivion of death would be the happy lot of both. Yet, as now the hours followed one another, as I heard them strike upon the bells of all the churches in this old city, and boom forth solemnly from the cathedral tower — wondering always, yet resignedly, when I should hear them for the last time; wondering, too, when the key would once more grate in the lock and I should be summoned to my doom—I cursed myself for never having penetrated Juan's disguise, for never having guessed she was a woman. Sir George Rooke had done so, I knew now; that was what he meant by his solemn warnings to me—fool that I was, not to be as far-seeing as he!

There were many things, which I now recalled, that should also have opened my eyes—her timidity, her nervousness, the strange power of mustering up courage at a moment of imminent danger; also the frequent change of colour; the remaining in the inn kitchen all one night; the shriek for assistance at the barrier encounter. And yet I had been blind, and thought it was a boy who rode by my side through all the perils we had passed.

I might have saved her had I but had more insight — might have refused to let her accompany me; have sternly ordered her to travel in some other way than along the danger-strewn path which I had come. She would have been safe now — what mattered it what had befallen me! — would have been free, with no hideous necessity of taking her own life to escape from the love which Morales forced upon her.

Yet, as I tossed upon my pallet, thinking of all this — thinking, too, of how fondly I had come to love this girl, so dear to me now that we were lost to each other forever — I knew, I felt sure, that no stern commands issued to her to turn back and quit my side would have been of any avail; that, as she had once threatened, she would have followed me like a dog, have lain upon the step of the house wherein I slept, would never have quitted my side.

For hers was the hot, burning love of the southern woman, of which I had often read and heard told by wanderers into far-off lands — the love that springs in a moment into those women's breasts, and, once born, is never quenched except by death — as, alas! hers was now to be quenched.

CHAPTER XXV.

"AS THE NIGHT PASSETH AWAY."

Still the days passed and I meditated on whether each as it came was to be my last. Wondered as every morning I watched the opening of the heavily clamped door, if, instead of my loaf and jar of water, that deaf and dumb jailer had come to summon me forth to my fate; and wondered again at what might cause the delay, since morning after morning his behaviour was ever the same, the bread always placed on the rough stone shelf that ran around the room, with the water by its side. That, and nothing more.

That Juana had gone by now with the Alcáide, I thought must surely be the case. I had taken since that night when last we met — and parted forever — to scoring with a nail a mark daily on the whitewashed but filthy wall, so that thereby I might keep some count of the days as they went by, and now there were six of such marks there. Surely she was gone—surely, too, I thought, Gramont's escape had taken place by now — yet they came not for me. What did it mean?

In my agony at the thought that by now, perhaps, Juana was dead by her own hand — I pictured her to myself using the small poniard I knew she carried, or the equally small pistol of which she was possessed — I groaned — nay! almost shrieked sometimes at my horrible picturings of her beautiful form and face stiff with death; in that agony I came to pray at last to God that the day or night which was passing over me might be my last. That He, in His supreme mercy, would see fit to inspire them with the resolve to make an end of me. Prayed that, by the time those never ceasing clocks without had struck once more the hour they were striking as I made my supplication, my soul might have left my body — that that body might be no more than a heap of ashes.

For I could bear my existence no longer. My thoughts — of my beauteous mistress lying in death's hideous grasp, of my poor old father, and the misery which would be his — not at my falling like a soldier, but at the mystery which would forever enshroud my death — were more than I could support.

But still another day passed — the sev-

ACROSS THE SALT SEAS. 345

enth—and still again at daybreak there was no summons to me to go forth and meet my fate. Yet, since by the increased pealings of the bells, and by the ringing of some sweeter sounding ones than those usually heard, I knew it was the Sabbath I wondered that my doom had not come. For the Sabbath was, I remembered, the day of execution in this land, because 'tis always a fête day, when the people are at leisure to be excited and amused.

That day passed, however, the night drew on, the dark had come; and still I was alive; had before me another night of horror and of mortal agony unspeakable to endure.

From my ghastly, silent warder I had tried more than once to obtain some hint, or information, as to when I might expect my sentence to be carried out—if I could have learnt that, I should have known also that Gramont was gone—was free—that, my God! Juana was dead, or near to her death. But as well might I have asked the walls of this cell in which I was, for a word or sign. I wrote on those walls with the nail a question—*the* question: "When am I to die?" and he stared as stolidly at it as though he were no more able to see than to speak or hear. Thinking, perhaps, that he could not read, I made signs upon my fingers to him, at all of which he shook his head, though what he meant to convey I know not. Yet, had my mind not been so distraught, I should have remembered that, perhaps, if he could not understand the one neither could he the other. Reflecting later on, however, I felt sure that he was able to do both — it was the only way in which one so afflicted as he was could have been made to understand his orders; and, still later, I knew that such was the case. And now, on that Sunday, as the horrid gloom of the winter night enveloped all the country around, while up from the pastures and fields there rose a vapour or fog, I took a terrible resolve, driven thereto by the misery of my reflections.

I determined that, if my death by the hands of the executioner came not to-morrow, I would take my own life. I could endure no longer, could think no more upon Juana as a dead woman, as one slain by her own hand.

"Oh! Juana, Juana," I wailed more than once, "my lost Juana. Then added, with fierceness, "Yet — no matter. We meet to-morrow at the latest."

Though they had taken my weapons from me ere they brought me here, there was enough of opportunity to my hand for accomplishing my purpose. There was the nail I had found — my sash, or belt — my cravat — either would serve for my purpose if I was brave enough to accomplish it.

"Brave enough — brave enough!" I found myself repeating. "Brave enough! Or," I whispered, "cowardly enough? Which is it? Which?"

And, as still the long hours of the night went on, and I lay on my pallet staring up into the darkness, listening to the hours told over and over again by the bells, until my soul sickened at their sound, watching a glint of the moon's rays on the metal roof of the cathedral, I answered my own question, reasoned with myself that self-destruction was the coward's, not the brave man's, act, and resolved at last to cast that awful resolution behind me, to endure and meet my fate like a man, as a gallant soldier should.

And so, eased — I scarce knew why — by my determination, I fell at last into a tranquil sleep, and dreamt that I was back in England, walking in my father's old flower garden in the Weald, with my love, Juana, by my side.

Some unaccustomed noise awoke me from that fair dream — something to which I was not used in the long silence of the nights—some sound which, as I raised myself on my elbow and peered around the cell, I could not understand; for in that cell there was no other presence, as for a moment I had imagined when I sprang up, half asleep and half awake; the moon, which had now overtopped the cathedral towers, showed that plain enough. Deep scurrying clouds were passing beneath her face swiftly—obscuring sometimes her brilliancy for some moments, 'tis true; yet, as she emerged now and again from them, her flood poured in and lit up the whole chamber. There was no one in it but myself!

What, therefore, was the sound I had heard? Stealthy footsteps outside?—those of my doomsmen, perhaps!—or was it some silent executioner about to steal in on me in the night, thereby to prevent the publicity of a death in the market place—a death which might by chance be reported to my own countrymen afar off, and like enough, if the war rolled down this way, be bitterly avenged? Was that it?

Again beneath the moon there passed heavy clouds, extinguishing her light so that for a moment my prison was once more steeped in darkness—I found myself thinking that there would be snow ere morning; that, if that morning brought my death, 't would be a bleak and wintry scene which the flames of the *braséro* would illuminate!—then through a break in those clouds a ray stole forth, a ray that glinted in through the iron bars of the window grate, across the stone-flagged floor, and onward to the heavily clamped door, then was arrested there—one spot shining out amidst those beams with the brightness and the dazzle of a diamond.

What was that thing, that spot on which the ray glinted so?

Creeping toward the door, as silently and lightly as I could go, I reached it, put out my finger and touched that gleaming spark, and found that it proceeded from the extremity of a key which was in the lock and which now protruded by a trifle into the room. It was the insertion of that key which had awakened me.

Yet—what did it mean, and why, when once in the lock, was it not turned; why not followed by the entry of one or more persons into the cell?

Were they coming back later to fall on me? Had the key been first inserted by some who had withdrawn directly afterward, so that, if the noise awakened me, I should sleep again shortly, when they could return to finish their work? This must be the true explanation—I was to be executed in the depth of the night when all were asleep in the old town, when no cry of anguish, no scream from one being done to death, would be heard.

"Yet," I thought to myself, "these precautions are useless. As well here as in the flames to-morrow. What matters where or how?"

At that moment my ears caught a sound—something was passing down the stone passage outside—something that was not the heavy tread of the jailer. Instead, a muffled sound—yet perceptible to me. A shuffling, scraping sound as though one who was shoeless was dragging each foot carefully along after the other.

Then I saw the end of the key which projected through the lock turn—I saw it sparkle in the moon's rays—once it grated harshly, creaked! And, slowly, a moment afterward the door opened inward, leaving the passage outside dark and cavernous. He who had so opened it with one hand carried no light in the other.

Stepping back from it, watching what should happen next—yet, I swear before heaven, with no fear at my heart—why should there be, since I desired to die and join my love? yet still with that heart beating loudly from excitement — I saw the blackness of the doorway blurred with a deeper intensity by a form standing outside it. I saw the moonbeams reach that form, lighting it up for a moment and glistening on the eyes of it. I saw before me the great figure and heavy, stolid face of my dumb, impenetrable jailer. The mute! Also observed that under his arm he carried something long — a sword.

His eyes upon me, he advanced into the cell — I seeing that his feet were bare except for thick, coarse stockings which he wore — yet making no motion as though to attack me, his action not such as would have rendered a more desperate man than myself resolved to defend himself. Then slowly, while I, my back against the farthest wall, stared at him more in wonder than in awe, he raised the arm under which the sword was not borne, and motioned to me with his finger, crooked somewhat, to follow him, pointing a moment afterward down the dark passage.

"So," I whispered to myself, drawing a deep breath as I did so, "the hour has come. He bids me follow him. I understand — it is to be done before daylight. Well, I am ready. God give me strength and pardon me."

Then I made ready to follow him, while he, observing this, prepared to lead the way.

All was profound and dark outside that cell when once we were in the passage — so dark that, ere I had barely reached it, I felt his great hand upon my arm, felt him clutching my sleeves between his fingers. And thus together we went on, he silent as a corpse, except for his breathing, which sometimes I heard — sometimes, too, felt upon my cheek — I going to my death.

One thing I noticed, even in these moments of intensity. We went the opposite way from that by which I had first been brought — the opposite way from which his footsteps, when he had been shod, had invariably sounded; also the opposite way from which my love had come to bid me a last farewell, and had been carried insensible after our parting.

Whither was I being taken?

The end of the corridor was reached in the darkness; I knew that by the fact that his grasp tightened perceptibly on my sleeve; also that, by a pressure of his fingers on it, he was turning me somewhat to the left; likewise, that grasp put a degree of curb upon me; a moment later seemed to signify that I was to go on again. And it felt to me that, in a way, I was being supported — held up.

Another instant, and I knew why. We were descending stairs — on the way down, doubtless, to some exit that should lead to my place of doom! Still I resisted not. One path to oblivion served as well as another.

By the manner in which the steps were cut I knew at once that we were in some tower, and that the stairs were circular; also my hand, which I kept against the side, told me the same thing. Moreover, there were *œillets*, or arrow slits, in the wall, through which I could see the moon shining on another wall, which seemed to be some fifty paces off — probably, I thought, the opposite wall of some courtyard built into, or by the side of, the huge ramparts.

Of sound there was none, no noise of any kind, no tramp of sentry to be heard, although I knew well enough that on the ramparts themselves soldiers were kept constantly on guard. Nothing; all as still as death, the death to which I was being led.

At last the stairs ended. My feet told me we were on the level now, a level into which they sank somewhat as I took step after step, whereby I judged that we were walking on sand, and wondered in what part of that prison, of those huge ramparts, we might be. Surely, I thought, some lowermost vault or dungeon, perhaps beneath the foundations of the structure, beneath the rocks between which the river flowed.

"My God!" I murmured to myself, "is this my fate? To be immured forever in some dark dungeon in the bowels of the earth, where neither light, nor sound — never hope — can come again. Better death at once, swift and merciful, than this. Far better."

Yet almost it seemed to my now frighted heart that this alone could be the case.

The air reeked and was clammy, as though with long confinement in this underground place, and by remaining ever unrefreshed from without by heaven's pure breezes was mawkish and sickly as the breath of a charnel house — perhaps 'twas one! — perhaps those who died here were left to fester and moulder away till their corpses turned to skeletons and their skeletons to dust; to die here, where no cry for help could issue forth, no more than any sound except a muffled one could penetrate, as I knew at this moment, for far above I heard a deep boom that seemed like the muffled roar of a cannon — a sound that was in truth the eternal bell of the cathedral telling the hour; also another broke on my ear — a swift, rushing noise, yet deadened, too — the sound, I thought, of the Minho passing near.

Then, all at once — as I knew that the sickly, reeking air would choke me, felt sure that ere many paces more had been traversed I must reel and fall upon that sanded floor — there blew upon my face a gust of air — oh! God! it was as though I had changed a monumental vault all full of rankling dead for some pure forest through which fresh breezes swept — far down toward where my dimmed eyes gazed I saw a glimmer of something that looked like the light of a coming dawn.

And I thanked heaven that, at least, these horrid vaults were not to be my prison or my grave; that, let whatever might befall me, my punishment was not to be dealt out here.

And ever still as I went on that stricken man walked by my side, held my arm with his hand, and directed the way toward the sombre light that gleamed afar.

CHAPTER XXVI.

WHAT HAS HAPPENED?

The light increased as we advanced; the space it occupied grew larger; also it seemed to be entering at what I now judged to be the mouth, or exit, of some narrow, vaulted passage, through which we were progressing and arriving at the end of; almost, too, it seemed as if this passage was itself growing less dark; as if now — as I turned my eyes to where the mute walked by my side — the outline of his form was becoming visible.

What was I to find at the end of this outlet — what to see awaiting me when at last I stood at the opening in the midst of the wintry dawn — a scaffold, or the *braséro?* Which? I perceived now — my eyes accustoming themselves to the dusky gloom — that this vaulted way, or corridor, was one hewn through a bed of rock, and roughly, too, blasted, perhaps, in earlier days; and that all along its sides were great slabs, or masses, of this rock, that lay where they had fallen. Perceived something else, also — a man crouching down behind one of the fallen blocks, his cape held across his face by one hand, so that naught but the eyes were visible; the eyes — and one other thing that shone and glistened even in the surrounding gloom — a huge gold earring, of the circumference of a crown-piece, which fell over the crimson edge, or guarding, of that cloak.

Where had I seen a man wearing such earrings as that before? Where? Then, even as I went on to my death, I remembered — recalled the man. 'T was he who had cried out to the Alcáide in the court, bidding him question Eaton as to how he knew so much of Gramont's past — yet — what doing here, why hiding behind that fallen mass? Was there some one within these dungeons whom he sought — some one for whom an attempted rescue was to be planned? I knew of none — knew of no other prisoner within these walls — since now Gramont was, must be, as far away as his unhappy child — my lost love, Juana. Yet, perhaps, it was not very like I should have known.

But now the end was at hand. I scarce cared to turn my eyes to observe whether or not the mute had seen the sailor shrinking behind the stone; instead, nerved myself, by both prayer and fierce determination, to meet my fate, to make my exit into the open as bravely as became a man; to let not one of my executioners see that I feared them or the flames that were to burn the life out of me.

So we drew near the mouth of the passage — moving through the gloom that was as the gloom of a shuttered and darkened house on some wintry morn — I seeing that, beyond and outside, was a sloping, stone-flagged decline that led down to a lane which ran out into the open country beyond. We were, therefore, outside the walls of Lugo, and I deemed that it was here, unknown to the towns-people, that I was to meet my fate.

We stood a moment later on that stone-covered descent, and I gazed around it startled — amazed! For here, upon it, was no hideous *braséro* piled up with logs of wood, and drenched with resin and pitch to make those logs burn more fiercely; no upright plank nor beam against which the sufferer's hand — my hand! — was to be nailed through the palm; no executioners clad in black from head to foot. Instead, a man in peasant's dress — green breeches, leather *zapátas* and a sheepskin jacket. A peasant holding by the reins two horses, one black, the other dappled grey.

I felt almost as though once more I should faint — felt as I had done in that reeking, mouldy corridor through which I had come — became sick, indeed, at the relief, even though 't were for an hour or so only, which was accorded me from instant death, since I knew that here that death could not be dealt out.

Then I turned to the deaf and dumb man — if such he was — who had now released my arm — had done so, indeed, since the half light had been reached — and implored him to tell me what was intended.

For answer — he guessed, no doubt, the import of my words — he pointed to the horses and made signs I should mount one of them. And I, incredulous, asking God inwardly what was meant, went toward the black one and seizing its reins and twisting a lock of its mane around my thumb prepared to do as I was bid, yet with my nerves tingling and trembling so that I scarce knew whether I could reach the saddle or not.

Then, ere the attempt was made, as I raised my foot to the iron, the mute touched my arm, felt in his belt with the other hand

and, producing a piece of paper, gave it to me.

It was from Juana; ran thus in English:

> Your road is through Samos, Caldelas and the other Viana. At Terroso you will cross the frontier. The jailer will guide you to us. Come quickly, so that thereby my fate may be decided.
>
> JUANA.

That was all. All — from her to me! From her to me! No word of love accompanying the message. Not one!

She had saved me in some way — had induced the Alcáide to bring about my escape also — had done this, yet could send me no greeting such as she must have known I hungered for. Was it shame, remorse, that made her so silent and so cold? Heartbroken, I thrust the letter into my pocket, and, at a sign from the mute, mounted the horse, he doing the same with the other.

Then, ere we gave them their reins, he leant across and put into my hands the sword he had carried under his arm since first he opened the door of my cell; a sword long and serviceable-looking, with a great hilt and curled quillon; one that I had seen another like somewhere, though where it was I could not recall.

* * * * * * * * * *

'T was over twenty leagues to Terroso,

I learnt in the course of our ride. Diminishing those leagues moment by moment, we went on and on, the black horse that I bestrode never faltering in its quick pace, the grey keeping close to it.

And I, my brain whirling, my heart beating tumultuously within my breast, my whole being — my soul! — shaken by the release from an awful death which had come to me, would have given all that I was possessed of if from that stricken, silent, terrible companion by my side I could have extracted one word — gleaned from him one jot or atom of information! Yet to my repeated exclamations he, seeing that I was speaking to him, shook his head persistently; when I made signs to him in the alphabet which I felt sure he knew, he turned his face away and rode on stolidly. Had a dead man, a spectre, been riding ever by my side, swiftly when I rode swiftly, halting when I halted, neither could have been more terrible to me than this living creature, so immutable and impenetrable.

I was sore beset — distraught, my mind full of fearful fancies! Fancies that I should find Juana dead — though, too, I imagined that she would not slay herself until she had made sure of my safety, else why her letter?—fancies that, since the letter contained no word or hint of love, she had forced herself to tear me out of her heart forever; forced herself to do so because now she knew she could never be aught to me again. These fancies, these thoughts, were awful in their intensity; were made doubly so by this silent creature who never quitted my side.

And once my agony of nerves grew so great that I turned round upon him—gesticulating fiercely—hating myself for my brutality in doing so against one who was, in truth, my saviour—shrieking at him:

"Speak! Speak! For God's sake, speak! Utter some word. Give some sign of being alive—a reasoning thing. Speak, I say, or leave me—else I shall slay you."

Then I shuddered and could have slain my own self at the man's action.

For he turned and looked at me—it was in the fast gathering twilight, as side by side always, we were slowly riding up a mountain path—looked—then, as I gazed, the tears rolled down his coarse face! And, poor unhappy, afflicted thing! those tears continued to trickle down that face till night hid it from my eyes.

I knew now that he understood at least, that he comprehended the words of pity

ACROSS THE SALT SEAS. 363

and remorse I poured forth before the darkness came; at least the touch I made gently on his sleeve was read aright by him. For on his broad, expressionless face, to me for so long a stolid mask, there came a placid smile, and once he returned my touch lightly as still we rode on, and on, and on.

We halted that night to rest our horses and ourselves at a miserable inn, high up in the mountains, a place round which the snow was falling in great flakes, that seemed, indeed, to be embedded in snow. A ghastly, horrid place in which, as I sat shuddering by the fire, while my companion and the landlord slept near it—wondering if by now Juana had accomplished her dreadful purpose, unable longer to bear the company of the man, Morales, to whom she had sold herself; or, almost worse still, the company of her sin stained father; wondering too, if by now that splendid form was stiff in death!—I almost cursed the escape that had come to me. In truth, I think that now, upon this night, amidst the horrors of this lonely mountain inn, I was almost a madman; for the soft beat of the flakes upon the glass of the window seemed to my frenzied mind like the tapping of ghostly fingers; as I fixed my eyes upon those flakes and saw them alight one by one upon the panes and then dissolve and vanish, it looked to me as though they were fingers that scratched at the window and were withdrawn only to return a moment later. Also the wind screamed round the house — I started once, feeling sure I heard a woman — Juana — shriek my name, plucked at the sword by my side and would have made for the door, but that the landlord laughed at me and pushed me back, saying that those shrieks were heard nightly and all through the night during the winter.

At last, however, I slept, wrapped in my cloak before the peat fire, the mute in another chair by my side. And so, somehow, the night wore through. The morning came, and we were on our road once more, ten leagues still to be compassed ere the frontier was reached, with, behind us, as now I gathered from my mutilated companion's manner in answer to my questions, the possibility that we might be pursued. That after us, in hot chase, might be coming some from Lugo who had discovered our escape.

The mountain water courses and rivulets hummed beneath the frozen snow bound over them by the bitter frost, the tree boughs waved above our heads and across our path as, gradually descending once more to the plain, the chestnuts and the oak trees took the place of the gaunt black pines left behind above; once on this bitter morning we saw the sun steal out from amidst the clouds—lying down low on the horizon as though setting instead of rising. Yet on we rode for our lives, with upon me a deeper desire than the salvation of my own existence—the hope that I should be in time to save Juana, to wrench her from Morales ere it was too late, to bear her away at last to happiness and love unspeakable. Rode on, my black horse stumbling once over a mass of stone rolled down from the heights above; the dappled grey coming to its haunches from a similar cause, yet both lifted quickly by a sharp turn of our wrists and rushing on again down the declivity, danger in every stride and only avoided by God's mercy.

The leagues flew by—were left behind—a long billowy plain arrived at, sprinkled with hamlets from which the cheerful smoke rose to the sky; the mute had passes which took us through that other town of Viana; the last spot of importance was reached—and passed!—that lay between us and the border—between us and Portugal and safety.

Then once more our beasts slackened in their stride, again the ground rose upward, once more the hills were before us, above them at the summit was the frontier, Terroso. Another hour and we should be there — Juana's and my fate determined.

To use whips — neither of us had spurs — was cruel, yet there was no other way; therefore we plied them, pressed reeking flanks, rode on and on mercilessly. And now the end was at hand; afar off I saw a cabin over which floated both the banner of Spain and of Portugal. We were there some moments later — the mute's papers again examined — our passage allowed.

We had escaped from Spain!

"You ride quickly," the Portuguese *aduanista* said; "seek some others, perhaps, who come before you?" and he addressed himself to my companion, probably because he bore the passports. Then continued: "If 'tis a señor and señora you desire, they are in the *fonda* half a league further on."

"*They*," he said, "'*They!*' God be praised!" I murmured. Had any tragedy occurred it would not have been "they."

Not waiting to answer, but briefly nodding my thanks, we went on, the last half league dwindling to little more than paces now.

And then I saw the *fonda*, a place no bigger than a wooden cabin. I saw a woman seated on a bench outside against its wall, her elbows upon her knees, her dark head buried in her hands.

She heard the ring of our horses' hoofs upon the road, all sodden as it was with half-melted snow, and sprang to her feet — then advanced some paces and, shading her eyes, looked up the way that we were coming; dashed next her hand across those eyes as though doubting what she saw, and ran down the road toward us.

"As I leapt from my horse she screamed, "Mervan!" and threw herself into my arms, her lips meeting mine in one long kiss, then staggered back some paces from me, exclaiming:

"How! How, oh, my love, how — how have you escaped — found your way here — to me?"

"How?" I repeated after her, startled at the question; startled, too, at the tone of her voice. "How! Do I not owe my salvation to you — to your power over him — the Alcáide?"

"My God! No!" she answered. "Never would he have aided you to escape." Then, suddenly, as some thought struck her, she screamed aloud: "Mervan — Mervan — where is my unhappy father?"

"Your father! Is he not here?"

"No! No! No! Oh, God! what has happened? Has he been left behind to meet his doom?"

And, as she spoke, she reeled and would have fallen had I not caught her in my arms.

CHAPTER XXVII.

"LIAR, I WILL KILL YOU!"

He had been left behind — and I was here! He whose escape had been arranged for was still a prisoner — I, whose doom had been fixed, was free.

What did it mean? What mystery had taken place?

One glance toward the *fonda* fifty yards away was sufficient to show that mystery there was — as unintelligible to another as to Juana. And more than mystery! — that my presence here was as hateful as unexpected, to one person at least. To Morales, the Alcáide!

For even as my love recovered sufficiently to be able to stand without my assistance, though still leaning heavily upon me, I — looking toward that *fonda* — saw Morales issuing rapidly from it, his sword carried in his left hand, his right hand plucking the blade from the scabbard. And — more ominous still of what his intentions were, as well as of his fury! — as he ran toward us he flung the now empty sheath away from him and rushed forward, the bare blade gleaming.

Then as he reached the spot where we both stood together, the mute behind us — while, even as I too plucked the sword the poor creature had furnished me with from its scabbard and stood upon my guard, I saw that his stolid face expressed not only fear but something else — astonishment! — Morales shouted, his words tumbling pell mell over each other so much as to be difficult of understanding.

"Wretches! Traitor! Traitress! 'T is thus I am deceived — hoodwinked! Tricked and ruined so that your lover may be restored to your false arms. So be it — thus, also, I avenge myself," and — horror! — he made a pass at Juana as she stood by my side. He was a Spaniard — and his love had turned to hate and gall!

Yet ere the shriek she uttered had ceased to ring on the wintry morning air, the deadly thrust that was aimed full at her breast was parried by my own blade; putting her behind me with my left hand, I struck full at him, resolved that ere another five minutes were over his own life should pay for that craven attempt; struck full at his own breast, missing it only by an inch, yet driving him back from me.

Back, step by step, yet knowing even as I did so that it was no odds on me in this encounter, that here was a swordsman who would dispute every thrust of mine; that it would be lucky if his long blade did not thread my ribs ere my own weapon found his heart.

It behooved me to be careful, I knew. Already, in the first moment, he had settled down to fighting carefully and cautiously; already one devilish Italian thrust was given—he must have crossed the Alps, I thought, to learn it!—that almost took me unawares; that, had my parry not been quick, would have brought his quillon hurtling at my breast, with the blade through me. Yet, it had failed! and with the failure the chance was gone.

"I know your thrust," I whispered, maybe hissed, at him; "'twill serve no more."

But even as I said these words it came to me that I should not win this fight, that he was the better man—my master—at the game—that I was lost. And as I thought this I saw—while we shifted ground a little on the sodden snow—the mute standing gazing earnestly, almost fascinated, upon us; I saw some people at the door of the *fonda*—a man and a woman—regarding us with horror-stricken glances—I saw Juana on her knees, perhaps praying! It might be so, since her head was buried in her hands!

And if he won, if he slew me, even wounded and disabled me, she was lost, too; with me out of the way, with her father dead or still a prisoner, nothing could save her. Her last hope would be gone.

That spurred me, egged me on, put a fierce and fresh determination in my heart, since I had not lost my courage, but only my confidence. That, and one other thing; for I saw upon the melting snow beneath our feet, even as we trod it into water, a tinge of crimson; I saw a few drops lie spotting it —and I knew that that blood was not mine. Therefore, I had touched him, had only missed his life by a hair's breadth; next time it might not be drops—might be the heart's blood of him who had sought that of my loved one!

Still, I could not do it, could not thrust through and through him. Every drive, every assault, was parried easily. Once, when I lunged so near him that I heard his silk waistcoat rip, he laughed a low, mocking laugh as he thrust my blade aside with a turn of his iron wrist; I could not even, as I tried, take him in the sword arm and so disable him.

Also, I knew what was in his mind, specially since, for some few moments, he had ceased to thrust back at me. He was bent on tiring me out. Then — then — his opportunity would have come, would be at hand.

"Disable him! Disable him!" Why did those words haunt my brain, ring through it again and again; seem to deaden even the scraping hiss of steel against steel. "Disable him!" What memory was arising in that brain of some one, something, long forgotten? A second later, even as I felt my point being pressed lower and lower by his own blade, knew a lunge was coming — parried it as it came — safely once more, thank God! — I remembered, knew what that memory meant.

Recalled a little, hunchbacked Italian *escrimeur* who used to haunt a fence school at the back of the Exchange in the Strand; a man whose knowledge of attack was poor in the extreme, yet who could earn a beggar's wage by teaching some marvellous methods of disarming an adversary. And I had flung him a crown more than once to be taught his tricks!

Now those crowns should bear interest!

I changed my tactics, lunged no more; our blades became silent; they ceased to hiss like drops of water falling on live coals or hot iron; almost they lay motionless together, mine over his, yet I feeling through blade and hilt the strength of that black, hairy wrist which held the other weapon. Also, I think he felt the strength of mine; once his eye shifted, though had the moment been any other the shift would have been unnoticeable.

That was my time! Swift as lightning, I, remembering the dwarf's lessons of long ago—why did I remember also the little sniggering chuckle he used to utter as he taught them?—drew back my sword an inch, then thrust, then back again with a sharp wrench, and, lo! Morales' sword was flying through the air three feet above his head—he was weaponless! My own was drawn back a second later, another moment I should have avenged his assassin's thrust at Juana—yet I could not do it. For he, recognising he was doomed, stood there before me, his arms folded over his breast, his eyes confronting mine.

"Curse you!" he said, "you have won. Well—kill me. At once."

No need for me to say that could not be. In the moment that I twisted his weapon out of his wrist I had meant to slay him, had drawn back my own weapon to thrust it through chest and lungs and back, and stretch him dead at my feet — yet now I spared him.

Villain as he was — scoundrel who would traffic with a broken-hearted woman for her honour and her soul as a set-off against her father's safety, and, in doing so, also betray the country he served — I could not slay a defenceless man.

His sword had fallen at my feet; one of them was upon it. I motioned to him now to return to the *fonda* — to begone.

"You have missed your quarry," I said; "'t will never fall to your lure again. Away!"

Yet, still standing there before us — for now Juana had once more flown to my side, and was sobbing bitterly, her wild, passionate words expressing partly her thanks to God for my double safety, and partly her bewailings that her father had gone to his fate — he had something to say, could not depart without a malediction.

"Curse you both!" he exclaimed once more. "Curse you! Had I known of your trick you should all have burnt and grilled on the *braséro* ere this — ay, even you, wanton! — ere I had let you fool me so."

Then he turned away as though to go back to the *fonda*, yet returned again, and, striding back to where the mute stood motionless, his expression one of absolute vacancy — as though, in truth, he was only now become dumb from utter surprise — he struck at him full in the face with his clenched fist.

"Dolt, idiot, hound!" he said. "Was it to aid in such treachery against me as this that I saved you from the Inquisition? God! that I had left them to take your useless life! Dumb fool!"

I, standing there, with Juana still clinging to my neck, as she had done since the duel was over, saw the man stagger back and wipe the blood from his lips; saw, too, his hands clench firmly; saw him take one step forward, as though he meant to throw himself upon Morales; then stop suddenly, and do nothing. Perhaps even now, after this foul blow, he remembered that he had been saved from death once by him who struck that blow.

But a moment later he approached the Alcáide, though now humbly, and like a beaten slave who sues for pardon, and entreats that no further punishment shall be dealt out to him, and, an instant after, began, with fingers and hands and many strange motions, to tell his master some-

ACROSS THE SALT SEAS.

thing — something in a dumb language that was, still, not the deaf and dumb language in common use, and which I myself chanced to know, yet one that none could doubt both of these men were in the habit of conversing in.

He was telling some strange tale, I saw and understood by one glance at my late opponent's face; neither could any doubt that who gazed upon it!

At first that face expressed amazement, incredulity — all the emotions that are to be observed on the countenance of one who listens to some story which he either cannot believe, or thinks issues, at best, from a maniac. Yet gradually, too, there came over the face of Morales another look — the look of one who does believe at last, in spite of himself; also there dawned on it a hideous, gloating expression, such as might befit a fiend who listens to the tortured cries of a victim.

What did it mean? What tale was that stricken creature telling him by those symbols, which none but he understood? What? What?

A moment later we knew — if Morales did not lie to us.

The mute had ceased his narrative, his hands made no further signs, and, slowly, he stepped back again to where the horses we had travelled on stood together, the reins of one tied to the other — and Morales turned to us, his features still convulsed with that horrible expression of gloating.

"I have wronged you," he said, raising his forefinger and pointing it at Juana, who shuddered and clasped me closer even as he did so; "and you," glancing at me. "The treachery was not yours, but another's; unless — unless " — and he paused as though seeking for words — "unless it should be termed otherwise. Say, not treachery, but — sublime sacrifice."

"What!" from both her lips and mine. "What!"

"Your father," he said, "had his chance " — and again that forefinger was pointed at her — "this poor fool, my servant, went to set him free; the horse was waiting for him — only, instead, it has borne *you* to safety " — and now he glanced at me — "also there was his sword for him — that by your side."

"My God! My God!" I heard Juana whisper on my breast.

"Only he — this buccaneer — would not accept it, not take it. He, stained deep with crime as he was, his name an accursed one through all the Indies — men spit upon the ground there, they say, with loathing when they hear it mentioned, even now — could bear all things but one. Shall I tell you what that one thing is?" and he glanced again at Juana, a very hell of hate in his look.

But she could only moan upon my bosom and murmur: "My father! Oh, my father!"

"He could not bear," Morales went on, "that his child should be what he knew she had become by now — my friend ——"

"Liar!" I cried. "I will kill you for this."

"Could not bear that she should bring deeper disgrace than even he had done upon your tainted names. Therefore he refused to come; therefore he preferred the flames to which he has gone" — a wild, piercing scream broke from Juana as he said those words — "and — so — so — that there should be nothing rise up to prevent him from going to his death, so that he should put away from himself all chance of salvation from that death and earn his oblivion from disgrace, he persuaded this fool that a mistake had been made — that 't was you, not he, who was to be saved, allowed to escape."

"You lie," I said again. "You lie. Some part of this story is true, some false.

Gramont never believed that she would give herself to you; knew that she meant to slay herself the instant she was assured of his safety. Spanish dog, you lie, and I will have your life for it."

"It is true," he said hoarsely, "as true as that an hour after you left Lugo he was led out and burnt at the *braséro*—the *braséro* that was prepared for you. Now," and once more he addressed Juana, "you have your lover back again—be happy in the possession; in the knowledge that his life is saved by the loss of your father's. Be happy in that."

CHAPTER XXVIII.

THE DEAD MAN'S EYES—THE DEAD MAN'S HANDS.

Was Juana dying, I asked myself that night — dying of misery and of all that she had gone through? God, He only knew — soon I should know, too.

Ere I had carried her to the *fonda*, Morales had disappeared, his afflicted follower with him — ere we reached the miserable room, in which she had passed the two nights that had elapsed since she had come here with him who had bartered for the sacrifice of her honour against her father's safety, I heard the trample of horses' hoofs, I saw from the inn window both those men ride swiftly away, their road being that which led on into Portugal.

It was not possible that I should follow him and exact vengeance for all that he had done or attempted to do against her, force him once more to an encounter, disarm him again — and, when he was thus disarmed, spare him no further. Not possible, because, henceforth, my place was by her side. I must never leave her again in life — leave her who had come to this through her love of me, her determination to follow me through danger after danger, reckless of what might befall.

She lay now upon her bed, feverish and sometimes incoherent, yet, at others, sane and in her right mind, and it was at one of such moments as these that I, sitting by her side, heard her whisper:

"Mervan, where is that man — Morales?"

"He is gone, dear heart; he will trouble you no more. And — and — remember we are free. As soon as you are restored we can leave here — there is nothing to stop us now. My journey through Spain and France can never be recommenced — we must make for England by sea somehow. Then, when I have placed you in safety, I must find my way across to Flanders."

For a while she lay silent after I had said this; lay there, her lustrous eyes open, and with the fever heightening and intensifying, if such were possible, her marvellous beauty. For now the carmine of her cheeks and lips was — although fever's ensign! — even more strikingly lovely than before; this woman on whom I gazed so fondly was beyond all compare the most beautiful creature on which my eyes had ever rested. As I had thought at first, so, doubly, I thought now.

Presently she moaned a little, not from bodily pain, but agony of mind, as I learnt shortly — then she said :

"Mervan, why do you stay by my side — why not go at once back to your own land? Leave me?"

"Juana!" I exclaimed, deeming that I had mistaken her state, and that, in truth, she was beside herself. Then added, stupidly and in a dazed manner: "Leave you!"

"Ay. Why stay by me? You have heard, know all, whose child — to my eternal shame!—I am. The child of that bloodstained man, Gramont. Ay," she said, again, "he, that other, Morales, spoke true. There is no name in all the Indies remembered with such hate and loathing as his. And I — I — am his child. Go — leave me to die here."

"Juana," I said, "can you hear me, understand what I am saying—going to say to you? Is your brain clear enough to comprehend my words? Speak — answer me."

For reply she turned those eyes on me; beneath the dark dishevelled curls I saw their clear glance—I knew that all I should say would be plain to her.

"Listen to my words," I continued therefore. "Listen—and believe; never doubt more. Juana, I love you with my whole heart and soul—before all and everything else this world holds for me. I love you. I love you. I love you," and as I spoke I bent forward and pressed my lips to her hot burning ones. "And you tell me to leave you, because, forsooth! you are his child. Oh! my sweet, my sweet, if you were the child of one five thousand times worse than he has been, ay! even though Satan claimed you for his own, I would love you till my last breath, would never quit your side. Juana, we are each other's forever now."

"No! No! No!"

"Yes, I say," I cried almost fiercely. "Yes. We are each other's alone. You are mine, mine, mine. I have no other thought, no other hope in all this world but you. If —if—our faith were the same I would send for a priest now who should make us one; there should be no further moment elapse in all the moments of eternity before you were my wife."

I felt the long slim hand tighten on mine for an instant, then release it a moment later; but she said no more for a time. Yet the look on her face was one of happiness extreme. After a while, however, she spoke again.

"The admiral knew," she whispered. "He had found out my secret."

For a moment I could not recall what she referred to — the incidents which had happened in such quick succession since we had quitted the fleet had almost obliterated from my memory the recollection of all that had taken place prior to that time. Yet now I remembered, and — remembering — there came back to me Sir George Rooke's strange diffidence after she had seized his hand and pressed it to her heart. Also, I recalled the deference with which he had treated her whom I thought then to be no more than a handsome, elegant youth, as well as my feeling of surprise at that deference.

And still, as I reflected over this, there was one other thing in connection with him which also came back to me; his words, to wit, that there were even worse things than shot or steel or death to cloud a brave man's career — that many a soldier had gone down before worse than these. And I knew now against what he had intended to warn me — against the woman now lying here sore stricken, the woman whom I loved and worshipped, the one who had been to me as faithful as a dog.

"So be it," I said to myself, "so be it. If I am to become bankrupt and shipwrecked through my love for her, I must be. Henceforth she is all in all to me, and there is nothing else in my life. Yet, up to now, the admiral's warning has been but little realised—I owe no ruin to her, but, rather, salvation."

For I could not but recall that 't was through her that any loophole of escape had come to me in the prison of Lugo; to her unhappy father that I owed, if Morales had spoken true, the absolute escape itself.

Even as I sat there meditating thus she moaned again: "My father. My lost, doomed father," and once more I heard her whisper: "His child! His child! The saints pity me!"

And now I set myself to place that lost father before her in a far different light than that in which she regarded him—to make her believe that, when almost all in the Indies who had their account with the sea had in their time been much as he had been, his crimes were not so black as they appeared to her; to also paint in glowing colours that sublime sacrifice—Morales had termed it truthfully!—which he had made in remaining behind whilst I escaped, in dying while opening to me the path to life and freedom.

"Juana, my sweet," I said, speaking low, yet as sympathetically as I could to her, "Juana, you deem his sin greater than it is. Also, remember, 't is almost certain Morales lies when he said he died because — because — of your flight with him. For, remember — what the vagabond forgot in his rage and hate! — remember, he knew of your resolve, your determination to pretend to give yourself to him in exchange for his safety."

As I said these words I saw her eyes glisten, saw her head turned more toward me on the pillow — in her face the expression of one to whose mind comes back the recollection of a forgotten fact, a truth.

"*Diós!*" she whispered, "it was so. He knew of my intention. 'T is true; Morales lied. Yet," she went on a moment later, "yet that cannot cleanse him from his past sins, purge his soul from the crimes with which 't is stained."

"Crimes!" I re-echoed, "Crimes! Think, recall, my beloved, what those crimes were. Those of buccaneer, 't is true, yet not so bad but that all like him were not deemed too sunken in sin to be refused pardon by Spain, by France, even by my own land. Those pardons were sent out to the Indies shortly before he was thought to be lost—had he returned to France, then he would have held a position of honour under Louis."

"How?" she asked—and now I noticed that in her face there seemed to be a look of dawning hope, a look too, as though with that newborn hope there was a return of strength accompanied by an absence of such utter despair as had broken her down. "How know you that?"

"I was there in the court when he was tried," I said, "I heard his words—and none who heard them could doubt their truth, no more than they could his fierce denouncement of that unutterable villain, Eaton. Juana," I said, endeavouring to speak as impressively as was in my power, to thrust home more decisively the growing conviction to her heart that Gramont was not the devil he had been painted, "you must teach yourself to think less ill of your father than report has made him. And—and remember, he could have escaped an he would; it was, as that man said, a sublime sacrifice when he went to his doom."

"But why?" she asked, "why?" Though even as she did so, I saw, I knew,

ACROSS THE SALT SEAS. 389

that in her heart there was the hope and wish to find something that might whiten his memory for her.

"Why," I repeated, bending near to her, speaking as deeply and earnestly as I could; above all, the softened feeling I was endeavouring to bring about in her heart toward that lost, dead father must be made to grow, until at last she should regard his memory with pity if naught else. "Why, because as I do believe, as I believe before God, he knew we loved each other, Juana——"

"Ah, Mervan!"

"Because his life was already far spent, because ours were in their spring; because, it may be, he knew that with him gone and me escaped in his place there was the hope of many happy years before you—with me— of years always together, of our being ever by each other's side until the end. Juana, my beloved, my love, think not of him as one beyond pardon and redemption, but rather as one who purified forever the errors of his life by the deep tenderness and sacrifice of his end."

I had won.

As I concluded she raised herself from the pillows on which she lay, the long shapely arms met round my neck, the dark curly head sank to my shoulder; soon nothing broke the silence of the room but her sobs. Yet ever and again she whispered through her tears: "My father, my unhappy father. May God forgive me if I have judged you too harshly."

Soon after that I left her sleeping peacefully and with, as it seemed to me, much of her fever gone — yet even as she slept I, sitting watching by her side, saw still the tears trickle forth from beneath the long eyelashes that fringed her cheeks, and knew that in her sleep she was dreaming of him.

But again I told myself that I had won; that henceforth the memory of her father's erring life would not stand between her and me, between our love.

The peasant who kept the miserable inn, and whose curiosity as to all that had taken place recently — the arrival of Juana and Morales, the duel, and then the rapid departure of him and the mute, while I remained behind in his place — was scarcely appeased by my curt and stern information that the lady above was shortly to become my wife, told me that there was no suitable sleeping place for me other than the public room. The other señor, he said, had had to make shift with that, since the one spare room which the señora occupied was the only one available in the house. He supposed, he added gruffly, that I, too, could do the same thing. There was a bench — and he pointed as he spoke to a rough wooden thing which did not promise much ease or rest — on which the other señor had slept; also a deep chair, in which one might repose easily before the fire. Would that do? Yes, I answered, either would do very well. I was fatigued, and could sleep anywhere. All I asked was that I should be left alone.

This was done, though ere the man and his wife departed to their quarters for the night the latter took occasion to make a remark to me. The lady, she observed, if she might make so bold as to say it, seemed to be of an undecided frame of mind. When she and the other señor arrived she had understood that he was the person to whom she was about to be married. It was strange, she thought, that the lady should elope over the border with one señor, to be married to another. However, she added, it was no affair of hers.

"It is no affair of yours," I said sternly once more. "Leave me alone and interfere not in our affairs. Your bill," I continued, "will be paid; that is sufficient." Whereon she said that was all that was required, and so, at last, I was left to myself.

Left to myself to sit in the great chair before the fire and muse on all that had lately occurred to make my journey toward Flanders a failure; to muse still more deeply on the love that had come to me unsought, unthought of; the love that, when I had at last accomplished my task and rejoined Marlborough, would, I hoped, crown my life.

Yet, as the snow beat against the window, for once more it was a rough night and the wind howled here as it had howled the night before, across in Spain — while as before the flakes falling on the rude panes seemed to my mind to resemble ghostly finger-tips that touched the glass and then were drawn off it back into the darkness without — I thought also of the now dead and destroyed man, the buccaneer who, all blood-guilty as he was, had yet gone to a doom that he might have escaped from.

And my thought prevented sleep, even though I had not now slept for many, many hours — my terrible reflections unstrung me — it seemed almost as if the spirit of that dead man had followed me, was outside the rough wooden door; as if, amidst those falling and swift-vanishing snowflakes on the glass, I saw his eyes glaring out of the blackness into the room. And soon I became over-wrought, the gentle beat of the snow became the tap of a hand summoning me to open and admit his spectral form — an awful fantasy took possession of me!

Was, I asked myself — as furtively I turned my eyes to those solemn, silent flakes that fell upon the window pane, rested there a moment gleaming white, then vanished into nothingness — was the lost soul of that man hovering outside the door or that window — the soul that but a few hours ago had quitted his body?

If I looked again at the casement should I see, as though behind some dark veil, the eyes of Gramont glaring into the room; see those flakes of snow take more tangible form — the form of a dead man's fingers scratching at the panes, tearing at them to attract my attention?

Distraught — maddened by the terror of my thoughts, fearful of myself, of the silence that reigned through the house, I sprang to my feet — I was mad! — I must go out into the gloom and blackness of the night ——

God! — what was that?

There *was* a tapping at the door — a footstep — next a tap at the window. The hands were there; I saw the fingers — the snow falling round them — on them. I saw, too, the eyes of Gramont peering in at me.

"What is it?" I cried hoarsely. "What? What?"

Then through the roar of the tempest without, through the shriek of the wind, above the loud hum of the torrent, I heard — or was I mad and dreaming that I heard? — the words:

"Open. To me — her father."

CHAPTER XXIX.

"LET US KISS AND PART."

As I unbarred the door that gave directly from the miserable living-room of the house to the outside he came in, the snow upon the shoulders of the cape he wore — some flakes even upon his face.

"You are alive! Escaped!" I whispered, recognising that this was no phantom of my brain, but the man himself. "Safe! Thank God!'

"Where is she?" he asked, pausing for no greeting, giving me none. "My child! Is *she* safe? Or — have I come too late?"

"She is here — safe. It is not too late."

His eyes roamed round the room; then, not seeing her, he continued :

"Where? I must see her — once."

"*Once?*"

"For the last time. After that we shall never meet again. The shadow of my life, my past, must fall on her no more. Yet — once — I must see her. Lead me to where she is."

"She has been ill, delirious—is crushed by all that has happened—by——"

"All that she has learnt," he interrupted, his voice deep and solemn—broken, too. "Yet I must see her."

"She is asleep above."

For answer to this he made simply a sign, yet one I understood very well—a sign that I should delay no longer.

"Come," I said, "come." And together we went up the narrow stairs to the room she occupied—stole up them, as though in fear of waking her.

Pushing the door open gently, we saw by the rays of the *veilleuse*, which I had ordered to be placed in the room, that she was sleeping; observed also that our entry did not disturb her; also it was easy to perceive that she was dreaming. Sometimes, as we standing there gazed down, the long, dark lashes that drooped upon her cheeks quivered; from beneath them there stole some tears; once, too, the rosy lips parted, and a sigh came from between them.

"My child, my child!" Gramont whispered to himself, "child of her whom I loved better than my life—that we should meet at last, only to part forever!"

And from his own eyes the tears rolled down—from his! He stooped and bent over her; his face approached hers; his lips touched that white brow, over which the short-cut hair curled in such glorious dishevelment, while he murmured:

"Unclose those eyelids once, look for the last time on me." Then he half-turned his head away, as though to prevent his own tears from falling on and awakening her.

Was he a sorcerer, I wondered, even as I watched—a sorcerer, as well as other things unnamable? Had he the power over his own child to thus reach her mind and brain, even though both were sunk in a deep, feverish sleep? In truth, it appeared so.

For, even as he spoke, those eyelids did unclose, the dark, dreamy eyes gazed up into his, while, slowly, the full, white, rounded arms encircled his neck, and their lips met, and from him I heard the whispered words:

"Farewell, farewell, forever. Oh, my child, my child!"

Yet—and I thanked God for it then, as ever since I have thanked Him again and again!—he had turned away ere the answering whisper came from her lips, had not heard the words that fell from them—the words;

"Mervan, Mervan, my beloved!"

Thanked God he had not known how, in her sleep, she deemed those kisses mine, and dreamed of me alone.

* * * * * * * * *

As the night went on the storm increased, the snow no longer came in flakes against the window of the room below, in which we sat, but, instead, lay thick and heavy in masses on the sill without—was driven, too, against the window by the fierce, tempestuous wind that howled down from the mountains above, and rocked the miserable inn.

"There is no going on to-night," Gramont said, coming in out of the storm after having gone forth to attend to the horse that had brought him from Lugo, and having bestowed it in the stables, where were the animals on which Juana and I had also ridden. "No going on to-night." Then, changing the subject abruptly, he said: "Where is that man?"

Not pretending to doubt as to whom he made allusion, I said:

"The Alcáide?"

"Ay, the Alcáide."

Whereon I told him of all that had happened since my arrival with the mute, and of his immediate departure further on into Portugal.

"You should have slain him," he said, "the instant you had disarmed him. You loved Juana and she you — she told me so when she divulged his scheme to me in the prison — you should never have let him go free with life."

"I *had* disarmed him. I could not slay a weaponless, defenceless man."

"One slays a snake — awake or sleeping. He merited death."

"Yet to him, in a manner, we all owe our lives. Juana — I — you."

"Owe our lives! Owe our lives to him! To one who trafficked with my girl's honour as against her father's freedom; a man who betrayed his trust to his own country as a means whereby to gratify his own evil desires! And for you — for me — what do we owe him? The chance of my escape came from another's hand than his."

"From another's! You could have escaped even without that vile compact made between — God help us — Juana and him?"

"Ay — listen. You stood by my side in the court when they tried us; you heard a voice in that court; saw the man who called out in loud tones to the man, Morales. You saw him, observed, maybe, that he bore about him the signs of a sailor."

As he spoke there came to me a recollection of something more than this — a recollection of where I had seen that man again, of how it was he who crouched behind the fallen masses of blasted rock in the passage beneath the bed of the river through which I had passed to freedom; also, I remembered the great gold rings in his ears, and the glistening of one upon the guarding of his cloak as he shrank back into the darkness.

"I remember him," I said, "very well — also, I saw him again, on the night that mute led me forth, helped me to escape."

"'T is so. That man saved me, was bent on saving me from the moment he saw my face in the court. He is a Biscayan — yet we had met in other lands; once I had saved his life — from Eaton. He — that doubly damned traitor — that monster of sin — had taken him prisoner in a pink he owned, yet had not captured her without a hard fight, in which this man, Nuñez Picado, nearly slew him. Then, this was Eaton's revenge: He bound him and set him afloat in a dismantled ketch he had by him, that to which Picado was bound being a barrel of gunpowder. And in that barrel was one end of a slow match, the other end alight and trailing the length of the ketch's deck."

"My God!"

"So slow a match that it would take hours ere it reached the powder, hours in which the doomed wretch would suffer ten thousand-fold the tortures of the damned. Yet one thing Eaton forgot — forgot that those hours of long drawn-out horror to his victim were also hours in which succour might come. And it was so. I passed that craft drifting slowly to and fro off Porto Rico. In the blaze of the noontide I saw a brighter, redder light than the sparkle of sun on counter and brass — when I stepped on board the ketch there was not a foot of the slow-match left — not an hour longer of life left to the man. Only, the bitterness of death was over for him then — he was a raving maniac, and so remained for months."

"He has at last repaid you in full."

"Ay! In full. He knew the secret way into the ramparts; all was concocted, all arranged for our escapes."

"For yours and hers?"

"For hers and mine. Had it not been that you had to be saved also — that the freedom which Juana had obtained from

Morales for me must be transferred to you, since I needed it not, she would never have been allowed to go forth with him. I or Picado would have slain him in the prison and escaped with her."

"I begin to understand."

"'T was best, however, to let her go forth unknowing — at least it removed him away from what had to be done — made it certain that he could not impede your escape. The rest was easy. I persuaded the mute that 't was you, not I, whom it was intended to save, that 't was for you her letter was meant, that it was I who was doomed."

"And Eaton? Eaton?" I asked.

"Eaton has paid the forfeit of his treachery," he said. "It has rebounded on his own head. The *brasero* thirsted for its victim — the populace for its holiday. They have had it. Trust Nuñez Picado for that."

He said no more, neither then nor later, and never yet have I learnt how that vilest of men was the substitute for those whom he had hoped and endeavoured to send to the flames. Yet, also, never have I doubted that it was done, since certain it is that from that time he has never again crossed my path.

"The storm increases," Gramont said,

as he strode to the window and peered out into the darksome night. "Yet—yet—I must go on at daybreak. I—I have that which needs take me on."

"Stay here with us," I cried, "stay here. Juana will be my wife at the first moment chance offers. Stay."

"Nay," he said. "Nay. She and I must never meet again. That is the expiation of my life which I have set myself —I will go through with it. In that last kiss above, I took my farewell of her forever in this world."

"What will you do?" I asked through my now fast-falling tears, tears that none needed to be ashamed of; tears that none, listening to his heart-broken words as they dropped slowly from his lips, could have forborne to shed. "What is your life to be?"

"God only knows," he replied; "yet one of penitence, of prayers for forgiveness so long as that life lasts. Thereby—thereby—I shall be fitter for the end. I am almost old now; it may not be far off."

Silence came upon us after that—a silence broken only by the howl of the wind outside the lonely house, by the thud of snow falling now and again from the roof and eaves—blown off by the fury of the tempest. But broken by scarcely aught else, unless 't was a sigh that occasionally, and all unwittingly, as I thought, escaped from that poor sinner's overcharged breast. Yet, for the rest, nothing; no sound from that room above, where Juana lay sleeping; nothing but sometimes the expiring logs falling together with a gentle clash in the grate.

Then suddenly, as I almost dozed on one side of those logs, he being on the other, I heard him speaking to me, his voice deep, sonorous and low — perhaps he feared it might reach her above! — yet clear and distinct.

"Evil," he said, "as my existence has been, misjudge me not. None started on life's path meaning better than I. God help me! none drifted into worse extremes. Will you hear my story — such as 't is meet you should know — you who love my child?"

I bowed my head; I whispered, "Yes." Once, because I pitied him, I gently touched his hand with mine.

"I was a sailor," he went on, his dark eyes gleaming tenderly at that small offering of my sympathy, "bred up to the sea, the only child of a poor Protestant woman. Later — when Louis the king first fell under the thrall of the wanton, De Maintenon, my mother died of starvation, ruined by the revocation of the Edict of Nantes, ruined ere that revocation by the shadow it cast before it on all of our faith. Think you that what was doing in the Indies by the Spaniards made me love the followers of the Romish church more?"

He paused a moment—again he went on:

"In the Indies to which I had wandered, I met with men who had sworn to extirpate, if might be, every Spaniard, every one of those who in their time swore that there was to be no peace beyond the line. That was their oath—we helped them to keep it, made it our watchword, too. All of us, Morgan, Pointis, Avery, Lolonois, your other countryman, Stede Bonnet, a hundred others, all of different lands, yet all of one complexion—hatred against Spain. And there *was* no peace beyond the line. You are a soldier, may be one for years, yet you will never know blood run as blood ran then. You may rack cities, even Louis' own capital, you will never know what sharing booty means as we knew it. Ere I was thirty I possessed a hundred thousand gold pistoles, ere another year had passed I owned nothing but the sword by my side, the deck I trod."

"Yet," I said, "when you were lost—

disappeared — you left your child a fortune — which Eaton stole."

"I did more," he answered. "I left her that — but — I left her another which Eaton could not steal. She has it now; it is, it must be safe. Do you know your wife brings you a great dowry?"

I started — I had never thought of this! — yet, ere I could say aught, he went on again.

"I pass over much. I come to twenty years ago. Eaton was my lieutenant; we were about to besiege Maracaibo, a gallant company three hundred strong. Well, let me hurry — see, the daylight is coming. I must away — Maracaibo fell, our plunder was great. Also, we had many prisoners. Amongst them one, a girl, young and beautiful; God! she was an angel!"

"Juana's mother that was to be," I whispered, feeling sure.

"Hear me. She was my prize — there were others, but I heeded them not, had eyes only for her. Her ransom was fixed at five thousand pistoles, because she was the niece of the wealthiest man of all, to be paid ere we sailed three days later. And I prayed that they might never be forthcoming, that I might bear her away with me, teach her to love me as I loved her."

"And they were not paid?" I asked breathlessly.

"We did not sail in three days' time; the money of the place had been sent away inland on our approach; also one-half our body were all mad with drink ashore. 'T was more nigh three weeks ere we were ready to depart."

"And the lady?"

"Her uncle had died meanwhile of a fever—yet—yet—the ransom was forthcoming. She was affianced to a planter; he came on board my ship, and with him he brought the gold."

"Ah!"

"My oath bound me to take it—had I refused, my brethren had the right—since we had laws regulating all things amongst us—to remove me from my command. I had to see him count the gold out on the cabin table, to tell her she was free to go."

"And she went?" I asked again, almost breathless.

CHAPTER XXX.

GONE.

"She went," he continued, "and I thought that she was gone from me forever, since, filibuster as I was, as I say, my oath to my companions bound me to set her free upon payment of the ransom. Yet, by heaven's grace, she was mine again ere long."

He paused, looking out of the snow-laden window through which there stole now a greyness which told of the coming of the wintry day; pointed toward it as though bidding me remember that his time with me was growing short; then went on:

"I was ashore for the last time before we sailed for Port Royal; those of us who were something better than brutish animals seeking for those who were wallowing in debauchery; finding them, too, either steeped in drink, or so overcome by their late depravity that they had to be carried on board the ships like logs. Then, as we passed down a street seeking our comrades, I saw her again—saw her lovely face at the grilled window of a house that looked as though it might be a convent; at a window no higher from the ground than my own head. And she saw me too, made a sign that I should stop, should send on my company out of earshot; which done, she said:

"'Save me. For God's sake, save me!'

"'Save you, Señorita,' I whispered, for I knew not who might be lurking near, might be, perhaps, within the dark room to which no ray of the blazing sun seemed able to penetrate; 'save you from what, from whom?'

"'From him who ransomed me — *Diós!* that you had not taken the money. I hate him, was forced to be affianced to him, am a prisoner here in this convent until to-morrow, when I am to become his wife.'

"'Yet, Señorita,' I murmured — 'how to do it? These walls seem strong, each window heavily grated, doubtless the house well guarded — and — and we sail at daybreak.'

"'Yet an entrance may be made by the garden,' she whispered in reply; 'the house is defended by negroes only — my room at the top of the stairs. Save me. Save me.'"

Again Gramont paused — again he

pointed at the day-spring outside — hurriedly he went on:

"I saved her. Twenty of us — that vile Eaton was one!—passed through the garden at midnight—up those stairs—killing three blacks who opposed us"—even as he spoke I remembered Eaton's ravings in *La Mouche Noire* as to the dead men glaring down into the passage; knew now of what his frenzied mind had been thinking on—"bore her away. Enough! three months later, we were married in Jamaica!"

He rose as though to go forth and seek his horse, determined to make his way on in spite of the snow that lay upon the ground in masses — because, as I have ever since thought, he had sworn to undergo his self-imposed expiation of never gazing more upon his child's face!—then he paused, and spoke once more:

"She died," and now his voice was broken, trembled, "in giving birth to her who is above; died when I had grown rich again — so rich that when I sailed for France, my pardon assured, my commission as Lieutenant du Roi to Louis in my pocket, I left her with Eaton, not even then believing how deep a villain he was; thinking, too, that I should soon return. Left with him, also, a fortune for her. What happened to her and that fortune you have learnt. Yet, something else you have to learn. Her mother's name had been Belmonte, and when Juana fled from Eaton, driven thence by his cruelty, she, knowing this, found means to communicate with an old comrade of mine, by then turned priest and settled at the other end of the island — at Montego. Now, see how things fall out; how, even to one belonging to me, God is good. 'T was in '86 I sailed for France, my commission in my cabin — nailed in my pride to a bulkhead — when, alas! madman as I was, I encountered a great ship — a treasure ship, as I believed. sailing under Spanish colours. And — and — the devil was still strong in me — still strong the hatred of Spain — the greed and lust of plunder. God help me! God help and pardon me!" and as he spoke he beat his breast and paced the dreary room, now all lit up by the daylight from without. Even as I write I see and remember him, as I see and remember so many other things that happened in those times.

"We boarded her," he continued, a moment later; "we took her treasure; she was full of it — yet even as we did so I knew that I was lost forever in this world, all chance of redemption gone — my hopes of better things passed away forever. For she was sailing under false colours; she was a French ship, one of Louis' own, and, seeing that we ourselves carried the Spanish flag, the better to escape the ships of war of Spain that were all about, had herself run them up. And we could not slay them and scuttle the ship—we had passed our word for their safety—moreover, an we would have done so 't was doubtful if we should have succeeded. There were women on board, and, though the men fought but half-heartedly to guard the treasure that was their king's, they would have fought to the death for them. Therefore, we emptied the vessel of all that it had—we left them their lives—let them go free."

"But why, why?" I asked, still not comprehending how this last attack upon another ship—and that but one of many stretching over long years!—should be so fateful to him, "why not still go on to France, commence a new life under better surroundings?"

"Why?" he repeated, "why? Alas! you do not understand. I, a commissioned officer of the French king, had made war on his ships, taken his goods; also," and he drew a long breath now, "also there were those on board who knew and recognised me — we had met before — knew I was Gramont. That was enough. There was no return to France for me; or, if once there, nothing but the block or the wheel."

"God pity you," I gasped, "to have thrown all chance away thus — thus!"

He seemed not to heed my words of sympathy, wrung from me by my swift comprehension of all he had lost; instead, he stood there before me, almost like those who are turned to stone, making no movement, only speaking as one speaks who encounters a doom that has fallen on him, as one who tells how hope and he have parted forever on wide, diverging roads.

"There were others besides myself," he continued, "who had ruined all by their act of madness, others of my own land who had gained their pardon, and lost it now forever, flung away all hopes of another life, of happier days to come, for the dross that we apportioned between ourselves, though in our frenzy we almost cast it into the sea. As for my share, though 'twas another fortune, I would not touch a pistole, but sent it instead to the priest I have spoken of — sent it by a sure hand — and bade him keep it for my child, add it to that which Eaton held for her; told him, too, to guard it well, since neither he nor she would ever see me more!"

"And after — after?" I asked.

"After, we disbanded — parted. I went my way, they theirs; earned my living hardly, yet honestly, in Hispaniola; should never have left the island had I not discovered that Eaton, who even then sometimes passed under the name of Carstairs — that was his *honest* name — and who had long since disappeared from my knowledge, was having a large amount of goods and merchandise shipped under that name in the fleet of galleons, about to sail as soon as possible. And then — then — knowing how he had treated the child I left in his care — the child of my dead and lost love — I swore to sail in those galleons, to find him, to avenge ——" He paused, exclaiming, "Hark! What is that?"

Above — I heard it as soon as he — there was a footfall on the floor. We knew that Juana was moving, had arisen.

"Go to her," he said, and I thought that his voice was changed — was still more broken — "Go; it may be she needs something. Go."

"Is this our last farewell? Surely we shall meet again."

"Go. And — and — tell her — her father — nay. Tell her nothing. Go."

O'ermastered by his words, by, I think, too, the misery of the man who had been my companion through the dreary night, my heart wrung with sorrow for him who stood there so sad a figure, I went, obeying his behest.

But ere I did so, and before I opened the door that gave on the stairs leading to her room, I took his hand, and whispered:

"It *is* our last farewell! Yet — oh, pause and think — she is your child. Have you no word — no last word of love nor plea for pardon — to send?"

For a moment his lips quivered, his breast heaved and he turned toward the other, and outer, door, so that I thought he meant to go without another sign. But, some impulse stirring in his heart, he moved back again to where I stood; murmuring, I heard him say:

"In all the world she has none other but you. Remember that. Farewell forever. And — in days to come — teach her not to hate — my memory. Farewell."

Then, his hand on the latch of the outer door, he pointed to the other and the stairs beyond.

While I, stealing up them, knew that

neither his child nor I would ever see him more, and, so knowing, prayed that God would at last bring ease and comfort to the erring man.

As I neared the door of the room in which she had slept she opened it and came forth upon the bare landing—pale, as I saw in the light of the now fully broken day, but with much of the fever gone; also with, upon her face, that smile which ever made summer in my heart.

"You are better," I said, folding her to me, "better? Have slept well? Is it not so?" Yet, even as I spoke, I led her back to the room whence she had come. She must not descend *yet!* "You have not stirred all through the night, I know."

"I dreamt," she said, "that you came to me, bade me farewell forever. Yet that passed, and again I dreamed that we should never part more. Therefore, I was happy, even in my sleep." Then broke off to say: "Hark! They are stirring in the house. Are the horses being prepared? I hear one shaking its bridle. Can any go forth to-day?" and she moved toward the window.

"Nay, Juana," I said, leading her back again, although imperceptibly, to the middle

ACROSS THE SALT SEAS. 417

of the room, "do not go to the window. The cold is intense — stay here by my side."

Not guessing my reason — since it was impossible she should understand what was happening below! — I led her back. Led her back so that she should not see one come forth from the stable whom she deemed dead and destroyed — so that she should not be blasted by the sight of her father passing away in actual life from her forever; then sat down by her side and led the conversation to our future — to how we should get away from here to England and to safety. Also, I told her not to bewail, as she did again and again, my failure to proceed further on my journey to Flanders and the army; demonstrated, to her that, at least, there had been no failure in the mission I had undertaken; that my secret service had been carried out — and well carried out, too — and, consequently, my return mattered not very much with regard to a week or month. The allies, I said, could fight and win their battles very well without my aid, as I doubted not they were doing by now, while — for the rest — had I not done my share both here and in Spain? Proved, too — speaking a little self-vauntingly, perhaps, by reason of my intense desire to soothe and cheer her and testify that she had been no barrier in my path to glory — that I, also, though far away from my comrades, had stood in the shadow of death, had been face to face with the grim monster equally with those who braved the bayonets, the muskets and the cannon of Louis' armies.

But all the time I spoke to her my apprehension was very great, my nerves strung to their bitterest endurance, my fear terrible that she would hear the man below going forth, that she might move to the window and see him — and that, thus seeing, be crushed by the sight.

For I knew that he was moving now — that he was passing away forever from this gloomy spot which held the one thing in all the world that was his, and linked him to the wife he had loved so dearly; knew that, solitary and alone, he was about to set forth into a dreary world which held no home for him nor creature to love him in his old age. I, too, heard the bridle jangling again; upon the rough boards of the stable beneath the windows of the *fonda* I heard the dead, dull thump of a horse's hoofs; I knew that the animal was moving — that he was setting out upon his journey of darkness and despair.

"You are sad, Mervan," she said, her cheek against mine, while her voice murmured in my ear. "Your words are brave, yet all else belies them."

"It is not for myself," I answered. "Not for myself."

The starry eyes gazed into mine, the long, slim hand rested on my shoulder.

"For whom?" she whispered. "For whom? For him? My father?"

I bowed my head—from my lips no words seemed able to come—yet said at last:

"For him. Your father." Then, for a moment, we sat there together, saying nothing. But soon she spake again.

"My thoughts of him are those of pity only, now," she murmured once more. "Pity, deep as a woman's heart can feel. And—and—my love—remember, I never knew who my father was until that scene in the inn at Lugo—thought always his, our, name was in truth Belmonte. The secret was well kept—by Eaton, for his own ends, doubtless; by my father's friend, the priest who had once been as he was, for his past friendship's sake. If I judged him harshly, a life of pity for his memory shall make atonement."

As she said these words, while I kissed

and tried to comfort her, she rose from where we were sitting and went to the window, I not endeavouring to prevent her now, feeling sure that he was gone; for all had become very still; there was no longer any sound in the stable, nor upon the snow, which, as I had seen as the day broke, had frozen and lay hard as iron on the ground beneath it.

Yet something there was, I knew, that fascinated her as she gazed out upon the open; something which—as she turned round her face to me—I saw had startled, terrified her. For, pale as she had been since we had met again here, and with all the rich colouring that I loved so much gone from her cheeks, she was even whiter, paler than I had ever known her—in her eyes, too, a stare of astonishment, terror.

"Mervan!" she panted, catching her breath, her hand upon her heart, "Mervan, look, oh, look!" and she pointed through the window.

"See," she gasped, "see. The form of one whom I deemed dead—or is he in truth dead, and that his spectre vanishing into the dark wood beyond? See, the black horse, that which he bestrode that night— oh! Mervan—Mervan—Mervan—why has his spirit returned to earth? Will it haunt me forever — forever — punish me because of my shame of him?"

And while I saw the horseman's figure disappear now — and forever — into the darkness of the pine forest, she lay trembling and weeping in my arms. To calm which, and also bring ease to her troubled heart, I told her all.

CHAPTER XXXI.

ALWAYS TOGETHER NOW.

The frost held beneath a piercing east wind which blew across the mountains that separated Portugal from Leon, so that now the snow was as hard as any road and there was no longer any reason to delay our setting forth. And more especially so was this the case because my beloved appeared to have entirely recovered from the fever into which she had been thrown by the events of the past weeks.

"I am ready, Mervan," she said to me the next day, "ready to depart, to leave forever behind these lands — which I hope never to see again — to dwell always in your own country and near you."

Wherefore I considered in my mind what was best now to be done.

That we were safe here in Portugal we knew very well — only it was not in Portugal that we desired to remain, but rather to escape from; to cross the seas as soon as might be — to reach England or Holland. Yet how to do that we had now to consider.

ACROSS THE SALT SEAS. 423

I had said we were safe here, and of this safety we had sure proof not many hours after her unhappy father had departed on his unknown journey; a journey that led I knew not where, no more than I knew what would be the end of it. And this proof was that, in the afternoon of the same day, the landlord of the inn came running in to us as fast as he could scamper across the already frozen snow; his face twitching with excitement, his voice shaking, too, from the same cause.

"Holy Virgin!" he exclaimed, while he gesticulated like a madman, his wife doing the same thing by his side, "who and what have I sheltered here in my house. Pirates and filibusters, gaol breakers and murderers, women whose vows are made and broken day by day. 'T is mercy we are not all stabbed to the death in our beds," and again he grimaced and shook and spluttered.

"You are as like," I said sternly, with a tap to my sword hilt, "to be stabbed to the death now, and at once, if you explain not this intrusion and your words, fellow." For he had roused my ire by bursting in on Juana and me in the manner he had done, and by frightening her, as I knew by the way she clung to me. "Answer at once, what mean you?"

"There are at the frontier," he said, speaking now more calmly, also more respectfully as he noted my attitude, while his wife ceased her clamour too, "some half dozen Spaniards from Lugo, all demanding where you are—and—and the wo—the lady; also asking for one they call their Alcáide, as well as another, who, they say, is a hundred-fold assassin. Likewise they vow they will have you back to Lugo."

"Will they! Well, we will see for that! Meanwhile, what say the frontiermen on this side, here in Portugal?"

"They dispute. They refuse. They say 't is whispered o'er all our land that the king has joined with the English brigands——"

"Fellow! remember." And again I threatened him.

"With the English nation against Spain and France. It may be so or not; I do not know. Yet I think you will be spared to—to—slay——"

Again he halted in his speech, reading danger in my glance, while I, turning to Juana, bade her keep calm and await my return from the border, to which I meant to proceed to see what was a-happening.

At first she would not hear of my doing this; she threw herself upon my neck, she besought me by our new-born love, by all our hopes of happiness in days to come, not to go near those men. Reminded me, too, that even now we were free to escape, to seize upon the horses, push on further into Portugal and to safety. Also she pleaded with me to remember that if aught happened to me, if I was taken again and carried back to Spain, all hope would indeed be gone, no more escape possible. Wept, also, most piteously, and besought me to recollect that if aught such as this befell she would indeed be alone in the world, and must die.

Yet I was firm; forced myself to be so. In my turn, bade her remember that I was a soldier, that soldiers could not skulk and run away when there was naught to fear.

"For," I said, whispering also many other words of love and comfort in her ear, "it may be true that the king has joined with us. For months it has been looked for, expected. And if 't is not even so, these people hate Spain and all in it with a deep hatred. They cannot harm us, certainly no half dozen can. 'T would take more than that. Let me go, sweetheart."

And gently I disengaged her arms from

my neck and went away amidst her prayers and supplications for my safety; amidst also the mutterings of the landlord to the effect that the *Inglés* seemed to fear neither devil nor man.

'T was not many moments to the border 'twixt the two countries, and I soon was there — seeing, however, as I hurried toward it, to the priming of my pistols, and that my sword was loose enough in its scabbard for easy drawing forth — and there I perceived that a harangue was going on between the Spanish and Portuguese frontiermen, while, on the side of the former, were also the half-dozen Spaniards, of whom the inn keeper had spoken. And amongst them I recognised two or three of those who had captured us in the inn garden at Lugo.

"Ha!" one of them called out as I approached. "Ha! See, there is one, the second of the brigands, though not the worst. *Assassinator!*" he shrieked at me, "we must have you back at Lugo."

"Best take me, then," I replied, as I drew close up, "yet 't will cost you dear," and as I spoke I whipped my sword from out its scabbard.

There was to be neither fight nor attempt to capture me, however; in truth, as you have now to see, my weapon had done its last work in either Spain or Portugal, since the men on this side meant not that the Spaniards should have their way.

"Back, I tell you," shouted the Portuguese chief, "or advance at your peril. We are at war; 't is known over all our land the *Inglés* are our allies. You have come on a bootless errand."

Now this, as I learnt later, was not the case in absolute fact, since Portugal joined not with us till the next spring had come, yet it served very well for my purpose; for these Spaniards did doubtless think that they would have got me—and, I suppose, Juana, too—bloodlessly, and have been able to hale us back to Lugo and its accursed *braséro*. But now they found out their mistake; they would have to fight to get me, and as, I think, they feared my sword as much as the four or five others of my new-found Portuguese friends, they very wisely desisted from any attempt. And so, after many angry words exchanged on both sides, in which I took no part, I went back to the inn, feeling sure that, unless I ever ventured into Spain again, I was free of its clutches.

* * * * * * * *

Once more, a few hours later, my love and I were on the road as travelling companions, only now we were lovers instead of friends, and the companionship was, by God's mercy, to be for the length of our lives. And sweet it was to me, beyond all doubt, to have her by my side, to hear her soft voice in my ears, and to listen to the words of love that fell from her lips — sweet, too, to me to make reply to them.

For one thing also I was devoutly grateful, namely, that I had not hesitated to tell her that her father still lived; that he had yet, by heaven's grace, many years before him in which to expiate his past; that he had escaped the awful end to which he had been doomed, and which, during some few hours, she imagined he had suffered — devoutly grateful that I had done this, because, now, the sorrow which she felt for the erring man was chastened by the knowledge that it was not too late for him to repent and obtain pardon, and that his death, whatever it might be, could scarce be one of such horror as that from which he had escaped.

After some consideration I had decided that 't would be best we should make our way to Oporto, where I thought 't was very like we might find some ship for either England or Holland — perhaps, also, since the trade of that town with England is of such extreme importance, some vessel of war acting as convoy for the merchants. Moreover, the distance was not great in so small a land as this, and by the chart I carried seemed not to be more than thirty or forty leagues, though to compass them we should have to pass over mountains more than once. Yet the horses were fresh — I rode now my own on which Gramont had come and had then exchanged for the black one on which I had escaped, it having been prepared for me ere I took his place — the snow was hard as iron; it was not much to do. And, much or little, it had to be done.

And so we progressed, passing through Mirandella and Murca, striking at last a broad high road that ran straight for Oporto — scaling mountains sometimes, plunging sometimes into deep valleys and crossing streams over shaking wooden bridges that by their appearance seemed scarce strong enough to bear a child, yet over which we got in safety. And, though neither she nor I spoke our thoughts, I think, I know, that the same idea was ever present to her mind as to mine, the idea that we might ere long come upon some sign of her father. For, now and again, as she peered down upon the white track we followed, losing more than once the road, yet finding it again ere long, she would rein in the jennet and look at the tracks frozen in the snow, then shake her head mournfully as we went on once more.

But of Gramont we saw no sign—nor ever saw him again in this world.

Going on and on, however, we drew near as I judged, to the coast, still climbing the mountains and still passing at other times through the valleys, over all of which there lay the vast white pall burying everything beneath it.

We heard also the great river that is called the Douro, rolling and humming and swirling beneath the roof of frozen snow which, in some places, stretched across it from bank to bank. In some places, too, where the road we traversed approached nearer to the stream, we saw it cleaving its way through banks so narrowed by their coating of ice that it o'erleapt and foamed above the sides, while with a great swish, such as a huge tide makes upon a shingly beach, its waters spread out with a hissing splash from their eddies and swept over the borders on either side. Yet, because the way this river rushed was likewise our way to peace and happiness—the road toward the great sea we hoped so soon to traverse—we regarded it with interest.

"See," I said to Juana, as now we rode close to it, so that at this time our horses' feet were laved by its overflow, "see how it bears down with it great trees from far inland, from where we have come; also other things, the wooden roof of some peasant's hut, some household goods too. I fear it has swept over the country, has burst in places from its narrow frost-bound sides."

'T was true—such must have happened —for even as I spoke, there went by the body of a horse—the creature's sides all torn and lacerated, doubtless by some narrow passage in which the spears of ice would be as sharp as swords' points; then, next — oh! piteous sight!—a little dead babe rolled over and over as the waves bore it along in their swift flight.

"Look, look," she murmured, pointing forward to where the river broadened, but out into the breadth of which there projected a spur, or tongue of land; "look! that catches much of what comes down— see! the dead horse's progress is stopped upon it—and Mervan, the little babe is also rolled on to that slip of land while there are many other things besides; more bodies of both men and animals."

There were, in solemn truth. As we rode nearer to that jutting promontory, we saw that much of what the Douro had brought down was stopped by it; upon the frozen tongue of land protruding were mixed in confusion many things. The dead horse and another which had preceded it; some poor sheep, a dog, the little babe which had just passed before our eyes, and two or three dead men; some on their backs, their arms extended on that frozen refuge — one on his face.

Mostly they were peasants; their garb told that, also their rough, coarse hands, which showed black against the leper whiteness of the ice and snow beneath them. But he who lay upon his face was none such, his scarlet coat, guarded with galloon, had never graced a peasant's back, no more than any peasant had worn that sword (with now both blade and scabbard broken) that was by his side.

And halting upon the little ridge which made the summit of that promontory and gazing upon that man, I knew as well as if I could see his down-turned face, whose body it was stretched out there upon its icy bier.

Also I saw that she knew, too. Neither scarlet coat nor battered weapon was strange to her.

"I will descend," I said, speaking in a low voice, such as those assume who stand in presence of the dead. "I will descend and make sure," whereupon she bowed her head in reply, making no demur. At that moment she, perhaps, thought it best to make sure that he who had sought her soul's degradation would never traffic with another woman's honour.

But as I went down on foot now to that tongue of land on which the drowned reposed, I had another reason besides this of making sure that the body was that of her tempter, the Alcáide. I desired to discover if 't was by the river alone that he had come to his death (borne down and into it by some streamlet nearer the Spanish border), and not by the avenging weapon of him who said that I should never have spared him, have never let him quit my side with life. For they might have met, I knew; the one who went first might have been belated on his road — snowbound; the second might have overtaken him, his vengeance have been swift and sure.

Stepping across the bodies of the drowned animals, avoiding those of the peasants, and putting gently aside that of the little babe, I reached him, recognising as I did so the coal black hair flecked and streaked with grey, the rings upon the hands stretched out, backs upward. Then I turned him over, seeing that the face was torn and cut by the jagged ice through which he had been hurried, also bruised and discoloured. But in all the body no sign of rapier wound, nor pistol shot, nor of avenging finger marks upon the throat.

So I went back to her and took my reins from her hands and once more we set out upon our way.

But the dark, lustrous eyes as they gazed into mine asked silent and unworded questions — so that I guessed my thoughts had been in her mind, too!— and when I answered with as equal a silence I knew that I had brought comfort to her heart.

CHAPTER XXXII.

THE END.

The early part of September, 1704, had been stormy and wet and very dismal, so that all in London feared that the great spectacle, which had been arranged with much pains and forethought for the seventh of that month, must be impaired if not totally ruined by the inclemency of the weather. And many there were who, during the night that passed away and when the dawn came, rose from their beds to peer out and see what the day promised.

Yet by great good fortune none were doomed to disappointment. For from away over the river, down by where the great ships were all a-lying dressed with flags, the sun came up in great magnificence and splendour; the clouds turned from purple to a fair pure daffodil; a sweeter autumn morning none had ever seen nor could hope to see.

And now from very early in the morning the crowd came in from far and wide, from north and south and east and west, from the villages along the river as far away as sylvan Richmond on one side, or Hampstead on another; while the gentry drove in from their country seats at Clapham or Kensington and on the road that leads to Fulham. Also those regiments at Hounslow, and the foot guards at Kensington, as well as the city militia from the east side, were all making their way into the town, with drums a-beating and flags streaming out to the fresh morning air and trumpets braying, while in the city itself my Lord Mayor was getting ready to proceed to Temple Bar, there to receive the queen and court.

For this day, the seventh of September, had been fixed for the thanksgiving for the victory of Blenheim which the Duke of Marlborough had recently won. The pity only being that, of those who were to take part in the great ceremony, my Lord Duke could not be there, he being still engaged on the Continent.

Nevertheless, from St. James' there set out so great a company for St. Paul's that 't is never likely any one then alive could expect to witness a more noble and imposing sight. For there were all the great officers of state, with, amidst them, the queen in a sumptuous coach drawn by eight horses, Her Majesty being ablaze with jewels. Alone she went in that coach excepting one companion, a lady dressed as quietly and simply as could be any lady in the land, there being neither at neck or bosom or throat, or in her hair, any single trinket to be seen.

Yet, I think, she was that day the proudest woman in all England, not even excepting great Anna, since she was the wife of the conqueror who had trampled Louis and his armies under foot; was Sarah, Duchess of Marlborough. Could any female heart have desired to be more!

In front of, as well as behind, and on either side of that chariot of state, there rode the Queen's Guards; yet ahead of those who rode behind — he being nearest to the back of the carriage — was one who yielded to none in thankfulness and gratitude for all which Providence had seen fit to do for him. An officer this, one handed, his left arm bound up — it having been nearly lopped off at Blenheim by one of the Elector of Bavaria's huge dragoons, whom that officer slew a moment later with his right hand — whose scarf, sword knot, richly laced scarlet coat and gold cockade proclaimed him a colonel of horse — myself.

From where we entered the Strand —

by the cross set up here — we saw that all the shops were boarded up and scaffolded, partly to resist the crowd and partly to furnish benches on which sight-seers might sit. On those benches, also in the shop windows, on the bulks and at the windows of the tradesmen's parlours above, was a noble and splendid company, the ladies of which had all adorned themselves with their choicest dresses and ribbons and laces, the more to do honour to those other two ladies in the great coach. Then, behind, came the lords of Parliament and the gentlemen of the Commons, also the Bishops in their wigs and lawn — each and all in coaches drawn by six horses — as well as many others of the nobility; while from the churches along the route, St. Martin's-in-the-Fields, St. Mary's in the Strand and St. Clement's Danes, the bells clashed and clanged, and, inside, the organs blew and anthems pealed.

At Temple Bar there was a great halt, since the gates were shut, yet opened as the queen came to them, whereon my Lord Mayor, surrounded by the aldermen and sheriffs, in their red robes and on horses richly caparisoned, received Her Majesty, the former handing to her the sword of the city, which she at once returned; after which we progressed once more toward St. Paul's, where, later, the dean preached a moving sermon.

And now my eyes were fixed and searching for a face—two faces—at a window beyond the Church of St. Dunstan's in Fleet street—which was all hung with banners and adornments stretched across from side to side—and presently I saw that which I sought for—a lady on a balcony holding up a little wee child in her arms, a lady dark and beautiful and dressed all in her best, her robe a rich brocade, with, at her breast, a knot of ribbons, the colours of the Fourth Horse—the woman who has ever been in my eyes the fairest, most lovely of her sex, my loved and honoured wife. And she stood there seeking for me, leaning over the balcony to wave and kiss her hand, took, also, our babe's little one in her arms and caused it to wave, too.

Riding by, I looked up and saw them, and blessed God — blessed God and praised His name, because He had seen fit to bring us safe through all the dangers we had encountered together, because He had seen fit to give to me for wife the sweetest woman the world held, and to bring us safe into haven at last.

For that, as well as all else, I blessed and praised His name, even as from roofs of houses and taverns the salvos roared forth, the bells pealed from the steeples, and we progressed through the city; companies ranged 'neath their banners, and, between the lines kept by the militia, the queen bowing from her side of the coach, the great, stately duchess from hers, the people shouting all the time, and crying but two names, "Anne" and "Marlborough," and women holding up their children, so that, in the days to come, when those children were old, they might say they had gazed on the wife of the greatest soldier in the world. And thus, at last, we came to St. Paul's and gave thanksgiving.

It was when night had fallen after Blenheim that my Lord Duke sent for me to his room in the inn, where he and the Marshal Tallard — who had led the French, and been defeated that day, and was now an honoured and well-cared-for prisoner of his Grace — were quartered, and spoke to me as follows:

"Colonel Crespin — for such you will be when the next gazette is published — if it were not that others have a prior claim, it should be you to whom I would confide my message to the queen and lords. For," and he smiled sweetly, as usual, though, to-night, a little wearily, "I have a recollection of your value as a bearer of despatches; yet, all the same, you shall go to England. You have a wife and child there, I know."

And again he smiled as I bowed before him.

"For which you have to thank me. By St. George, I never thought when I sent you on that journey you were going sweetheart hunting, too."

Whereby you will perceive that his Grace knew very well all that had befallen me two years before, when I set out for Spain to find, if might be, the English fleet. It would be strange, indeed, if he had not known it, for my story had been told all over the forces from the moment I returned and joined my regiment; nay, more than once, I had told it to Marlborough himself.

"I shall not be far behind you," he continued, "the New Year should see me home, too. Yet I have messages for the queen and my own wife. You shall bear them. It will give you an opportunity of seeing your own wife. She is, I hear, vastly beautiful."

"In my eyes, my lord Duke, the most beautiful woman in the world."

"That is as it should be. So," he continued simply, "I think of mine. But, also, you must see the queen. She has heard of your adventures, wishes she had seen you when you were on leave in England. Tell her all — tell her as bravely in words as you can be brave in action — and you will not stop at the command of a regiment of horse. See also my wife; her influence is extreme — our enemies say 't is a bad influence — yet she will help you."

And I did see the queen on my arrival in England, also the great duchess, Sarah, on the night before we went to St. Paul's; after which I wondered no more how every one loved the former, spoke of her, indeed, as the "Good" Queen — a title, I think, as dear and precious as that of "Great," which Elizabeth had worn. She was very ruddy, I noticed when I stood before her, her beautiful red-brown hair bound most matronly above her brow, while her arms — which were bare, to show, as I have heard, their extreme beauty — were most marvellous to behold, as well as her hands. Yet, queen as she was, and a well favoured one, too, it was more on the other lady who stood behind her that my eyes rested; for she was beautiful beyond all I had imagined, so that I wondered not that report said the duke loved her as fondly as when they were boy and girl together, she only a maid of honour, and he an ensign. Yet, also, I thought that beauty marred by an imperious haughtiness which made her seem the queen and the real queen seem her subject.

"So, Colonel Crespin," Her Majesty said to me, "I set eyes on you at last — you of whom I have heard so much. Well, I am vastly proud to know so brave a gentleman. Later, I must also know your wife — whom I hear you wooed and won in a strange fashion." Then changing the subject swiftly, while her kindly eyes rested on me, she said: "Your father must be very proud of you."

Not knowing what reply to make to such a compliment, I could but bow again, whereon she continued:

"Your arm is bound up, I see — I hear you got the wound at Blenheim. 'T is very well. In after years it will be as great a distinction to have had that wound as any honours or titles that may come to you. It does not prevent your riding?"

I murmured that it inconvenienced me but very little, whereon Her Majesty said:

"That is also well. To-morrow I desire you follow my coach to St. Paul's. I love my people to see those who have served me bravely," whereon, with a gracious inclination of her head, accompanied by a sweet smile upon her honest, kindly face, she turned and left the apartment, the duchess bowing too, though somewhat more haughtily than the queen had done. Yet she whispered a word in my ear as she passed out; a word appropriate enough to one as proud as she.

"You have served *him* well," she said. "Those who do that are my friends forever."

And now the rejoicings for our victory at Blenheim were over — the siege and taking of Gibraltar three weeks before, by my other friend, Sir George Rooke, being not forgotten — the crowds had dispersed, the great banquet to be given by the city was near at hand and the illuminations of London were beginning.

Yet I had no desire to be feasting in the midst of that great company — instead, I was seated in the room from the balcony of which I had seen my wife that morning; her head upon my shoulder, her lips murmuring words of love inexpressible in my ear; words in which, amongst the rest, I caught those that told me how proud she was to have won me from all other women, how proud and happy in knowing that we were each other's forever in this world.

* * * * * * * * *

What need to set down more — what more have I to say?

Only this. That never would she hear of redeeming any of that second fortune which her unhappy father had left in the custody of the priest in the Indies who had once been as he himself was; and consequently, that from the time we became man and wife no further intercourse was ever held between us and those far-off islands from which she came. Nor was that fortune wanted — God has ever been good to us; I have prospered exceedingly in my soldier's calling; all is very well.

Of him, Gramont, we have never heard more. Yet that, somewhere, he is, if still alive, expiating his past I have never doubted. The truth was in the man's eyes as he spoke to me on that morning when he went forth broken-hearted from the house which held his child; the truth, and a firm determination to atone by suffering and hardship for all that he had done. And what stronger or more stern resolve could any sinner have taken than that of his? The determination to tear himself away forever from the companionship of his newly found daughter, and to remove thereby from her forever the shame of his presence.

"Come, Mervan," she said to me, as now

the autumn evening turned to night, and from every house in Fleet street the illuminations began to glisten. "Come, you must prepare for the city banquet."

"Nay," I said, "nay. I need no banquets, would prefer to stay here by your side."

"And so I would you should do. Yet you must go. I will not have you absent from so great a thing. You! my hero—my king. And while you are gone I will watch over our child, or solace myself with this."

And as she spoke she went over to where the spinet was, and touched a smaller instrument that lay upon it—the little viol d'amore from which we have never parted, and never will.

THE END.

www.ingramcontent.com/pod-product-compliance
Lightning Source LLC
Chambersburg PA
CBHW022142300426
44115CB00006B/310